FCL070000021

D0586647

Cyrano

Cyrano

Adventures in space and time with the legendary French hero

ISHBEL ADDYMAN

London · New York · Sydney · Toronto

A CBS COMPANY

First published in Great Britain by Simon & Schuster UK Ltd, 2008
A CBS COMPANY

1 3 5 7 9 10 8 6 4 2

Simon & Schuster UK Ltd
Africa House
64–78 Kingsway
London WC2B 6AH

www.simonsays.co.uk

Simon & Schuster Australia
Sydney

PICTURE CREDITS
1, 13, © RMN
2, 12, © Photos12
3, 11, 18, 24, © Bridgeman Art Library
4, 14b, © Alamy
5, 16, © Mary Evans
6, 7, © Getty
8, 17, 20, courtesy of author
9, courtesy of Collection David-Sertillanges, www.cyranodebergerac.fr
10, 15, 21, © Corbis
14a, © Wellcome
19, © Lebrecht
22, © Ronald Grant Archive
23, © Rex
25, © Advertising Archives
26, © Scala Archives

A CIP catalogue for this book is available
from the British Library.

ISBN: 978-0-7432-8619-0

Typeset in Bembo by M Rules
Printed and bound in Great Britain by
Mackays of Chatham Ltd

For my Mother
with love always

Contents

'The joy of a spirit is the measure of its power'

Ninon de Lenclos (1620–1705)

'Failure is always a proof of freedom'

Jacques Brel (1929–1978)

PROLOGUE

Lieutenant de Cavais to Marshal de Gassion – 1642

Honoured Sir,
I am given to understand that, after the report made to you by Monsieur de Bourgogne, you wished to have further information regarding the incident that took place at the de Nesle gate, at which I was also present. I am sensible of the honour you do me in requesting my account. I dare to hope that the following will serve the purpose, it is as faithful and as detailed a description as I could make it.

It was late afternoon when we eventually left the tavern. I don't think anyone apart from me took his suggestion seriously. As usual, he had drunk much less than the rest of us and, while we spilt out into the sunshine, stumbling over one another, he was a still point at the centre of the rabble. Most of the others laughed off his invitation to come and watch what would happen. In the end only four of us followed him towards the de Nesle gate. It is an area I would normally avoid but I was determined to witness his humiliation. He had angered me that day with several clever witticisms at my expense, and I admit that I was eager for revenge. Setting off, I was elated that his hour was finally come. I was praying for him to fail, to be silenced. As we got nearer and the sound of voices began to reach us, I felt the first squirt of fear through my guts. My fellow officers had insisted on accompanying him in order to protect him and I knew that I might also be expected to step in. When we caught the first sight of the crowd of villains waiting for us, there was no doubt in my mind that this was not a fight I wanted any part in; we were outnumbered at least ten to one and by a crowd of the most ungentlemanly ruffians. He turned and asked to us to wait behind him, and under no circumstances to attempt to interfere. It was a suicidally stupid thing to say and I almost laughed, but the sound died in my throat. One of the men hurled an obscene insult in our direction and I felt all their eyes on us, sizing us up. It was at that moment that I realized I had lost all my previous envy of him. My corrosive desire to be a spectator at the moment of his bloody and ignominious death had vanished.

He walked towards them and drew his sword. I remember that he spoke but not the words, which were quickly drowned out in any case by coarse mocking laughter and howls of almost hysterical derision. It was clear that the men had been drinking and one or two of them seemed to be finding the situation increasingly comic. That this single, lean figure should step forward to challenge them all was preposterous indeed. I no longer wished to witness the moment when they would sweep over him like a pack of wolves and tear him to shreds. But I was compelled to keep looking. He continued advancing towards them at an unhurried pace. The tension in this moment of calm while both sides waited to see what the other would do was making the hairs on the back of my neck itch and I felt my armpits and groin suddenly prickle with sweat. My former enemy, beckoned the nearest of the gang to come towards him. The ruffian responded with a sarcastic jibe and, laughing back over his shoulder to his companions, he swaggered forward. Most of them seemed to be armed with thick clubs or glinting knives but the first to fight was unsheathing a heavy sword. All the others watched hungrily as the two figures came within reach of one another. The next thing I saw was the impossible brightness of the blood arching from the lackey's neck and seeming almost to hang a moment in the air along with his suddenly awkward form, before both fell to earth together. The brilliant redness oozed all around the man's lifeless body, soaking through his grubby clothes and seeping into the ground. The reaction from the watching rabble was swift and varied; some rushed forward yelling furiously, others were already beginning to edge away. With extraordinary agility and speed, their opponent was already on the move, and had leapt across in order to position himself on the fallen rubble in such a way that the ditch protected him from attack from the rear and the masonry prevented his adversaries from being able to rush or crowd him. If they wanted to fight him, they would have to do so according to his rules, each man individually. What followed was a simply dazzling display of swordsmanship. There were moments when I was convinced he was lost. He received a powerful blow from a cudgel which ought to have felled him, but he recovered in time to deliver a swift slashing riposte. His assailant screamed and ran off cradling his arm. Shortly after, I saw his sword catch in one fellow's eye-socket and seem to stick there – it looked as though the extraordinary duellist would be disarmed and left defenceless in the face of the howling mob, but he calmly used his gloved left hand to dislodge the blade with a sharp downwards tug. Later, he almost fell amongst them, when, scrabbling for purchase, he slipped on the severed finger of one of the knife-wielding attackers, but he regained his balance just in time. Soon the unruly crowd had dwindled to almost nothing. Half-a-dozen inert forms were strewn about and others were limping and stumbling away, aided by their fellows. The most craven were already long gone, having fled at the sight of a man's throat being opened. My companions rushed over to tend to their exhausted hero, while I inspected the fallen men. Two were already corpses, rapidly cooling, and I counted another seven incapacitated and weeping or groaning in their agony. I have seen my share of such slow, lingering deaths on the battlefield and the sound of their suffering brought back insistent and terrible memories. I drew my dagger thinking to dispatch them to a swifter end. In an instant he was beside me, his hand was on mine and he said to me, 'No, leave them, they will tell the story.' I observed him bend to each of the wounded men in turn and say, 'We have not yet been introduced; my name is Monsieur de Cyrano de Bergerac.'

This is the true and faithful record of my observations and I hope that my humble testimony will prove useful to your honour. If I may serve you further in any way possible, I dare to hope that so noble a military leader will not disdain the unworthy but unfailing loyalty of one of his devoted subordinates. I remain your humble servant,

Monsieur de Cavais

Introduction

Over three and a half centuries ago, a lone swordsman stepped out of the shadows of obscurity and into the light of lasting legend. His 'duel with a hundred men', as it became known, was a defining moment in the career of a man whose insane daring made him a legend in French history. At the time, the story blazed through the taverns and back streets of seventeenth-century Paris and brought Cyrano de Bergerac to the attention of Marshal de Gassion, one of the highest military commanders in the land. As a result, Gassion attempted to hire the hero of the hour for his own company, but his offer came too late. The invincible swordsman had already decided to leave his military career behind.

The precise details of Cyrano's single-handed battle against a gang of hired thugs have been lost in the tide of admiration and exaggeration that such a feat naturally provoked. There is no surviving documentary evidence recording the incident directly: the letter with which this book opened is a fiction. But the eyewitness, Monsieur de Cavais, is not himself an invention. Although neither Cavais nor Bourgogne left a written account, their names are known to us (along with that of a third witness, a soldier named

Cuigy) thanks to another man, Cyrano's loyal friend and fellow officer, Henri Le Bret. Le Bret was by his side at the de Nesle gate, and in 1656 he published his version of the story. He only offers the barest outline of the tale, but it is one of the highlights of the first ever biography of Cyrano de Bergerac.

Today, the name Cyrano is known to most of us as that of a fictional character: the eponymous hero of a five-act tragi-comedy in verse, *Cyrano de Bergerac* by Edmond Rostand. The play has won over audiences around the globe and Rostand used the duel with one hundred men in order to establish his hero as a man of phenomenal courage and death-defying, swashbuckling talent. The story of the duel has to be the single element of the play that one would least expect to have any basis in historical fact, and yet it was not invented by the poet Rostand, but drawn from the life story of a real person, as recounted by one of his closest friends.

Before the hero there was a man, and before the legend there was a life. Born in Paris in 1619, the real Cyrano de Bergerac came from an inauspicious bourgeois background. He was uncompromising, unconventional and eccentric to the last, and yet the real Cyrano was also on some level a slave to the social conventions of his time. Determined to efface his comparatively humble origins, Cyrano worked hard to transform himself from Savinien de Cyrano, the grandson of a Sardinian fishmonger, into Cyrano de Bergerac, the supposed scion of a great family of Gascon noblemen. To this day, despite his well-documented Parisian immigrant roots, the Gascon town of Bergerac in the south-west of France proudly proclaims Cyrano as its most famous native son. The centre of this pretty, small town is graced by not one, but two statues of him. In the course of his life, Cyrano determinedly eclipsed his true history. His flamboyant manipulation of his own image was so successful that ultimately the legend blotted out the reality altogether. Like a shadow, his image is distorted and stretches far beyond its original source. He also inadvertently sparked off a chain reaction which has seen his extraordinary story told and re-told in the centuries since his death, in versions which range from the sublime to the ridiculous.

The phenomenal success of Rostand's fictionalized version of Cyrano's life has been so overwhelming that today it is a surprise to many to learn that Cyrano de Bergerac really existed. The play is full of inaccuracies and anachronisms but it undoubtedly captures the spirit of the original Cyrano. The real Cyrano de Bergerac and Rostand's hero share certain points of contact, but in the end the truth is infinitely more intriguing than the fiction. While the stage Cyrano is an undeniably appealing creation, the man himself was considerably more complex and more impressive. The scarcity of evidence in piecing together the biography of the real Cyrano has tended to favour those writers who use the absence of proof as an encouragement to invention. The tendency to want to fill in the mysterious gaps in Cyrano's life story with suitably dashing and romantic episodes is both natural and profoundly unhelpful. For the entire period 1641 to 1648 (almost the whole of Cyrano's twenties) only one document has so far been found relating to the great swordsman. Hard evidence about the life of the real Cyrano is scarce and in order to make the most of the fragments that we have, it is essential to consider each element with forensic caution. The illumination provided by setting each detail in its historical context is vital. An investigation of such scraps of proof as have survived the passage of time is perhaps the only way to finally unearth the untold story of this unsung hero. The fictional Cyrano looms large, and a process that attempts to reveal a little of the human weaknesses and complexity behind a heroic façade might have been one of increasing disillusionment and disappointment. Instead, the real Cyrano, source of a legend, stands revealed as a man who richly deserves the respect, the attention and the affection currently only given to his fictional counterpart.

The real Cyrano wrote letters, plays and poetry and his stylistic range covered satire, tragedy and comedy. His masterwork was an innovative science fiction novel, a delirious, fantastical adventure in outer space, in which he imagined the hot air balloon, talking books, rocket propulsion, the eerie sensations of zero gravity and the lunar landing years ahead of their time. His work served as an important inspiration to other illustrious writers: Molière, Voltaire, Jonathan Swift, Jules Verne and H. G. Wells all owe a debt to Cyrano. Yet attempts to define this extraordinarily talented and daring individual quickly run into difficulty: murderous pacifist, serious comedian, frivolous intellectual, honest deceiver. Cyrano de Bergerac has always been a profoundly paradoxical figure: in his lifetime the real Cyrano, a difficult, daring and dangerous individual, provoked extreme responses, he was much loved and much hated. As a result opposing accounts of the man struggled for dominance, no single version was strictly factual or entirely objective. In the writing of both Cyrano's detractors and his apologists fact and fiction are interwoven and the outlines of the man and the legend haze and blur. In the late nineteenth century, these confused elements of Cyrano's story suddenly crystallized into two distinct accounts: the first saw the unadorned facts presented by a diligent academic and in the second the romantic legend was blazoned abroad by a playwright at the height of his powers. A new division emerged, which has since grown and deepened.

Today there are two distinct figures who share the name Cyrano de Bergerac. One, a fictional character with an enormous nose is celebrated, admired, even adored, while the other, the original, is forgotten, dismissed or ignored. A fiery, fascinating individual is now remembered only as a romanticized burlesque figure. The story of Cyrano has appeared in poems, novels, plays, on film, as an opera and even as a ballet. There is, however, only one element of the story which is common to each of the myriad versions of the man and the legend – all accounts agree that Cyrano de Bergerac was an invincible duellist. In a letter written by the man himself, he made light of his extraordinary sword-fighting reputation and came up with a neat summary of the paradoxical polarization of opinion he provoked, declaring: 'In truth, it is a very great consolation to me to be hated because I am loved; to find enemies everywhere because I have friends everywhere.'

I

A grain of truth

The play *Cyrano de Bergerac* by Edmond Rostand premiered in Paris on 28 December 1897. Audience and actors alike were immediately caught up in the delirious storm of a *succès fou.* At two o'clock in the morning all the lights were still blazing in the Théâtre de la Porte St Martin, the auditorium was still packed to capacity and outside in the surrounding streets crowds of curious onlookers had gathered. The final ovation lasted over an hour and after the first forty curtain calls the stage manager gave in and simply left the curtain raised. An account of the night's events appears in the memoir of Rostand that his wife Rosemunde published after his death. She claims that the emotional impact of the play had been so overwhelming that friends who had been at each other's throats for years suddenly threw themselves into one another's arms. Whether the production really did put an end to decade-long feuds or not, its success was undeniably phenomenal and enduring. At the age of twenty-nine, the poet Edmond Rostand had produced his masterpiece.

Cyrano de Bergerac not only transformed its author overnight into the darling of literary Paris, winning him the prestigious Croix de la Légion d'honneur, it also endured beyond all expectation. The play has never really lost its original extraordinary popularity. Over one hundred years have passed since the extravagant success of that opening night and *Cyrano de Bergerac* has been translated into many different languages and continues to be performed all over the world. Cyrano made his first appearance on the silver screen in 1900 and since then a variety of films have featured the legendary swordsman. Recent adaptations range from the lavish French costume drama directed by Jean-Paul Rappeneau to Steve Martin's updated Hollywood comedy *Roxanne*, complete with happy ending. From the very first, admirers of the real Cyrano scented the danger that Rostand's work represented. As early as 1898, the academic Pierre Brun predicted that: 'The legendary Cyrano will absorb the real Cyrano over the centuries', adding rather sadly, 'I have ceased to fool myself about this.'

When Edmond Rostand wrote his box-office smash he didn't create the legend of Cyrano, he merely added new fuel to a fire that had already been burning fitfully for over two hundred and fifty years. Tales of some of Cyrano de Bergerac's more extreme exploits had filtered down through the generations, taking on greater and more heroic proportions as time passed. Much the same could be said of Cyrano's nose, which had also swollen to epic proportions, thanks to the operation of time and exaggeration. The increasing inaccuracy of the Cyrano legend was in direct proportion to the increasing length of Cyrano's nose – Pinocchio-like, the longer the nose, the bigger the lie. We may be fairly certain that few members of the audience who attended the opening night had more than a hazy notion of the reality behind the legend. In the late nineteenth century Cyrano de Bergerac had become a grotesque caricature. Two and a half centuries after his death he was still remembered, but was variously dismissed as a dangerous lunatic, or a laughable eccentric.

Edmond Rostand created his own moving version of Cyrano's

life, which echoed the fairy tale 'Beauty and the Beast'. Like the authors of all the best fairy tales, he didn't allow facts to stand in the way of romance. Rostand's father was a successful barrister who wrote poetry in his spare time and he seems to have envisaged a similar career for his son. He financed Edmond's law degree, keen to see his offspring suitably qualified for a respectable, lucrative career. However, Rostand junior abandoned his legal training to devote himself entirely to poetry. It is hardly surprising then that this headstrong young man was uninterested in establishing the truth behind the legend of Cyrano de Bergerac. He longed to write dramatic, inspirational verse, to 'give lessons of the soul', not to replicate the accuracy and precision of dry legal documents.[1]

The stage Cyrano is a burlesque figure, a man whose nose is so disproportionately vast that his hideousness renders him savage. He has fought countless duels, and is reputed to be capable of killing a man just for looking at him askance. However, this fearless, ferocious Cyrano falls madly in love with his beautiful cousin Roxane. Cyrano's passionate devotion to Roxane exerts a powerful humanizing influence, rendering the bestial soldier vulnerable. Cyrano's desperation to be close to his beloved and his need to express his love (without risking her scorn) famously leads him to embrace an opportunity to woo her by proxy. He allows the Baron Christian de Neuvillette, an attractive, young cadet from his own regiment, who has caught his cousin's eye, to speak for him. Christian is so entranced by Roxane's beauty and wit that he cannot find the courage to speak to her himself and consequently he is happy to accept Cyrano's offer to write his love letters for him, and even allows Cyrano to make a moving speech on his behalf from the shadows beneath Roxane's balcony, pleading for a kiss. This balcony scene deliberately recalls Romeo and Juliet, and the action of the play unfolds in similarly tragic vein.

Directly after their hastily improvised wedding ceremony, Roxane's new husband, the Baron Christian de Neuvillette, is sent away from her to Arras on the orders of the Count de Guiche who is his jealous love rival. While they are besieged at Arras, Cyrano continues to write love letters to Roxane, braving enemy fire to cross the siege lines in order to send daily letters to his beloved. Roxane in turn risks her own life to follow her husband to the battlefield. Intoxicated by the letters, she determines to beg Christian to forgive her for having loved him at first just for his beauty. But her attempts to reassure Christian of the purity of her love for him backfire horribly. In her insistence that it is his soul, as revealed to her in his letters from the battlefield, that she loves so passionately, she unknowingly betrays to him the fact that it is Cyrano who has won her heart. Christian is killed by enemy fire before he can force Cyrano to admit the deception and ask Roxane to choose between them. The action of the play then skips forward fourteen years. The final act takes place in the courtyard of the convent where Roxane has shut herself away from the world to mourn the loss of her beloved husband. In the final scene a wounded and dying Cyrano arrives for his weekly visit to his 'old friend', he finally admits to Roxane that he was the one who wrote the letters but that he felt constrained to keep silent because although the tear stains on the final farewell letter were his own, the bloodstains were Christian's. The truth having finally been revealed to her too late Roxane laments,

> *I never loved but one man in my life.*
> *Now I must lose him twice.*[2]

The play itself is undeniably romantic and beautifully written, but its initial startling success was also underpinned by some extremely canny marketing. Rostand was fortunate that, as a charming and personable young poet, he had managed to find his way to the heart of the close-knit theatrical and literary community in *fin de siècle* Paris. He benefited from a close association with some of the leading figures in French theatre. In particular Rostand was spectacularly fortunate in his choice of leading man. Benoît-Constant Coquelin would play the title role over four hundred times in the course of the initial fourteen-month-long sell-out run of *Cyrano de Bergerac*. Coquelin also played the role in London and in the United States and was the first actor to play Cyrano on film. He was one of the most celebrated and successful actors of his generation, adored by the public and critics alike. Contemporary reviews of his performance praise 'the extraordinary brilliancy of M. Coquelin's action and delivery', giving a clear idea of the significance of Coquelin's skill in creating the role of Cyrano.[3] The distinguished English theatre critic C. E. Montague was unequivocal in his admiration of Coquelin's powers: 'the sheer comic force with which he embraced and enjoyed the idea of what he was acting. The communicable energy of his joy in all the contents of human nature was incomparable; no comedian in our time has glowed with a more radiant heat of life and delight.'[4]

In 1897, Coquelin was fifty-six years old and a highly experienced actor. In the first published edition of the play Rostand acknowledged the significant contribution that his talented lead had made to the creation of the play in a characteristically lyrical dedication. 'I had intended to dedicate this poem to the spirit of Cyrano. But since his soul has passed into you, Coquelin, I dedicate it to you.'[5] Rostand owed an additional debt of thanks to Coquelin for an open letter to the poet that the actor had written and which had appeared on the front page of *Le Petit Parisien*:

> In his work he does something that few men of today even among the most illustrious know how to do, he writes with his heart. Above all he is a sincere being . . . I am proud to have lived to come into contact with such a man and I am happy to have the chance to say so here: Cyrano has been the most wonderful creation of my career and the greatest joy of my existence.[6]

Another imposing figure who offered Rostand crucial support and exposure was the legendarily talented and eccentric actress Sarah Bernhardt. Bernhardt, who was known as 'the eighth wonder of the world', dined regularly with Rostand and his beautiful young wife and the poet had penned an earlier play *La Princesse Lointaine* specifically for her. *La grande Sarah* was at the height of her powers in 1897. At the age of fifty-three she had a distinguished career behind her and was the proprietor of her own theatre. Her endorsement was an extremely important seal of approval for a new work. Bernhardt also had a genius for publicity; early on in her career as a tragedienne she had let it be known that, convinced she was destined to die young, she had ordered herself a beautiful silk-lined coffin that she kept in her bedroom and occasionally slept in. She was constantly surrounded by a court of admirers and a menagerie that included a wolf, a leopard and a monkey named Darwin. She dispensed her patronage with regal aplomb. *Cyrano de Bergerac* represented a collaboration between a poet she considered a charming protégé and a fellow thespian who was one of her oldest colleagues and dearest friends. Bernhardt recognized immediately that the combination of Rostand's sublime poetry and Coquelin's overwhelming charisma would make for theatrical magic. She gave the production her blessing in typically extravagant fashion. The following letter to Coquelin was published in *Le Figaro* on the day after the premiere.

> I can't begin to tell you my joy for your triumph of yesterday and of this evening. What happiness, my Coq! What happiness! It is the triumph of Art, and of beauty. It's your immense talent! It's the genius of our Poet! I am so happy, oh! so! I send you my love, my heart beating with the purest joy and the sincerest friendship, Sarah.[7]

Sarah Bernhardt's ebullient lust for glory had enabled her to become an internationally recognized celebrity. Despite her dubious social status as an unapologetically unmarried mother she had embarked on successful tours of England and the United States; her trailblazing paved the way for a similar tour later undertaken by the cast of *Cyrano de Bergerac.*

Edmond Rostand was not just a dreamy romantic he was also an astute observer of the zeitgeist and he had recognized that the time was ripe for his swashbuckling sonneteer. The late nineteenth century was an uncomfortable period in French history, the economy was static, social welfare was failing, labour-management was increasingly problematic and the birth rate was falling. In 1870, Bismarck's Germany had defeated the French Army in the Franco-Prussian War, triggering the collapse of Napoleon III's Second Empire. In 1894, the nation was gripped by a profoundly divisive scandal, when the anti-Semitism underpinning the conviction of Captain Alfred Dreyfus for treason was revealed. Looking back, to an age when matters of honour were settled swiftly and decisively, sword in hand, allowed audiences to escape the uncertainties of the present and revel in a heroic past, when life was less complicated and heroes were unequivocally noble and dashing. This romantic fascination with the age of the musketeers had begun some fifty years earlier with a flowering of fictional re-creations of the seventeenth century. Most famously Alexandre Dumas had achieved enormous success with his series of novels detailing the daring escapades of d'Artagnan and the Three Musketeers: *Les Trois Mousquetaires* (1844), *Vingt Ans après* (1845) and *Le Vicomte de Bragelonne* (1848–50). Edmond Rostand shrewdly rewrote history and transformed Cyrano from an anti-establishment rebel into a national hero.

Just three years before the opening of the play, a rather different version of Cyrano's life story had appeared, with considerably less fanfare. In 1894, the academic Pierre Brun had published a complete edition of the works of Cyrano de Bergerac, accompanied by an account of his life. The work had begun as Brun's doctoral thesis at Montpellier University and the full title of the published version was *Savinien de Cyrano Bergerac – his Life and his Works drawn from previously unpublished documents*, which is admittedly a bit less snappy than Rostand's *Cyrano de Bergerac*. Brun's biography had been painstakingly pieced together from various sources that he had managed to unearth from the obscurity of parish records and the dark depths of the Bibliothèque Nationale. The aim of Brun's six years of dedicated research was to establish a clear, factual picture of the real Cyrano, unclouded by the exaggerations and rumour that his extraordinary career had always attracted. Ironically, Brun's new edition of Cyrano's life and works may very well have been a key element in drawing Rostand's attention to the subject.

Sadly, for the unassuming academic, his work was quickly overshadowed by Rostand's popular success and the adulation of enraptured critics who declared: 'We do not want realism we want fantasy.'[8] The reviewers also advised the public not to be disenchanted by Pierre Brun's book, but to go to the theatre and 'forget about Brun for an evening'.[9] Given the way in which the public readily embraced this advice, Brun could be forgiven for bitterly resenting Rostand and his creation. In fact, he remained remarkably calm and patient as six years of hard work, attempting to replace the legendary Cyrano with the real, were swept away on a tide of enthusiasm. Although clearly terribly disappointed, Brun refused to rage against Rostand. He understood and appreciated the powerful appeal of Rostand's lyrical distortion of the true story of Cyrano de Bergerac. An eager young academic named Émile Magne was quick to step into the breach, and shortly after the play opened Magne published a pamphlet in which he attacked the historical inaccuracies of Rostand's work. Brun refused to be drawn, however, affectionately dismissing Magne's study as unnecessary: 'With the bold intolerance of youth . . . he makes use of an enormous tome to crush a brilliant butterfly.'[10] Clearly the kindly old academic had a healthy sense of proportion.

Émile Magne may not have particularly impressed Brun with his account of the numerous factual errors to be found in the play, but his outspoken attack certainly succeeded in riling the playwright. The second edition of Magne's work contains a reproduction of Rostand's handwritten letter to the author furiously repudiating Magne's criticism. It seems that Edmond Rostand took great offence at his shaky grasp of history being highlighted in this way and promptly launched a misguided campaign to defend himself. However reluctant he was to criticize Rostand's work, which he greatly admired, Brun was not above enjoying a quiet revenge. He published a second academic study on the same theme as the first, and included a brief but cheerfully scathing reference to the poet's undignified response to Émile Magne's pamphlet. He also expressed disappointment that his own painstaking research would inevitably be overshadowed by the romantic appeal of Rostand's creation, and the works of the real Cyrano ignored by readers dazzled by the fictional hero: 'I had hoped that the real Cyrano would eventually replace the legendary Cyrano entirely. I had hoped – touching illusion – that I might have corrected various errors and approximations . . . It was not long before I was disenchanted.'[11]

Brun's second study of Cyrano was entitled *Savinien de Cyrano de Bergerac – Parisian Gentleman, the history and the legend*. His inclusion of the phrase 'Parisian Gentleman' in the title was significant, because one of the most basic errors about Cyrano, further propagated by Rostand's work, was the idea that the great swordsman was a Gascon nobleman from the Périgord region in the south-west of France. In fact the estate from which the family took their name was not the large prosperous Gascon town of Bergerac but a small rural estate just outside Paris. Far from belonging to the highest ranks of the Gascon nobility, the family were originally a pretty lowly bunch of Sardinian immigrants. The family name Cyrano was simply a French version of the Italian surname *Cirano*. Cyrano's first name, as Brun's title reveals, was Savinien. He was named after his paternal grandfather, who had begun life as a fishmonger.

The continued confusion over Cyrano's origins still persists today, despite the fact that Brun had published the parish records of Cyrano's baptism, proving incontrovertibly that he was born in the heart of Paris. This simple error is one of the most persistent and with good reason; it originated with that master of misinformation, Cyrano himself. If the family had owned the estate or *seigneurie* of Bergerac in Gascony, then they would necessarily also have been far richer and more influential than they were. It was no accident that Cyrano chose to join the most famous Gascon regiment of his day, the Cadets de Carbon de Castel-Jaloux. Not only did Cyrano join a Gascon regiment but he made quite sure to outdo them all in fulfilling the stereotype of a Gascon noble. He was fiercely independent and gained renown as a 'demon of bravery'. History is silent on the question of whether he also assumed the distinctive thick Gascon accent. Personally, I like to think he would have made that little extra effort. Despite Brun's attempts to situate his historical Cyrano in a detailed context the legend was too vigorous to be confined by the recitation of facts and dates. But it is to facts and dates that we must return in order to retrace the origins of the legend and understand its extraordinary vigour.

2

The time of games

In 1707 Abel-Pierre de Cyrano (the nephew of the great swordsman) ran into some legal trouble. In the course of his defence he confirmed the family's Sardinian origins. More recently, it has been discovered that on their arrival from Italy the family had originally settled in the provinces. The parish records of the town of Sens over 100 kilometres to the south-east of Paris, reveal details of a baptism in 1532 of one Savinien Cyrano, as well as later property transactions under the same name.[1] This is almost certainly Cyrano's grandfather, and it shows the dynamic head of the family selling up his interests in Sens and moving to the capital to seek his fortune. Cyrano's namesake, his grandfather Savinien greatly improved the family's lot by securing lucrative court appointments. It must have taken extraordinary amounts of confidence and charm to make the leap from the fish market to the royal court. Social mobility did exist in the seventeenth century but only in rare cases. Money talked, then as now, but on the whole if you were born a fishmonger you died a fishmonger and so did your children. Having seduced and married a nobleman's daughter, Savinien, the seafood-selling son of a Sardinian, had used her contacts to go on to become *secrétaire du roi*. This was a minor administrative position in the court of Henri IV, and Savinien would have paid good money for the privilege. He negotiated the cut-throat world of the court with wit and aplomb. After just two years he secured another even more lucrative sinecure, becoming *auditeur à la cour des Comptes*. This was another role similar to the first, with responsibility for assisting in the administration of the king's income from the complex system of taxes and duties. The salary for such a post was minimal; it was tacitly understood that in going about their duties, courtly administrators would naturally have ample opportunities to line their own pockets. In addition, appointees were exempt from taxation.

Savinien had used his gains to purchase the estates of Mauvières and Soub-Forêts in the idyllic setting of the valley of Chevreuse just outside Paris. It was partly thanks to his father's dynamism that Savinien's eldest son, Abel, Cyrano's father, was able to make a very advantageous alliance. In 1612, at the comparatively advanced age of forty-five, Abel married Espérance Bellanger. Espérance was worth waiting for. She was a minor heiress (her parents and all her siblings having died before her marriage) who came from a wealthy family of financiers. Abel and Espérance were married on the 3rd of September at the church of Saint-Gervais in the heart of Paris. An inventory of all the goods belonging to each of them was made at this time, as part of the financial settlement between the two, and although Espérance's half is lost we have a detailed list of Abel's possessions. It provides an interesting glimpse into the household into which Cyrano was born. The inventory includes a library of over a hundred fine-bound volumes of works, mostly in French and Italian but featuring Greek and Latin texts as well. The high proportion of books in Italian would seem to confirm the Cyrano family's Sardinian roots. The books themselves also suggest a cultured and intelligent readership – they cover a diverse range of subjects from legal texts to Rabelais, to Pliny's *Natural History*. This library would have been the original source of Cyrano's lifelong love affair with the written word. An interesting range of *objets d'art* also lend weight to the picture of a family not indifferent to the arts. Several sculptures and paintings of mythological subjects are listed, along with more domestic subjects: a little boy, a flute-player, a villager and his wife, a horse, two dogs, a bull and a lion. It is also noted that Abel owned half a horse; he shared the animal with his brother Samuel. There was a fine pearl necklace which must have made a welcome wedding gift for Espérance. The list also includes a life-size bust of Henri IV and thirteen medallions featuring the king and his queen.

The inventory builds a picture of the Cyranos as successful, cultivated members of the minor gentry, with strong ties of loyalty to the king. However, the family's fortunes did not continue to thrive. The root cause may perhaps be connected to the dramatic assassination of King Henri IV in 1610. Henri was stabbed to death by a mad monk, who leapt into the royal carriage. At the time of the king's sudden death, his baby son was still too young to rule the country and a regency was established to govern during the new king's minority. Many of Henri IV's underlings would have found themselves abruptly displaced by favourites of the new regime. Abel had not inherited his father's forceful personality and gift for diplomacy and so he had to live off his small legal practice and the income from the family's estates, being either incapable of regaining his father's position in the vicious, precarious world of the court, or unwilling to try. He did, however, manage to marry very well indeed. Although Abel would not achieve any spectacular social ascension, some of the relations on his new wife's side of the family rose to lucrative positions of great prestige and responsibility.

Cyrano's parents had already been married six years by the time he was born on 6 March in 1619. Their eldest son, Denis, had been born on 13 March 1614. In vivid contrast to Cyrano, Denis was devout and serious. He showed an early propensity for theological study and eventually entered the priesthood. Two more sons followed in quick succession, Antoine born 11 February 1616, and Honoré born 3 July 1617; both Antoine and Honoré died very young. Cyrano also had a younger brother named Abel born around 1624. He had at least one sister, Catherine, whose date of birth is lost to us. Altogether, Espérance gave birth at least six times, but only four of her children lived into adulthood and only Abel II went on to have a family and children of his own. It is quite possible that Cyrano also had other siblings whose names and dates of birth are lost to us, the baptismal record is far from reliable and in the seventeenth century death in childbirth was terrifyingly commonplace and infant mortality rates were cruelly high. In an age before vaccination small children had virtually no protection against the virulent epidemics that regularly swept through the community and mothers often succumbed to deadly post-natal infections.

In the larger towns and cities such as Paris, where Cyrano spent the first three years of his life, living conditions were unsanitary and filthy. There were no proper drains and no organized method of rubbish disposal, so infectious diseases were readily transmitted. The greater population density exacerbated the problem and consequently epidemics were more frequent in urban areas. Leprosy, typhoid, cholera and diphtheria were all common and usually fatal. Throughout Cyrano's lifetime terrifying outbreaks of the plague would also periodically strike the city, leaving thousands dead. The historian J. L. Flandrin, having looked at the way in which levels of infant mortality began to fall in the eighteenth century, comes to a distinctly disturbing conclusion, arguing that since, 'it cannot be explained by reasons of medicine or hygiene; we had simply ceased to let children die or to help them to die when they were not wanted.'[2] Whether one accepts this allegation of seventeenth-century infanticide or not, it is at the very least vividly apparent that attitudes towards children and family life were significantly different from our own. In a work published in 1622, when Cyrano was three years old, a young mother about to give birth to her sixth child is offered the following consolation by a friendly female neighbour: 'Before they are old enough to give you much trouble you will have lost half of them, or maybe all.'[3]

A child's initial chances of survival were reduced still further by the bourgeois practice of sending new-born babies away to be looked after by a wet-nurse who would breast-feed them until they were weaned, at which point they would be returned to the family home. A professional wet-nurse would be a woman from the lowest rank of society, and as a result the living conditions in which the baby would spend its earliest weeks of life would be the poorest it might ever experience. Fortunately, Cyrano was a strong and healthy baby and it was perhaps to reflect this vigour that he had been named after the dynamic head of the family, his paternal grandfather Savinien.

Despite the fact that the loss of a young child was a far more common occurrence than today, for every tiny unmarked grave there were also significant memorials to these brief lives erected by those privileged enough to be able to afford to indulge their grief. In contrast to portraits from previous centuries, seventeenth-century family groups often included images of children who had died in infancy. These little phantoms were generally immortalized in such a way as to render them indistinguishable from their surviving siblings; such paintings give no hint that certain of the subjects had died years before the painting was executed. In spite of the resignation in the face of high infant-mortality rates expressed by authors such as the great philosopher Montaigne, who remarked, 'I lost two or three children in their infancy, not without regret but without fuss', it is natural to assume that privately many families experienced this harsh fact of seventeenth-century life with a grief that was no less agonizing for being commonplace.[4]

In his prose masterpiece *The Voyage to the Moon* (1656) Cyrano seems to rebel against his humble origins, reflecting bitterly on the fact that a man's birth is the only aspect of his destiny over which he has absolutely no control. One of his central characters launches a surprisingly vehement attack on the biblical commandment 'Honour thy father and thy mother'. The hero is also confronted with the first great injustice of existence – the fact that in the moment of conception the baby, who is after all the one for whom the occasion has the greatest importance, is also the one with the least say in the matter. 'Alas! In an affair in which you were the only one concerned, you were the only person whose opinion was not consulted!'[5] Cyrano introduces the novel idea that rather than gratitude for having been brought into existence, a son owes his father resentment for having denied him the possibility of a more impressive birthright in a more illustrious family. In the superior rational society of the moon, as Cyrano's imagination saw it, the inhabitants recognized that the traditional 'tyrannical authority' of fathers was both unjust and unreasonable. He conjures up a vision of a nation in which the young men rule the family and take all important decisions without consulting the wishes of their elders, treating their parents with disrespect that borders on disdain.

Cyrano deliberately took the argument to its extreme, and Dyrcona the space-travelling hero of *The Voyage to the Moon* is given the following disturbing advice by his lunar protector: 'Tread on the belly of the father who engendered you, trample on the bosom of the mother who conceived you.'[6] The shocked hero is later reassured by his mentor that some degree of exaggeration had been necessary in order to correct the wrong-headedness of the poor misguided earthling. He compares his technique to that of a gardener attempting to straighten out a tree that is growing twisted: 'I was obliged to act like one who wishes to straighten a crooked tree; twisting it to the other side so that between the two contortions it grows straight again.'[7] This vivid explanation is also the perfect metaphor for Cyrano's satirical writing; it serves as a useful warning to the reader not to take any of the ideas expressed too literally. The extreme nature of Cyrano's attack on the parent-child relationship is far from providing proof that Cyrano had an unhappy childhood or a troubled relationship with his parents, it is a typical moment of provocation. But some documentary evidence does suggest that, whatever may have been the case when Cyrano was a child, in later life his relationship with his father did degenerate alarmingly. It is impossible to recover the fine detail of Cyrano's boyhood but a minimum of investigation serves to cast doubt on the rosy vision of a cosseted aristocratic background which Edmond Rostand imagined for his hero.

In a poignant early scene between Cyrano and Roxane the two cousins evoke an idyllic picture of their shared childhood.

Roxane: But, for the confession I have come to make,
I need to find in you my almost-brother
With whom I played in the park, by the lake.
Cyrano: Yes, you came to Bergerac every summer.
Roxane: You used reeds for your swords in those days.
Cyrano: And you used corn-silk for your doll's hair.
Roxane: It was the time of games.[8]

The real Cyrano did have a cousin named Madeleine Robineau, who may have served as the model for Roxane, but she was ten years older than her swashbuckling relative; of course the pair may still have played together in their childhood, but not in the landscaped grounds of a stately chateau in Bergerac. As we have seen, Cyrano had lived in the heart of Paris until the age of three. In 1622, the family moved out to the manor house on the estate of Mauvières near Chevreuse, to the south-west of Paris on the road to Chartres. The house was beautifully situated beside a river in the thickly wooded splendour of the Valley of Chevreuse, an area currently protected for its outstanding natural beauty. The estates were not large; there was a working watermill and a few farm buildings attached, but no elegant park or ornamental lake in sight. The chateau was completely rebuilt in the eighteenth century so the only original traces of Cyrano's childhood home that survive today are the watermill and a very pretty dovecote. The name Bergerac had attached to the lands in the late fourteenth century when they were awarded as a gift from King Charles V to Ramond de la Rivière de la Martigne for his bravery in regaining that city from the invading English. La Rivière was originally from Bergerac and so renamed the meadows to the west of his land in honour of his home town and of his achievement, so that the seigneurie became known as de Mauvières et de Bergerac.

Rostand's duet of shared memories is perfectly pitched to serve the dramatic needs of the scene; it establishes the harmonious counterpoint of two voices which will then be abruptly broken. In the play Roxane has summoned Cyrano to a private rendezvous in order to confess to him her love for Christian. She hopes to enlist his help in protecting the young Baron (who has just joined Cyrano's own regiment) and also in passing on the flattering news of her interest in him. The exchange is cleverly constructed to reveal to the audience, but not to the embarrassed and oblivious Roxane, that a deeply smitten Cyrano is expecting her proposed avowal of a secret passion to concern him rather more directly. His heroic attempts to conceal the pain caused by the abrupt discovery of her feelings for Christian are subtly underplayed; only as Roxane leaves him with a parting compliment on his extraordinary bravery in fighting alone against one hundred armed men does he allow himself the sardonic reflection: 'I've done better than that since then.'[9]

As we have seen, Rostand's version of Cyrano's life was criticized in his lifetime for the inaccuracies and anachronisms which abound in the work. Émile Magne, the young academic who put his criticisms into print, objected to the 'hybrid' nature of historical fiction. He highlighted the fact that Rostand's *Cyrano* was at times appallingly inaccurate and at others a perfect reflection of the original.[10] As the older and wiser academic Pierre Brun pointed out, it is a pointless exercise to look for academic precision in a work of fiction. Rather than focusing on the numerous occasions when Rostand chose inspiration over historical investigation, it is more interesting to consider the elements of the life of the real Cyrano which did make it onto the stage.

Certain details in the play reveal that Rostand had paid close attention to Cyrano's own writing. For example, when the fictional Cyrano looks back with longing on a childhood spent in the countryside, climbing trees and eating unripe blackberries he voices a deep attachment to the rural landscape, which appears time and again in the writing of the real Cyrano. In a letter 'On a house in the Country' the absent host is reproached for staying away from his 'enchanted palace'. Cyrano waxes lyrical about the myriad beauties of a landscape scented with violets and wild roses, where a stream whispers the story of its journey to the pebbles, and the trees towering above him seem to carry the whole world suspended from their roots. Cyrano's delight in the countryside is unequivocal, 'I have found the Garden of Eden, I have found the golden age and the source of eternal youth . . . here one laughs with one's whole heart.'[11] His unfailing fascination with animals, birds and plants and his keen eye for the details of the natural world were to provide some interesting highlights in his satirical writing, not least in the moment in *The Voyage to the Sun* (1662) when the hero, Dyrcona, is put on trial for the crime of being human by an enlightened parliament of birds.

Since Cyrano's entire adult life was spent in the city of Paris (with the obvious exception of his time on the battlefield) it seems that his passionate relationship with the natural world must have begun in childhood. Cyrano's family moved to the countryside when he was three, just as he reached an age to be able to appreciate it. His increasing awareness of his surroundings coincided with a new-found freedom. Released from the confines of a town house in the heart of a bustling city, he would have been able to toddle about and explore this newly expanded world. Although the real Cyrano retained a lifelong affection for the scenes of his childhood, Rostand's nostalgic vision springs from a nineteenth-century romantic idea of childhood. The reality is likely to have been much darker.

In 1618, the year in which Cyrano's mother became pregnant, events were taking place elsewhere in Europe that would eventually impact on the destiny of her unborn child. On the morning of the 23rd of May, the power struggle between Catholic and Protestant factions in Northern Europe erupted in a small-scale violent confrontation that would have extremely wide-ranging consequences. Members of a Protestant assembly in Prague had come to the conclusion that a provocative confrontational act was required if their concerns were to be taken seriously. At around 9 a.m., a group of armed men forced their way into the Hradschin Castle and up to a council room where they found four of the ten regents appointed by the Catholic Habsburg Emperor Matthias to rule the kingdom of Bohemia. Two of the four, namely Vilém Slawata and Jaroslav Martinitz were known to support a plan to re-Catholicize Bohemia. First Martinitz and then Slawata were hurled bodily from a high castle window. Slawata managed to cling to the sill but his grip was loosened by a couple of vicious blows from a knife handle. Finally, a scribe was thrown out after the two regents. The dramatic events of 'the defenestration of Prague' (as the incident became known) precipitated Bohemia and the Habsburg Empire into a conflict that would gradually encompass most of Western Europe. The power struggle between Protestant and Catholic factions already smouldering away throughout Europe was ignited by this spark and raged on for thirty blood-soaked years. All three of the men thrown out of the window actually survived. Opinion was divided at the time as to what it was that saved them. The Catholics insisted that the men were rescued by ministering angels, whereas the Protestants offered the more prosaic explanation of a soft landing in a giant pile of manure. In Cyrano's lifetime, France would in turn be drawn into the Thirty Years War. He lived through a turbulent era when the nation was periodically ravaged by war and violence was endemic in society.

One particularly notable event in Cyrano's early childhood was the explosion of a dramatic scandal at court. The execution of the dashing young duellist, Comte de Montmorency-Bouteville, in 1627 caused a huge public outcry. Cyrano was only eight at the time but the execution was the culmination of a long-running, notorious controversy of the sort uniquely fitted to appeal to the imagination of a small boy. It certainly seems to have marked him strongly and may even have been instrumental in dictating certain elements of his future career. In February 1626, shortly before Cyrano's seventh birthday, King Louis XIII had issued an edict designed to reinforce the ban on duelling. Cardinal Richelieu, the king's ambitious advisor and the most powerful politician of the era, had hoped to eradicate the aristocratic practice of settling quarrels over matters of honour with bloody swordfights. The statesmen of France had been trying for years to wipe out this fatal craze but to no avail. Richelieu himself had personal experience of the damage a duel could inflict – his father had killed a man in a duel and his eldest brother died in another. Duelling was already illegal, having been banned by laws passed in 1566 and 1579. Nevertheless, the young nobles continued to slaughter one another.

The edict of February 1626 had imposed heavy penalties on duellists. The act of issuing the challenge to a duel was rendered punishable by the loss of offices, the confiscation of half of the challenger's property and his banishment for the period of three years. If the challenger or the defender did not die in the duel they could both be stripped of their noble status, or even executed. The illegal art of the duel therefore carried a double death penalty – if your opponent didn't kill you there was a chance that the king might. One man in particular bitterly resented this attempt at royal interference in what was deemed to be an established right of the nobility. Comte François de Montmorency-Bouteville was twenty-eight years old, and already the successful champion of twenty-two duels, when he determined to stage a dramatic public protest against the edict. On the 14th of May 1627, he arranged for duels to take place between six noblemen in the middle of the Place Royal in broad daylight. One well-known noble, Bussy d'Amboise, died in the duel and another man was gravely wounded. Comte de Montmorency-Bouteville and his cousin Comte des Chapelles, who had both survived the contest, fled Paris. They were soon hunted down and brought back to the capital, where they were imprisoned in the Bastille. Montmorency-Bouteville's family, the illustrious Montmorency-Luxembourg clan, were one of the highest in the land, and they attempted to close ranks to get Montmorency-Bouteville and des Chapelles pardoned.

At the trial, the influential Duc de Montmorency and the Prince de Condé appealed for clemency alongside the Comtesse de Montmorency-Bouteville and other aristocratic ladies. Despite the intercession of these influential figures and the emotional testimony given by the countess, Montmorency-Bouteville's young wife, who was pregnant at the time, the king remained unmoved. The two men were publicly executed in the Place de Grève on the 22nd of June 1627. The king's only comment was 'I pity the woman but I must defend my authority.'[12] Public opinion was outraged. The people of Paris had followed the details of the case avidly, from the first dramatic moment when the young count had publicly demonstrated his contempt for the anti-duelling law in such spectacular fashion. There were huge crowds present at his execution. It is unlikely, however, that he and des Chapelles gained much comfort from the fact that *le tout Paris* had gathered to register their anger at the king's harsh decision. Richelieu responded by producing propaganda pamphlets, designed to convince the people of the justice of the punishment and the iniquity of duelling.

To a young boy, the story must have been endlessly fascinating. Later in life, Cyrano paid homage to his boyhood hero in a letter, recounting a vivid dream about a journey through the afterlife in which he described hearing Montmorency-Bouteville's voice. The count's ghost is heard raging against his solitude. His isolation is explained as the result of the fear that his duelling prowess inspires in all those around him: 'I distinguished the voice of de Bouteville, who was thundering on about the fact that everyone refused his company; but his anger did him no service: no one dared to approach him for fear of a quarrel. That man carried solitude with him.'[13] Cyrano would eventually become as notorious and skilful a practitioner of the illegal duel as the flamboyant count himself. Another effect of the scandal would become apparent much earlier on, when the young Cyrano, tremendously impressed by Montmorency-Bouteville's fierce independence and flagrant disregard for authority, began to imitate his hero's determined defiance in his own private rebellion.

When he was about seven years old Cyrano was sent away from home to be taught alongside other boys his age by the local country curate. It was here that he first met Henri Le Bret. Their friendship would last a lifetime and Le Bret would prove to be Cyrano's most loyal and devoted ally. Cyrano's friend would also eventually become his first editor and biographer. It was common practice for families to send their sons away to be educated at around the age of seven or eight, and until that age Cyrano would have been taught the rudiments of reading and writing at home, spending all his time with his mother and siblings. At around seven years old, a boy was supposed to have left the earliest phase of childhood behind and had to be ready to assume the beginnings of an independent existence outside the nursery. Monsieur Héroard, the doctor who was in charge of supervising the education of the future King Louis XIII, kept a meticulous diary detailing his supervision of the prince's upbringing which makes for intriguing and occasionally disturbing reading. In the diary Héroard describes the moment when he informed the young prince that he must leave his nursery playthings behind and start behaving like an adult, 'You must not play with these little toys any more . . . you are big now, you are no longer a child.'[14] Louis was six years old.

Apart from a couple of lines penned by Le Bret in which he describes the curé with whom he and Cyrano lodged as 'a good country priest who took in little boarders', there is no surviving record of Cyrano's early education.[15] Rostand's vision of a high-spirited young Cyrano leaping around brandishing a reed for a sword may well be perfectly accurate, but it is also obviously incomplete. The curé who looked after the young Cyrano left no records but some years later a curé, in a similar country parish, began a journal in which he recounted the everyday details of his existence and that of his parishioners. The journal of Alexandre Dubois makes for eye-opening reading; rather than a rural paradise the parish is revealed as a decidedly dangerous place. Henri Platelle who edited a modern edition of the diary remarks on 'the spirit of violence which seems to reign in the village'.[16] The very first entry tells the story of a dangerous criminal who had burned down the vicarage several years earlier. The unnamed arsonist had also murdered one Hubert Couteau the censor from a nearby town and the parishioners took it upon themselves to ensure that vengeance was swift. 'He was killed himself in the most tragic manner, more than twenty villagers having dipped their hands in the blood of this murderer, immediately after he had bathed his own in the blood of the poor censor.'[17]

The priest's diary is packed with incident; some children spot a group of Spanish soldiers hiding in the wheatfields and the enemies are duly hunted down and killed. A brawl breaks out in front of the church which leads to blood being spilt in the graveyard. A pregnant girl and her unsuitable lover refuse to submit to the authority of her male relatives and the lover ends up shooting the girl's brother. The pair then run off to get married leaving the brother to die of his wounds. Inseparable friends both called Pierre destroy their friendship and themselves in a row over a woman which ends in another fatal shooting. Dubois also gives a particularly lively thumbnail sketch of a honey-tongued criminal who ends up being hanged, leaving behind a pregnant wife and three small children. 'He was a hypocrite who stole everyday, and who, when his curate admonished him, responded with such fine words that if you didn't know him you would take him for a saint.'[18] In another entry a marauding soldier (not an enemy but one of the French troops) was caught stealing a chicken and shot. We have no way of knowing whether similar events took place in the parish in which Cyrano's schoolmaster was curé, but none of the incidents inspires any degree of surprise or outrage in the priest and his resigned attitude gives some indication that such incidents were far from being isolated cases and the parish far from unusual. The boys would inevitably have seen and heard a great deal as the curé was the focal point of the community. The priest's responsibility for collecting the church tax, administering the last rites, and recording births and deaths made him a figure respected and resented in about equal measure.

Dubois complains frequently about the reluctance of his parishioners to attend divine services and even mutters darkly about the 'blackness of their souls'. Cyrano and Le Bret would have had no option about attendance and the inescapable close-up view which Cyrano had of the church as a small boy may well have contributed to his determined atheism in later life. An extract from a contemporary sermon written by one Father Lejeune and entitled 'On the duty of Fathers' gives an indication of the attitude towards education encouraged by the moral leaders of the community. Lejeune insists that regular beatings form an indispensable part of the correct upbringing of children and in particular of boys. His rationale is that any amount of physical suffering is far preferable to the spiritual agony which ultimately awaits youngsters who are left to their own devices. 'If you do not punish your children they profane the churches . . . when they form the habit of swearing, lying, cursing . . . when they haunt meetings of girls . . . if you knew the evil which would result for them you would prefer to break their arms and legs.'[19] It was hoped that the mortification of the flesh would lead to the purification of the soul. Educational discipline was often the result of an attempt to achieve, not just good conduct from pupils, but also moral and spiritual improvement. That the result of such practices was the raising of generations of devout and pure-minded young men seems decidedly unlikely. In Cyrano's case at least we may be certain that the theory was an abject failure. In such a context his provocative attack on paternal authority suddenly becomes rather more understandable.

Le Bret's account of the boys' early education leaves little doubt that the young Cyrano was simply too clever for his own good. He describes Cyrano's 'aversion' for the pedantic professor and his lack of respect for the curé's learning, which Le Bret admits was minimal. He reveals that Cyrano considered his first schoolmaster incapable of teaching him anything at all, and that he paid little attention to his lessons as a result and still less to his teacher's corrections. The precocious little troublemaker was not, however, as unremittingly obnoxious as his extravagant contempt for the curate might suggest. In fact, he won the love and admiration of at least one of the adults who knew him as a small boy. In 1628, when he was nine years old, Cyrano's godmother, Marie Feydeau, died. Her will made special provision to leave him a legacy of six hundred *livres*. This legacy was in the form of an annuity, which was to be used, initially, to help fund Cyrano's studious older brother Denis as he made his preparations for the priesthood, but was ultimately to be given to Cyrano in its entirety on his parents' death, with no restrictions as to its intended use. It was by no means a matter of course for a godparent to single out their godchild for a generous bequest of this nature and it seems to imply that the mischievous young Cyrano had won his godmother's heart. As a little boy Cyrano was already capable of inspiring great affection and loyalty in those closest to him.

Le Bret reveals that Cyrano's rebellion against the regime in the home of the country curate was ultimately successful. He managed to persuade his father to move him back to Paris.

> He paid so little attention to his lessons and to his corrections that his father, who was a good old gentleman but fairly indifferent to the education of his children, and too credulous of Cyrano's complaints suddenly took him away; and without verifying whether his son would be better elsewhere he sent him to this town [Paris] where he left him to his own devices until the age of nineteen.[20]

The fact that Le Bret criticizes Cyrano's father for indulging his son and giving in to his request to leave the home of the curate suggests that he may have resented being left behind for a certain time to face the uninspiring lessons alone. This would have been particularly galling because Le Bret was a couple of years older than Cyrano. It seems probable given their enduring friendship that Cyrano and Le Bret were eventually reunited in one of the colleges in the centre of Paris where the sons of the gentry traditionally went to finish off their education. There is no surviving written record to prove Cyrano's attendance at a particular college but it seems likely that he would have followed the traditional educational path and his writing reveals a strong link with one college in particular, the Collège de Beauvais.

Cyrano's first success as a professional writer was a comedy entitled *Le Pédant Joué.* This play was not performed in public until 1645, when Cyrano was twenty-six years old, but certain scenes seem to have been composed much earlier. It is entirely possible that Cyrano began work on the play while still at college. The central character is a pedantic college principal named Granger. The principal of the Collège de Beauvais was an erudite and pedantic professor of Rhetoric named Jean Grangier. The real Grangier was legendary for his avarice and for his vicious treatment of the young pupils in his charge. He had a longstanding affair with one of the college servants who had several children by him. When he reached an age where it became clear that no legitimate offspring were going to be forthcoming, thanks to the failure of various attempts on his part to find a respectable bride, he decided to legitimize his existing children, by marrying their mother. This sparked off something of a scandal, not because of the relationship, or the resulting children, such liaisons were commonplace and were accepted as such provided those concerned were vaguely discreet. Rather, it was the attempt to make such a relationship respectable and to change the status of the woman concerned that was seen to be perverse and dishonourable. Grangier had to apply for special dispensation from the church authorities for the marriage to be allowed.

During this time a rebellion broke out at the college. The students accused Grangier of enriching himself at their expense through the corrupt administration of college funds. The professor was famously miserly and certainly didn't use the money paid by the college parents to keep the boys in grand style. It is likely that the scandal of Grangier's wedding had played a significant part in igniting the student rebellion. However, the students were unable to prove that Grangier had been misappropriating college funds and the rebellion was soon quashed.

The plot of Cyrano's *Le Pédant Joué* reworks a familiar theme of seventeenth-century comedy, in which a profoundly unsympathetic central character is duped and outwitted by his subordinates, to the great delight of the audience. The title of the play, which translates as 'The Pedant Duped', highlights this theme and promises the audience the pleasure of seeing an authority figure brought down a peg or three. The basic plot concerns the attempts of the pedant of the title to win the hand of the beautiful young heroine Genevote de la Tremblaye. In the course of the action the professor is constantly outwitted and undermined by his own son; Granger junior is his rival for Genevote's affections and is aided by a particularly crafty manservant named Corbinelli. The heroine has no intention of allowing herself to be shackled to the repellent old man; she has fallen in love with his rebellious son. At the end of the play the young people triumph and the pedant is forced to agree to their marriage. At which point the son whisks his new bride off to bed, leaving the professor to the consolations of philosophy.

The pedant's hapless pursuit of the feisty Genevote may perhaps have been inspired by one of Grangier's own doomed attempts to find a respectable bride. Cyrano's play also depicts the professor as a miser, which recalls the suspicion of the students of Beauvais that the original Professor Grangier was hoarding their fees rather than spending them appropriately on the college and the students. In one notable scene Genevote launches into an exhaustive, insulting description of Granger senior to his face; she pretends to welcome the pedant's attentions, while simultaneously asking him to join her in laughing at a particularly horrible, old college professor that she claims to have heard about. Even when he recognizes himself in her insulting description the professor does not give up hope of winning her hand. The insults in question read exactly like the kind of scatological invective a vengeful fourteen-year-old might concoct, being rather laboured and heavily reliant on schoolboy humour. The pedant is likened to a legendary tree that, in its various parts, can provide all the necessities of life for an entire nation. A brief extract will be more than enough to give an idea of the whole,

> Genevote: . . . his sores provide the meal, his ears the sails of the windmill; his arse the wind to make the sails turn, his mouth the bread oven; and his person the donkey to carry the flour. As for his nose, well it's just asking for us to have a dig. This wonderful nose arrives everywhere a quarter of an hour before its master; ten reasonably fat cobblers could take shelter from the rain underneath it to do their work.[21]

Ironically, this impassioned outpouring of bile would come back to haunt its creator. Edmond Rostand borrowed the nose gags from this passage and had his fictional Cyrano use them against himself. In an early scene in Rostand's play, the stage Cyrano attacks a man who has insulted his nose. Deriding the other's pathetic lack of imagination, Cyrano promptly reels off a series of far more creative insults. Although Rostand may have played with the facts he caught the spirit of Cyrano; this was a man who, even in his teens, was already immensely proud of his satirical creativity, and who relished the challenge of devising increasingly elaborate and inventive insults. The teaching methods of the seventeenth century did not allow for the expression of imagination or individuality by pupils, and this may be the reason why Cyrano first began to write creatively. Cyrano's response to the repressive religious regime, which was standard educational practice at the time, was an unrelenting anti-authoritarian stance. He would retain an element of that adolescent rebelliousness throughout his adult life.

3

A dangerous tendency

In the legend of Cyrano, the rebelliousness that marks the hero's character and the fact that he 'carries solitude with him' (like the Comte de Montmorency-Bouteville) are attributed to his physical difference and the sense of isolation that this imposes. The single fact about Cyrano de Bergerac that most people remember is that he had a big nose. On stage Cyrano's hypersensitivity about his appearance is the axis around which almost all of the dramatic action turns. The historical Cyrano does not seem to have been plagued by any such morbid dissatisfaction with his own appearance. In fact, there is evidence to suggest rather the reverse. There is a portrait of Cyrano that was engraved in the year before his death. It shows him in three-quarter profile, his eyes soulfully downcast. This pose hardly seems the most likely to be adopted by a man who wished to minimize the impact of his supposed 'disfigurement' since it throws his considerable snout sharply into relief. The portrait reveals that the real Cyrano was not hideous and that, although he did have a fairly long beaky nose, he definitely didn't have a complex about it. If anything Cyrano was rather proud of this distinguishing feature and made various jokes about it being a sign of superiority to have a large nose. These same jokes would ultimately be turned against their creator in the process of his transformation into the legendary grotesque.

In *The Voyage to the Moon* the hero is surprised to learn that a big nose can be a particularly useful attribute. When he asks a lunarian to tell him the time he is bewildered that the man simply lifts his head a little and turns a broad fixed grin upon him. It is only later that he learns that the men in the moon tell the time in this manner, using the shadow cast by their noses on to the dial of their teeth as a rudimentary sundial. He is also later informed that on the moon small nosed people are not allowed to breed; his host explains the logic of this 'barbarity' by revealing that: 'We have observed over thirty centuries that a large nose is like a sign above the door of our corporal homes that says "Herein dwells a man who is witty, prudent, courteous, affable, generous and liberal".'[1]

Apart from the odd passing allusion to his supposed noble Gascon origins the fictional versions of the legendary Cyrano generally depict a mature man, whose story is taken up only at the height of his career, presupposing an unremarkable youth. In fact the real Cyrano died at the age of thirty-six, and at the high point of his swashbuckling heyday he was only twenty years old. This quirk of chronology in the transformation from life to legend springs from Rostand's original casting of the portly 56-year-old Coquelin in the lead role. Ever since, representations of Cyrano on stage and screen have all tended to take their cue from Rostand, and Cyrano is often played by a mature man, while Roxane and Christian are interpreted by younger actors. Rostand's decision to pass over Cyrano's youth in dignified silence was perhaps also inspired by his awareness that a mysterious shadow hung over Cyrano's adolescence. The end of the 1630s, when Cyrano was in his late teens, was a distinctly enigmatic point in his career. Despite his confident declaration in later life that, 'it would be better to allow young people to govern their families rather than the elderly',

Cyrano's own early youth seems at first glance to have been a far from illustrious time.[2] In Henri Le Bret's brief biography of his friend, the author expresses mild resentment on the subject of Cyrano senior's laissez-faire attitude to his son's education and his decision to allow Cyrano to spend his teenage years in Paris unsupervised. Le Bret's criticism seems to spring, not just from the fact that for a time he was left behind in the country without his friend, but also from the fact that eventually Cyrano's father seems to have regretted allowing his son such freedom.

The roots of the quarrel that would erupt between father and son lie not only in Cyrano's questionable conduct as a headstrong youth, but also in the fact that the pair had very different priorities and fundamentally different temperaments. Savinien the elder, Cyrano's grandfather, had never been content with his lot as a bourgeois tradesman and had worked hard to escape his humble origins. Cyrano inherited this desire to achieve nobility at any price. Abel on the other hand had none of his father's restless determination to improve the family's social standing. This indifference to aristocratic pretension was evident in Abel's decision to sell the family estates of Mauvières and Bergerac. In 1636, Cyrano's father signed over the land to Antoine Balestrier, seigneur d'Arbalestrière, for the princely sum of 17,200 livres. Abel had grown up in the city and was content with the comfortable existence of the urban bourgeoisie. He may have preferred the ready money that the sale provided to the surface appearance of gentility, which the possession of land could bestow. Abel de Cyrano was unusual in the family for his lack of pretension to nobility. When he sold off the family land and returned to the centre of Paris, the whole family should, by rights, have ceased using the names de Bergerac and de Mauvières and the associated crests, since they no longer had any legal claim to do so.

Despite his father's chosen course of action, Cyrano was not about to abandon his dignified title and return to the homely

Savinien de Cyrano. Not only did Cyrano continue to use the name de Bergerac throughout his life but he also occasionally assumed more heroic-sounding christian names: Alexandre, for the great warrior king Alexander the Great and Hercule for the invincible hero of Greek legend.

The practice of appropriating key signifiers of noble rank was to become increasingly common among the wealthy urban elites of Cyrano's time. In his comic epic *Francion*, first published in 1623, the novelist Charles Sorel jokes about a 'fat rogue' who calls himself *le Sieur de Guillaume* not realizing that the noble sounding 'de' needs to appear before the name of a seigneurie and not before a christian name and that calling himself the Lord of William is not going to convince anybody.[3] Significant tax exemptions made noble status all the more desirable and the numbers of the fraudulent nobility were so overwhelming that the king was eventually forced to take action. In 1666, Louis XIV ordered a nationwide investigation that lasted eight years. Those claiming noble rank were required to present documentary proof of their claims or cease all pretension to nobility and pay up on their outstanding taxes. The royal crackdown came into effect after Cyrano's death and his nephew was fined for continuing to use the name associated with the estates sold by Cyrano's father some forty years earlier. The sale took place when Cyrano was seventeen years old, at the high point of his carefree existence as a student in the capital. It has been alleged that the young Cyrano had run up gambling debts so great as to force his father's hand in the sale, but no documentary evidence exists to support this claim. The loss of the family's estates would have hit Cyrano particularly hard; he had always been happiest in the countryside and his later works reflect this passionate love of the natural world. Although as an adolescent he was intent on tasting all the indulgences that the city had to offer, in later years he would look back with regret to the lost Elysium of the countryside.

Cyrano's anger at his father's decision to sell off the country estates and his conviction that he could have handled the family's fortunes better himself, may help to explain the theme of father–son conflict which runs throughout his works. In *The Pedant Duped* the main orchestrator of the professor's downfall is his own son. Another contemporary example of a father–son dispute provides a vivid illustration of the high-handedness of parental authority in action. After an argument with his son and the exchange of angry letters on both sides, Henri de la Trémoille's son (a near contemporary of Cyrano) refused to apologize to his father and, as a result, he received the following letter.

> Know then, ingrate, that you do not deserve to be treated like the least of my servants, who has not merited as you have, every sort of punishment . . . learn that except for my mercy you ought to demand nothing but leave to die . . . the parricide committed by Cromwell and his colonels is a lesser crime than the ingratitude of an unnatural son, since it touches a father more keenly than the executioner's axe.[4]

La Trémoille junior did not respond favourably to this fire and brimstone, and the two were never reconciled. The story represents a parallel to that of Cyrano and his father whose relationship could so easily have fractured in similar fashion. Cyrano, or more accurately Savinien junior, had inherited his paternal grandfather's restless spirit; at first this echo of his own father may well have been a source of pride to Abel. But once the sale of the land brought the two into direct conflict it is likely that Abel would have reacted with anger and resentment that his son should presume to criticize his decisions.

When Le Bret came to write his biography of Cyrano he passes over the period marked by this family dispute in haste, but not without dropping an intriguing veiled hint at unspecified debauchery: 'That age at which human nature is more easily corrupted and the great freedom he had to do whatever he pleased led him to a dangerous tendency . . .'[5] Le Bret goes on to say that having finished his own studies and resolved on joining up he decided to persuade Cyrano that they should join the king's army together. The decision to enlist was a stroke of genius on the part of Le Bret. The army was the perfect solution to Cyrano's crisis. Through deeds of military daring, a young man could earn himself the gratitude of his monarch, and in so doing ascend the dizzying heights of the nobility far more rapidly than by any other route. All new recruits at officer level were automatically ennobled and entitled to style themselves *écuyer* (squire). In the military, Cyrano would find, not only the discipline necessary to control a decidedly eccentric and wayward spirit, but also an outlet for his extraordinary energy and courage. As so often in his life, the dominant theme directing Cyrano's career was to be friendship. Without the steadying influence of his best friend, Cyrano could easily have found himself abandoned by his family, disinherited and disowned. If Le Bret had not been there to save him from himself, his writing career might never have been, and his star might have faltered and faded before he even reached adulthood.

Henri Le Bret's tantalizing hints of decadence and corruption have inspired the curiosity of almost all who have taken an interest in Cyrano. Le Bret gives no detail about the specific nature of the 'dangerous tendency' from which his friend needed rescuing. There is no way to conclusively ascertain what Le Bret is referring to and as a result the temptation is to allow the imagination to run riot. In 1834, Théophile Gautier wrote an article for the review *La France Littéraire*, ostensibly in order to rescue Cyrano's neglected literary reputation. Gautier succumbed to the temptation to fill in the gaps in Cyrano's intriguing biography. His interpretation of Cyrano's 'lost years' is particularly appealing and seems to have had a certain influence on Rostand. 'The good old days of beautiful, poetic courtesans, the time of balconies climbed, of silken rope-ladders, of ballets and masquerades, of that Spanish gallantry solemn and delirious at the same time, devoted to the point of inanity, ardent to the point of ferocity.'[6] His account of these 'beautiful adventuresses', the poetic courtesans, is tinged with both fear and lust; they were 'voluptuous and proud creatures loving gold, blood and perfumes with an equal love'.[7] In his imagination Gautier conjures up a heady mix of danger and desire. Then, carried away with his own invention, he declares it inevitable that Cyrano should have strayed awhile among such irresistible temptations. A survey of all the distractions on offer to a young man in seventeenth-century Paris may cast useful light on the mystery of Cyrano's time amid 'dangerous' temptations and lend a little more substance to Le Bret's veiled hint.

Thomas Overbury, an English traveller to France who published his *Observations* on his return, commented disdainfully on the common French tendency to abandon academic study at an early age. 'The Gentlemen are all good outward men, good Courtiers, good Soldiers, and knowing enough in Men and businesse, but meerly ignorant in matters of letters, because at fifteene they quit bookes and begin to live in the world.'[8] It is unclear at what stage Cyrano left the Collège de Beauvais, but it seems probable that he did so reasonably early on, being jealous of his freedom and determined to live the life of a young nobleman with appropriate abandon. A certain dalliance with the seamy underworld of the city was considered as something of a gentlemanly rite of passage. François Lhuillier, the father of one of Cyrano's closest friends (a young man known as La Chapelle) joked with an acquaintance who wished to arrange an appointment to visit him at home, 'No, don't come that day, it's my brothel day.' Lhuillier also took his son along with him on one notable 'brothel day', in order to arrange for the boy to lose his virginity. Which was either the *ne plus ultra* of adolescent parental embarrassment or the best birthday present ever. Above all it may have been the result of a bit of shrewd practical thinking on the part of Lhuillier senior – by introducing the boy to an establishment where he knew that he could trust the staff, he may in fact have been trying to protect his son and to prevent him from falling into the hands of some of the city's most dangerous and unscrupulous criminals.

Without the benefit of this paternal introduction a stranger in the city often found that the temptations of the flesh could prove fatal. An anonymous English author recounting his *New Journey* through France towards the close of the seventeenth century warned that the haunts of highwaymen and footpads were not the only parts of the city to be avoided on pain of death. 'It is as dangerous to pick up a whore, or go into a Bawdy-House; for they most commonly strip a man both of his money, clothes and life, giving him the House of Office for a grave.'[9] We can deduce from the indignant tone of this warning that our anonymous British traveller clearly expects his audience to consider the whore and the 'Bawdy-House' as standard conveniences of continental city life. Despite the overwhelming evidence that attitudes to prostitution and the sex-trade were decidedly flexible, the cynicism of Lhuillier senior's parenting technique can still seem slightly surprising. However, it should be noted that the whole idea of childhood as a sacred time set apart from the realities of adult life is a modern construct and would have been entirely foreign to the families of the time.

Consider the education of the king himself. Louis XIII was born in September 1601 and would rule France for a significant part of Cyrano's lifetime. At the age of three the future king was encouraged to take part in a joke whereby his father would ask him, 'Who is father's darling?' To which the prince would reply by pointing to his chest. Then his father would ask, 'And who is the infanta's darling?' (the infanta being the six-month-old Spanish princess to whom Louis was already formally engaged) to which

Louis would reply by pointing to his crotch, cue roars of laughter all round.[10] The modern isolation of children from adult sexuality is a relatively recent phenomenon. As the historian François de Dainville points out in his study of the Jesuit influence on education in Cyrano's time, the modern idea of the respect due to childish sensibilities was entirely unheard of at this time: 'In front of them nothing was forbidden: crude speech, lewd actions and situations; they heard and saw everything.'[11] This was not only true for families where the constraints of economic pressure meant that the whole family slept together in one room. Louis XIII shared his bed chamber with his nurse, and she shared her bed with her husband.

To some extent the foreignness of such attitudes may be explained by the contemporary conviction that very young children were naturally innocent and protected by their pre-pubescent ignorance of sexuality. The point where this issue becomes rather hazier is at the age of puberty; in the seventeenth century it was still common for girls to be married as young as eleven years of age, although the average age for wedlock was nearer to twenty-five. Equally revelatory of the sexual mores of Cyrano's adolescent years (and equally disturbing to a modern audience) is Montaigne's flippant remark that 'one hundred schoolboys will have caught the pox before having reached Aristotle's lesson on Chastity'.[12]

If the emotional landscape of Cyrano's time seems decidedly unfamiliar, the physical landscape was equally unrecognizable. Peter Heylyn, another British traveller who recorded his impressions of seventeenth-century France paints a delightful portrait of the streets of the most romantic city in the world:

> As it is now the least rain maketh it very slippery and troublesome; and as little a continuance of warm weather, stinking and poisonous. But whether this noisomenesse proceed from the nature of the ground, the sluttishness of the people in their

> houses, or the neglect of the Magistrates in not providing a sufficiency of Scavengers, or all, I am not to determine. This I am confident of, that the nastiest lane in London, is Frankincense and Juniper, to the sweetest street in this city.[13]

Like Overbury's 'observation' of the ignorance of the average Frenchman, Heylyn's prose is clearly coloured by jingoistic exaggeration but his account is by no means unusual. Another seventeenth-century traveller, James Howell, recounts a saying current among the Parisians themselves, 'That an ill name is like the Crot (the dirt) of Paris, which is indelible'; Howell leaves nothing to the imagination, 'besides the stain this dirt leaves, it gives off also so strong a scent that it may be smelt many miles off'.[14]

The filth and stench of poor sanitation was far from the worst that the scenery of Cyrano's lifetime had to offer. That robbery and murder were rife does not prove that the era was lawless – in fact, just as in England, the authorities had vigorous and enthusiastic recourse to judicial punishments ranging from torture to execution. The death penalty was used on a grand scale. In order to serve the double purpose of punishment and warning all such events took place firmly in the public eye and the results were often kept on display for a considerable length of time with predictably gory results. The author of *A New Journey*, on passing through a peaceful woodland on the outskirts of Orléans 'perceived the Trees were loaded with very ungrateful Fruit, so rotten that I was forced to hold my nose from the confounded stink that proceeded from it; the spectacle was very hideous, being above twenty Highwaymen, that were hung to the branches of the trees *in Terrorem*.'[15]

The young Cyrano would have been used to such sights and would almost certainly have frequented the *cabarets*, drinking joints, haunted by many a future tenant of the scaffold. The cabarets were the equivalent of English taverns and they were much despised by the religious authorities for their destructive influence on the parishioners. As one contemporary author put it: 'The debauched young person can see his chances of pleasing the Lord escaping out of the windows of the brothels and cabarets.'[16] A curate determined to help his flock, much against their wishes, often struggled in vain to limit the opening hours of the cabarets, in the hope of limiting the worldly distraction available to the less than high-minded customers. The bishops, who had the authority to enforce such measures, were reluctant to do so, recognizing that over-zealous interference from the local clergy should not be allowed to go too far, for fear of provoking outright revolt. The sons of the nobility delighted in the contrast between these rough places and their own pampered lives. Certain cabarets were also the haunt of literary men. In particular, the infamous taverns the Pomme de Pin (The Pine Cone) and the Chêne Vert (The Green Oak) may well have been where Cyrano first encountered the free-thinking poets, playwrights and authors who were to form his turbulent inner circle as he took his first steps towards a literary career.

Cyrano was the true heir of his talented grandfather, both Savinien senior and junior were vigorous social climbers, who placed great importance on striving to live nobly. In the seventeenth century, social mobility was not just a question of money, but also of codes of honourable or 'honest' behaviour. In 1630, when Cyrano was eleven years old, Nicolas Faret had published a handbook of aristocratic behaviour entitled *The Honest Gentleman*, subtitled 'the art of pleasing at court'. Faret's book was enormously popular with numerous sell-out editions appearing throughout Cyrano's lifetime. The book's extraordinary appeal is partly explained by that subtitle 'pleasing at court', the art at which Cyrano's grandfather had excelled, and the key to wealth and advancement. Faret gave his readers a detailed account of the essentials of noble conduct. Those who wished to achieve the aristocratic ideal would find invaluable instruction in its pages.

Living nobly was not solely a question of being born into the right family. This was made explicit in another, rather more radical book than Faret's entitled *Traité de la Sagesse* (On Wisdom). The author, Pierre Charron, drew a distinction between two different types of nobility. On the one hand, there was the 'natural' nobility, determined entirely by birth, but Charron also described a second category, 'personal and acquired' nobility which he saw as based on virtue. The most important of the noble virtues, as Faret's title revealed, was honesty. Of course, more often than not, it was money rather than virtue which allowed the successful bourgeois tradesman to aspire to the trappings of nobility and snobbish English travellers were particularly scathing about the ease with which the ranks of the aristocracy could be infiltrated by such upstarts. Peter Heylyn quips 'Heaven hath not more stars than France Nobles' and in his memoirs one John Reresby ends a sycophantic account of the impressiveness of the French dukes with the supercilious observation that, 'This title is the only one at this day considerable in France, those of earl, marquis, baron and knight being so common, a man needs not lands to acquire them; good clothes and a splendid equipage creates them daily.'[17]

Molière, the great comic writer (and plagiarist of Cyrano) satirized this contemporary trend in his comedy *Le Bourgeois Gentilhomme*. The play's humour is largely reliant on the comic ineptitude of the bourgeois gentleman of the title and his increasingly desperate attempts to pass himself off as a true aristocrat. The foremost signifier of social superiority was the lack of visible means of support. Trade was irredeemably bourgeois and incompatible with noble 'honesty'. This is probably a fairly shrewd assessment of the realities of seventeenth-century business practice. Although the 'honesty' of the parasitic alternative, namely living off the sweat of the peasants, is another question. One of the most obvious privileges of the aristocracy was being so unimaginably rich that money ceased to have any real meaning. The extravagance and excesses of the French aristocracy are legendary and we all know what they eventually led to. The downside of joining the ranks of the pseudo-aristocracy was the need to assume an indifference to excessive expenditure that many could ill afford.

The nineteenth-century novelist Alexandre Dumas vividly depicts the consequences of noble liberality in *The Three Musketeers*. The heroes live a hand-to-mouth existence, treating one another to sumptuous feasts with vast quantities of expensive wine when in funds and going hungry when fortune is less kind. In one scene Athos confirms his status as the most noble of all the musketeers by playing a high stakes game of dice with some grasping Englishmen and reacting with supreme courtly indifference when they successfully (albeit fraudulently) strip him of all his money and possessions and those of his friends as well. The accuracy of this presentation of gambling as a mark of high noble status may be judged by the words of the same contemporary author who warned against the debauchery of brothels and cabarets. The Maréchal de Caillière, in his own aristocratic handbook – which was specifically aimed at the aspiring class of *gentilhommes particuliers* to which Cyrano certainly belonged, comes to the following somewhat startling conclusion: 'I have always esteemed the love of gaming as one of nature's benefits, I have often recognised its usefulness . . . I would argue that it is natural to us to love gambling.' He goes on to explain this conviction with the argument that gaming gives access to the best company and can provide a reasonable living to a talented player, he also warns that rich people should avoid the temptation, since they have more to lose. Finally, he makes a suggestion, which to a modern reader is distinctly unexpected, coming from a determinedly devout and pious author: 'I advise a man who knows how to play and who enjoys games of chance, to risk his money there, since he has little to lose he doesn't risk much and he could win a great deal.'[18] In spite of Caillière's unmixed approval, gambling was officially illegal. Although largely tolerated by the authorities the cabarets which served as gambling dens were notoriously attractive not just to the idle rich and the hopeful poor, but also to thieves, beggars, prostitutes and loan-sharks.

Among this seething mass of temptation and debauchery it is small wonder if Cyrano lost his way for a time. The question remains, what exactly did Le Bret mean by a 'dangerous tendency'? It is possible that it was around this time that Cyrano first came into contact with the man who was to become his nemesis. Charles Coypeau Dassoucy, the self-styled 'emperor of the burlesque', was the son of a lawyer. His mother was a musician of Italian descent, a feisty and impulsive woman who was, according to Dassoucy's own account of her, so wildly unfaithful that he was not at all sure that he was his father's son. His parents separated early after a turbulent marriage that apparently included a duel fought over a passage in Justinian. Once separated, his father soon gave him a serving girl for a stepmother, a fact that he seems to have bitterly resented. Dassoucy was a successful composer, who would have made a handsome living from his musical talents were it not for his tendency to gamble. He frequently referred to music and gambling as the two central passions of his life, but his semi-autobiographical novel *Adventures of M. Dassoucy* reveals that his other main passion was a choirboy named Pierrotin, whom he labels the 'evil spirit' of his life. Having been forced to flee the court and the capital, in order to avoid prosecution and imprisonment for blasphemy and sexual offences, Dassoucy spent some years in the provinces and in Italy touring with his music and his choirboy performers. In 1673, he was imprisoned in Paris, but he won his release with an eloquent plea addressed to Pope Clement IX. He died in Paris in 1677 on the 29th October at the age of seventy-two.

Dassoucy was charming and intelligent with an endearing line in self-deprecating humour. He was also a poet, a talented composer and musician, who earned his living writing comic songs to entertain the king. Dassoucy was at the centre of a lively circle of musicians, poets and playwrights all struggling to make a living from their art. Such company would have been enormously appealing to the young Cyrano, but Dassoucy was not only charming and seductive, he was also an alcoholic and addicted to gambling. Above all, Dassoucy was a sexual predator, who preyed upon a succession of vulnerable young men and boys. The vexed question of Cyrano's tortured relationship with Dassoucy (whom he began by comparing to Orpheus and ended by threatening to murder) is one to which we will return later on. Whether Le Bret would really have congratulated himself on 'stopping' a homosexual Cyrano by taking him off to live in an all-male establishment seems rather doubtful. It may be that he saw the need to remove Cyrano from Dassoucy's pernicious sphere of influence and that he saw the beginnings of an abusive relationship developing between the two, observing the combination of manipulation and seduction that was the hallmark of all Dassoucy's involvements with impressionable young men.

Dassoucy's homosexuality may have been the least of Le Bret's worries, since he was also a notorious 'libertin', one of the godless group of intellectuals for whom sedition and blasphemy were the proofs of 'free thought', whose debauchery and disrespect of authority led more than one of their number to perish in prison or at the stake. The royal family had included more than one obviously gay member in the past and in Cyrano's lifetime the king's brother would surround himself with a coterie of 'mignons', gorgeous male companions who squabbled among themselves for the prince's favour. 'The Italian vice' as it was known was a commonplace and less dangerous tendency than the thought-crime of 'libertinage'. The contemporary moralists Father Garasse and Father Mersenne both write at length about libertinism as a terrible 'danger' to the youth of the country and if there was one thing that attracted the young Cyrano beyond any other it was danger.

4

The temptation of heroism

Henri Le Bret had chosen to enlist and he succeeded in persuading Cyrano to join him in this new adventure. For the young Cyrano, there was a specific appeal to such a potentially lethal step. In his bestselling book of useful advice for the aspiring noble, Nicolas Faret highlights the social advantages of a career in the armed forces. 'Since every man has to choose a profession . . ., it seems to me that there is none more honourable or more essential to a gentleman than that of arms . . . Nobility is acquired by arms.'[1] In an earlier, similar work, Olivier de la Marche had identified five possible paths to greatness. The first, the possession of 'an office appointed by the crown', was the route taken by Savinien senior, Cyrano's ambitious grandfather, whose purchase of court appointments secured the family both money and prestige.[2] No matter that in the early eighteenth century the types of court offices purchased by Savinien senior would become known as *savonnette à vilain* (soap for scum), in the early seventeenth century such appointments were a solid path to respectability.

If the offices bought by Savinien senior had been filled by the family for two generations or more, the Cyranos would have been assured their place within the *noblesse de robe* (nobility of the gown). Cyrano's father, however, had chosen the second option in de la Marche's list, the deceptively simple sounding 'honest life of noble gentlemen'.[3] Since the family owned the estates and the seigneurie of Mauvières, Abel simply had to preside as lord of the manor and this in itself would be all the proof needed of the family's standing. Whether as a result of poor management, or distaste for the rural life, Abel had abandoned this path, selling off the family estates and returning to Paris. This left three other options theoretically open to Cyrano, since a return to either of the first two would have required significant investments of capital. The third and fourth options, 'general service of the prince' and 'letters patent of nobility accorded by the monarch' both depended on gaining direct access to the king. Such access was both limited and hotly contested and, as an unknown adolescent of dubious social standing, Cyrano had no hope of rubbing shoulders with Louis XIII. This left one remaining path for him to try: 'the career of arms'.[4]

Cyrano's time as a member of the 'honourable profession' was comparatively short-lived. He served as a member of the noble corps of cadets under the aristocratic commander Carbon de Castel-Jaloux for just short of two years between 1638 and 1640. The name cadets derives from the tradition that it was the younger brother or *cadet* who was destined for the army. The oldest son, being the heir to the family fortune, was too precious to be risked on the battlefield and was kept at home, where he would learn to manage his estates and be groomed for a life as lord of the manor. Younger sons, with no such glittering prospect to look forward to, were expected to forge a path for themselves. The church and the army were the two main career prospects open to the nobility. Cyrano would not have got far as a priest. There was also the option of studying law, as many of Cyrano's male relatives and fellow authors chose to do; but poring over legal documents and resolving the petty disputes of his neighbours was apparently not a sufficiently enticing prospect. Whatever his initial enthusiasm for the military may have been, Cyrano's experience of the armed forces nearly killed him and would scar him for life in more ways than one.

In spite of the brevity of Cyrano's time as a soldier, today it is perhaps the best-known fact of his career. Naturally, this is largely due to Rostand's vision of the cadets. The playwright seems to have taken his cue from Henri Le Bret's depiction of Cyrano as the ultimate soldier-poet: 'I saw him one day, in the guardroom, working on an Elegy with as little distraction as if he had been in a study far removed from all the noise.'[5] Le Bret's brief biographical note may not be definitive, but it is at least the testimony of someone who was there. Not only that, but the evidence of Cyrano's works also seems to support Le Bret's vision of a poet whose passionate concentration allowed him to blot out the myriad distractions of a noisy crowd of guardsmen in order to focus on the work of creation. He was not the most polished wit of the era, nor, perhaps, the most talented, but an undeniable vein of high-voltage imaginative intensity is a consistent and distinctive feature of Cyrano's style. Le Bret's testimony in this instance has a ring of truth. The snapshot it affords us of the young Cyrano also serves to confirm that his compulsion to write was a lifelong trait and not solely a feature of his later years. The real Cyrano was only temporarily a soldier but he was always a poet.

Rostand took this brief glimpse of Cyrano, seen at the heart of his regiment, yet at the same time far removed from his fellow recruits, and fashioned from it the portrait of a fictional Cyrano, who is, at once, loved and feared by the other cadets. His distance from them is palpable throughout the play and it is this distance that both isolates and elevates him. Rostand's cadets are ostensibly Castel-Jaloux's men, but when the hardships of the siege of Arras force the men almost to the point of revolt, the commander is forced to call on Cyrano for help. Castel-Jaloux asks Cyrano to cheer the men up to calm their aggressive despair; instead Cyrano's successful strategy is to depress them still further. He asks the regimental piper to play an air from the old country and to the melancholy sound of the music he conjures up a poetic vision of Gascony. In this way he manages to pacify the men by transmuting their suffering into a 'nobler hunger', nostalgia. He reminds the men of the peaceful, edenic splendours of 'the green softness of evenings on the Dordogne' in terms which recall the real Cyrano's letter to his friend singing the praises of an 'enchanted palace' in the countryside. There is no evidence to support Rostand's view of Cyrano as the true leader of the regiment, in fact his distaste for following orders and his frustration with his subordinate position probably hastened his withdrawal from the army. But Rostand's departures from historical reality serve to infuse the real Cyrano's passion for the pastoral and the unexpected into the behaviour of his theatrical shadow.

It was at the point of his enrolment with Castel-Jaloux's men that Cyrano introduced the element of ambiguity about his origins that was to prove so enduring. Firstly, by his use of the name Cyrano de Bergerac, rather than the more accurate Savinien de Cyrano, and secondly, by his affiliation to an almost exclusively Gascon regiment. Le Bret specifically states that the guards were nearly all Gascons. It was not just the consequent convenient assumption that his family were a more significant land-owning presence than they really were that Cyrano stood to gain from this association with a company of Gascons. The region was famed for producing particularly courageous soldiers and Tréville, the captain of the king's personal regiment (known to us as the Musketeers) was himself a Gascon, who favoured the promotion of his fellow countrymen. Thanks to the popularity of the novels by Alexandre Dumas the term Musketeer has come to be indissolubly linked to the elite regiment captained by Tréville and later by d'Artagnan himself. In practice, at the time, it signified anyone armed with a musket and was thus applicable to many other troops. Cyrano and Le Bret were both musketeers in the cadets.

Tréville, the son of a merchant, was a page to the king at fourteen, then a cadet in the *regiment des gardes françaises*. He entered into the company of the king's musketeers as a second lieutenant and became captain in 1634. By joining the cadets Cyrano identified himself with men who revelled in a proud tradition of loyalty and courage. The Gascon soldiers were such a strong and charismatic presence in Paris that they too engendered a legend which would outlive them and ensure immortality to certain key figures. If Rostand chose to depict Cyrano as a Gascon, it was not because he didn't know any better – as he would protest angrily when challenged on this point. In fact Edmond Rostand had realized that a Gascon Cyrano made for a better story. A fashion for historical novels set in the seventeenth century and featuring heroic Gascon noblemen had swept the nation in the nineteenth century and Edmond Rostand understood and hoped to emulate the popularity of these evocations of a golden age of chivalry and adventure.

The most famous of the swashbuckling epics to feature a Gascon soldier as its hero is Alexandre Dumas' 1844 novel, *The Three Musketeers*. Dumas's book begins with a wily literary hoax intended to add spice to a tale of high adventure and intrigue. In his introduction Dumas describes how he had been working in the Bibliothèque Royale doing some research for his history of Louis XIV when he stumbled upon the 'Mémoires de M. d'Artagnan', which, he explains, had been printed in Amsterdam to avoid French censorship of the scandalous truths found within. Fascinated by the characters appearing in the memoir, Dumas pursued his researches further and discovered an unpublished manuscript, for which he even goes so far as to give the library code as 4772 or 4773. The manuscript is entitled *Memoirs of Monsieur the Count of La Fère, concerning certain events that took place in France towards the end of the reign of King Louis XIII*, and in its pages

Dumas is delighted to discover the names of the three Musketeers who feature in d'Artagnan's memoirs: Athos, Porthos and Aramis. With this wealth of factual material he is able to construct a historical novel which is directly drawn from the true confessions of the principal figures. The Count of La Fère being none other than the superbly aristocratic Musketeer, Athos himself. Sadly, manuscript 4772 (or 4773) was a pure invention, but the three-volume memoirs of d'Artagnan do actually exist and are still available in print today. These memoirs, which served as Dumas's most important source, were themselves a seventeenth-century literary hoax. They were written not by d'Artagnan but by one Gatien Courtilz de Sandras and first published in 1700, nearly thirty years after d'Artagnan's death. Dumas' claim that the memoirs were published in Amsterdam in order to avoid French censorship was entirely accurate. However, the 'truths' contained within the memoir are not so certain. Courtilz had served as a musketeer, and so was able to pass himself off as a member of d'Artagnan's inner circle. In reality, he was unlikely to have had any significant contact with d'Artagnan as he had actually served in a different troop from that commanded by the great Musketeer, and his 'memoirs' were simply a wildly racy and inventive collection of anecdotes, loosely intertwined with a few basic facts of d'Artagnan's actual career.

Having no personal fortune, the career soldier Courtilz had turned to his pen to make a living after being forced to abandon the sword when his regiment was disbanded following the peace of Nimègues in 1678. His new speciality was controversial historical pieces like the d'Artagnan memoirs – the incendiary political criticisms that Courtilz included in his work did not spring from a dedication to any particular cause. On seeing the success and the scandal surrounding the memoirs he promptly penned an anonymous pamphlet in which he attacked his own publication and contradicted every controversial opinion expressed in the original. This neat trick enabled him to cash in on both sides of the furore he had caused. Courtilz's impudence and imagination earned him two lengthy periods of imprisonment in the Bastille, the second and longer of which ultimately killed him. Courtilz and Cyrano were kindred spirits but sadly their paths almost certainly never crossed, since Cyrano died when Courtilz was just eleven years old. As for the three musketeers, Cyrano's membership of a Gascon regiment means that he may very well have come into contact with Isaac de Porthau, Henri d'Aramitz and Armand de Sillègue d'Athos d'Auteville. The three were almost his exact contemporaries and were all serving in the Musketeers by around 1641.

Cyrano and d'Artagnan fought side by side at the siege of Arras and were both wounded in the fray. Their paths may well have crossed, but it seems unlikely that they ever became close. The real d'Artagnan was actually about a decade older than Cyrano and the three musketeers. Born in 1611, his full name was Charles de Batz de Castelmore, but he chose to style himself Count d'Artagnan (a name taken from his mother's side of the family) when he left Gascony at the age of sixteen to seek his fortune in the army. Unlike Cyrano, d'Artagnan was a skilled courtier and rose rapidly to occupy a trusted position within the king's personal guard (the Musketeers). The real d'Artagnan was also sent on spying missions to republican England. He had two sons, both of whom he named Louis, after the king, in an act of blatant crawling that Cyrano would have been unlikely to admire.*

The author Théophile Gautier had helped to draw Rostand's attention to Cyrano as an interesting subject with an 1834 article that featured his imaginative vision of the young Cyrano dallying with perfumed courtesans, amid scenes which could have come straight from Courtilz's pages. Gautier also wrote a historical novel

* It was common in the seventeenth century to reuse a name when a child died young so it is unlikely that the two little boys, both called Louis, were alive at the same time.

set in the seventeenth century whose hero was (like Dumas' d'Artagnan) an impoverished Gascon noble. The story of *Le Capitaine Fracasse* follows the adventures of the Baron de Sigognac, who leaves his ruined chateau behind to follow a troupe of travelling players to Paris, where he becomes involved in a series of picaresque adventures. Gautier's portrait of the Baron owes much to the legend of the noble Gascon and not a little to Cyrano himself. Slightly cruelly, his only acknowledgement of this debt is in the portrait of Lampourde, an expert duellist who is hired by the villain of the piece to assassinate the Baron. Jacquemin Lampourde is a mercenary, not a nobleman, and his appearance is decidedly unprepossessing. He has long monkey arms, heron legs, a bony chest and worst of all, 'a prodigious nose that recalled that of Cyrano de Bergerac, the pretext for so many duels . . . Lampourde consoled himself with the popular axiom: "A face is never spoiled by a big nose."'[6] After further detailing Lampourde's excessive ugliness the description of his face ends with the reflection that 'nevertheless no one ever cared to mock him, his expression was too worrying, sardonic and ferocious'.[7] Gautier's portrayal of Lampourde seems to have been partly inspired by the attacks on Cyrano, which began to appear after his untimely death. Rostand had been familiar with Gautier's vision of Cyrano since childhood; when he was a schoolboy his teacher had read both *Le Capitaine Fracasse* and *Les Grotesques* to the class.

Cyrano's decision to join the cadets may have been partly prompted by a pragmatic desire to improve his lot in life, but it was above all a decision to seek death or glory. Jacques Prévot, the author of a critical study of the life and works of Cyrano de Bergerac published in the late 1970s, opens his discussion of the poet's life with the discouraging reflection that 'the biography of Cyrano evades all investigations'.[8] His thoughtful analysis of Cyrano's *oeuvre*, nevertheless, outlines a vision of the soldier-poet striving to surpass himself, to overcome the limitations of the world he inhabited. For Prévot, the real Cyrano was continually succumbing to 'the temptation of heroism'.[9] It is perhaps this distinctive feature of the man above all else that gave rise to a legend which would not only outlive him but grow and transform with extraordinary vigour for centuries after his death. At the beginning of his adult life, the evidence of Cyrano's surrender to the temptation of heroism is clear. In the seventeenth century, opportunities for reckless heroics abounded. Across Europe, taking into account both civil and international wars, only two years in the entire century could be counted as entirely peaceful: 1669 and 1670. In *The Courtiers Guide* of 1606 a similar (if less popular) book to Faret's *The Honest Gentleman*, the author reflects on the thoughtless enthusiasm of young nobles for the aristocratic rite of passage that was going to war. He describes young noblemen muttering resentfully about the peace and the fact that it prevents them from proving themselves on the battlefield.

Cyrano's opportunity to show what he was made of came with a conflict that had been raging throughout central Europe since before his birth. The Thirty Years War had begun in 1618, the year of Cyrano's conception. In 1635, France had finally become officially involved in the conflict, declaring war on the Spanish and on the Empire. By 1636 things were not going well for the French and an important defeat at Corbie-sur-la-Somme led to panic in the capital, as fears of invasion swept the city. The king (or perhaps more accurately his trusted advisor the brilliant politician Cardinal Richelieu) realized the crucial importance of strengthening France's military defences and an urgent recruitment drive was set in train.

In the course of Louis XIII's reign France's army would swell from around 30,000 men to around 250,000. The recruitment methods used in Cyrano's lifetime were both unsophisticated and ineffectual. In 1635 an official request was made for men to present themselves to the *prévôt de Paris* within twenty-four hours of the call in order to join up and receive in return 12 livres pay, of which 6 were to be paid in advance. Levels of desertion in the armed forces at the time have been estimated at 50 per cent rising to 75 per cent at the end of campaigns as winter approached. Richelieu commented in his memoirs that he always divided in half any numbers he was given for the size of France's troops for precisely this reason. The recruitment request was designed to be a sort of amnesty, aimed at luring back deserters and rounding up vagabonds and masterless men in the hope of transforming the layabouts and troublemakers of the realm into a useful commodity – cannon fodder. Of those that turned up, most sensibly took the money and ran. A profound discrepancy existed between the noble ideal of the soldier, as outlined in popular works of the time and the reality, which was that the greatest percentage of France's military forces were, of necessity, made up of violent and unreliable malcontents. In his time with the cadets Cyrano found himself confronted by this clash between the idealized fiction of warfare and the stark reality.

The year of Cyrano's enlistment had seen some exciting developments for the French nation and a new mood of optimism was the result. After twenty-three years of childless union, the king and queen had finally produced their first child, a baby boy. Until this 'miraculous' birth, the lack of a direct male descendant had meant that the threat of a disastrous power vacuum hung over the nation. King Louis XIII's health was never strong and his death would have seen the crown pass to his younger brother, who had already staged rebellions in an attempt to seize power prematurely, with the backing of his unpopular mother, Marie de Medici. Such a failure of the direct male line all too often triggered internal power struggles. A nation prey to the infighting of warring factions was a nation one step away from bloody civil war. As such, the celebrations that marked the birth of the Dauphin were both dramatic and heartfelt. The little boy came to be known as Louis Dieudonné in recognition of the seemingly miraculous nature of his arrival after more than two decades of disappointment. The birth of the future Sun King Louis XIV was hailed as quite literally 'a gift from God' and Parisians celebrated the gift in style. Fountains flowed with wine, fireworks and festivities were organized and the nation breathed a collective sigh of relief.

As it turned out, the collective rejoicing was somewhat precipitate, since Louis XIII's death just five years later would leave France subject to the violent unrest of the uprising known as the Fronde. This rebellion, or more accurately this series of rebellions was largely due to the unpopularity of a regency in which France was ruled by two foreigners: the Spanish queen mother Ann of Austria and Richelieu's replacement the Italian Cardinal-Minister Giulio Mazarini, known as Mazarin. In the meantime, the positive mood was unsullied by any indication of the storms to come and Cyrano must have experienced an initial rush of pride in the thought that he was going to risk his life for king and country. In order to join the regiment Cyrano's family would have had to pay for his commission as one of the cadets and also for his equipment. A contemporary text gives a list of the items he would have required: strong boots, stockings and breeches, two or preferably more thick shirts, a stout leather doublet, a waterproof greatcoat, a large felt hat. It was suggested that clothes should all be on the large size and feature a bare minimum of stitches, as seams were the favourite residence of fleas and lice. For the same reason the author advised against fur as too attractive to parasites. Cyrano would also have been expected to provide his own musket and sword and his own horse.

It was during the seventeenth century that military uniforms were first introduced and in certain regiments the commanding officer would gift his men with a uniform. There was an element of showmanship involved in dressing one's troops, just as in the expensive liveries worn by the servants of great lords. As such the king's Musketeers had a suitably flashy uniform, graced with the fleur de lys (which they had to hand back as property of the crown when Cardinal Mazarin disbanded the regiment in 1646). For troops who did not wear uniforms, it was traditional to include a colourful mark of some kind to aid mutual recognition.

At first, Cyrano would have spent some time with the unit in Paris undertaking some basic training before beginning the long march to the campaign grounds. Pierre Charron's comment on military training gives a hint of the challenge facing the young Cyrano, unaccustomed to serious physical hardship. Charron reflects that training should harden the men against suffering, sweat and dust. Charron was concerned that recruits ought to be selected on the basis of a predisposition to withstand the hardships of warfare. In his *Treatise on Wisdom* Charron suggests to the king that certain environments are more likely to produce men hardy enough for the horrors of war. 'They should be taken from the fields, the mountains, sterile places, nourished on all kinds of hardship . . . Because those from the towns, nourished in the shade on pleasure and gain are more cowardly and insolent, effeminate.'[10] Cyrano had joined a troop in which most of his fellow cadets came from the mountainous regions of the Pyrenees and who therefore fulfilled Charron's criteria. Despite being an indolent, spoilt Parisian and therefore liable to abandon himself to 'to delights and to women' at any minute, Cyrano would belie this accusation of the cowardice of city dwellers. He may very well have proved the point about insolence though.

On joining the cadets Cyrano found himself plunged into a world very different from anything he had ever known before and surrounded by men, many of them as young as him, but all of whom must have seemed more assured and more at ease. The Gascons shared a common heritage, common ideals and common experience. In order to survive in this new environment Cyrano had to choose between keeping a low profile and trying to surpass the courageous Gascons – predictably, he went for the latter option.

Faret's invaluable book offers a word of advice as to what are the legitimate ambitions of a young nobleman: 'It seems to me, therefore, that the greatest ambition of he who carries a sword is to be considered a man of boldness and courage.'[11] The simplest way to fulfil this ambition was to fight duels and within his first few days with the company Cyrano was to throw himself headlong into the fray.

The call of adventure and the desire to mark oneself out by individual acts of courage was a noble French tradition with roots in the age of chivalry. An edict of 1600 had even ratified the link between military prowess and aristocratic distinction. Above all the warrior-hero was a literary staple and one of the biggest successes to sweep the capital in Cyrano's youth was a play based entirely on this notion of bravery and military success as indicators of nobility of soul. *Le Cid* by Pierre Corneille was first performed in 1637; Louis XIII, not normally a great patron of the theatre, commanded three private performances at the Louvre. In his enthusiasm for the piece, the king ennobled Corneille (a demonstration of the fourth of Olivier de la Marche's paths to greatness in action). In fact it was Corneille's father who was accorded the letters patent of ennoblement so that the playwright's honour should not be sullied by nobility too freshly acquired. Richelieu, who was a passionate devotee of the arts, also personally accorded the playwright a stipend. This worldly success provoked jealousy and a vicious flurry of pamphlets known as *La querelle du Cid* in which both the play and the author were attacked. The most important crime Corneille had committed was that of innovation. *Le Cid* was denigrated for failing to conform to the Aristotelian rules of tragedy, notably in its failure to conform to the three unities and to the norms of the genre. It was further alleged that Corneille had stolen the work outright from a Spanish author, Guillen de Castro whose play *Las Mocedades del Cid*, based on the life of the eleventh-century Castilian knight Rodrigo of Vavar, first appeared around 1599.

Corneille had freely admitted taking his inspiration from de Castro's text and termed his play a tragicomedy because despite its tragic register (there aren't any jokes) the action ends happily with a marriage, the traditional conclusion of a comedy. Richelieu himself was eventually forced to step in to defend his protégé personally.

In *Le Cid* Corneille depicts the dilemma faced by the various protagonists forced to choose between honour and love. The heroine, Chimène, finds herself in a similarly unenviable position to Shakespeare's Ophelia, her father having been killed by her beloved. Chimène refuses to be broken by her predicament. Her unhesitating response to the news that her fiancé Don Rodrigue has slaughtered her father in a duel is to choose duty over love. She is unwavering in her conviction that Don Rodrigue must die to avenge her family honour. In spite of the pain it causes her, she appeals to the king for the execution of the man she loves. This leads to the central dilemma of the play since the king refuses to execute Don Rodrigue as by rights he ought to do. The king's decision is based on a pragmatic realization that he cannot afford to punish the courageous Don Rodrigue, because, in the interim, the young hero has taken the place of the murdered count and saved the city from the threat of invasion. The king cannot afford to execute so talented a military commander, the safety of his kingdom depends on it.

This was the image of the very real dilemma faced by Louis XIII. His edicts against duelling all too often went unenforced because the duellists were the military heroes of the nation. Louis could not afford to sacrifice his rebellious nobles to the scaffold. He needed them to spill their blood for him on the battlefield rather than in fighting duels amongst themselves. Corneille's play vividly illustrates the problem faced by the monarch: how to distinguish between the courage required for military success, and the courage required to settle personal differences 'honourably' by duelling, when the two are inextricably linked in the minds of the heroes themselves? Another contemporary text, the *Catéchisme royal* by Pierre Fortin de la Hoguette, attempts to provide a model for the king to follow, but conspicuously fails to address the issue of the intrinsic link between the two forms of courage. In the dialogue it is the monarch himself who recognizes the duel as an honourable proof of noble courage:

> The King: But if we take away the duels how will the nobility prove their courage?
> The Governor: In your armies, Sire.
> The King: And if there is no war?
> The Governor: If there is no war is it reasonable to suffer civil war to rage between them in order to satisfy this curious itch for honour?[12]

The governor's dismissal of the 'curious itch for honour' is both glib and facile, clearly an attempt to minimize and ridicule the duel, in order to lessen its power and, despite emphasizing the rebellious nature of the act by likening the duellists' encounters to 'civil war', the governor has not really answered the king's question. Pierre Corneille's phenomenal success with *Le Cid* did not arise because he was able to present the king with a solution to the problem of the duel but rather because he observed and reflected back to the society of the time one of its most fascinating and complex preoccupations.

Pierre Corneille was just thirteen years older than Cyrano, but his glittering career provides a stark contrast to that of our hero. Setting aside the question of their respective artistic merits, it remains undeniable that an unbridgeable gulf existed between Cyrano de Bergerac, whose writing gained him neither honours nor worldly success and whose two plays would languish unperformed and unpublished for many years and Pierre Corneille, who knew how to court royal favour and who was ennobled and richly rewarded as a result. A key moment from *Le Cid* may serve to illustrate this. As the venerable old man Don Diègue attempts to calm the anger of the hot-headed count, he evokes the absolutist nature of Royal authority:

> Don Diègue: But we owe this respect to absolute power,
> To question nothing that is the King's desire.[13]

These lines are interesting in that they highlight a central problem which would later confront Cyrano in his attempts to make his way in the world – the need to subject oneself 'unquestioningly' to the authority of one's superiors was to prove an insurmountable barrier for him. Cyrano's constant struggle was to submit to no superiors of any kind and thus he would never pay the necessary respect to those who could have assisted his advancement.

As an adolescent Cyrano could hardly have avoided seeing at least one performance of *Le Cid*, if not more; it was the most celebrated and controversial play of his youth. He would certainly have been attracted by its theme of duelling and family honour and he may well have been inspired by the high ideals of courage and duty depicted on stage. In particular, as a headstrong nineteen-year-old, keen to make his mark in the world he may have been struck by the character of Don Rodrigue: the young hero of the play, a historical figure who demonstrates his greatness on the battlefield and in two dramatic duels. No doubt Don Rodrigue's proud reflection that 'Valour does not wait upon the number of years' chimed with the fearless youth. Cyrano's next step would not see him sagely attempting to emulate the concrete successes of his fellow author, but rather risking life and limb to defend his nation and his honour in emulation of the theatrical hero whom all Paris was talking about. *Le Cid* was an inspirational example of the way in which a life could become the stuff of legend.

5

A demon of bravery

On first joining his new regiment, Cyrano was a nobody. As we know, he had no influential connections and no conspicuous personal wealth. In order to distinguish himself as a hero, he first needed to overcome his own insignificance. In Corneille's later comedy *Le Menteur* (1643) the character Dorante, the 'Liar' of the title, confronts the same problem: how to make the most of a less than impressive background? Dorante is desperately anxious to transcend his inexperience and lack of importance in order to convince those around him that he is nothing less than the model nobleman.

> Dorante: Tell me, do you think I make a good cavalier?
> You don't see anything about me that smacks of the
> schoolboy do you?[1]

Fresh from school, dressing up as a soldier for the first time Cyrano must have worried, like Dorante, that his inexperience would shine through and his new clothes be shown up as just a costume. In his determination not to seem like a provincial nobody, Dorante spins an elaborate web of lies that draws him to the brink of catastrophe.

Cyrano opted for a much simpler method to compensate for his lack of money or social standing. Le Bret describes how in Cyrano's first few days with the guards, rather than hoping to impress his fellow recruits with invented glories he decided to win their respect on their own terms. He would fight his way into their approval: 'Duels which in those days seemed the single, fastest way to make oneself known rendered him so famous in so few days that the Gascons, of whom the regiment was almost exclusively made up, considered him as a demon of bravery, and reckoned him as many duels as he had spent days in the company.'[2]

Cyrano's ambition to 'make himself known' took the simplest and the most extreme form possible: every single day he fought a new duel and, within a very short time, his fearsome reputation was established. Fencing would have been a part of Cyrano's education at the Collège de Beauvais – the art of swordplay being considered an essential gentlemanly accomplishment. The right to carry a sword was in itself a noble privilege. Books of the period, outlining the details of a gentlemanly education, are insistent on the importance, not just of fencing, but also of the fundamentals of military training. In Cyrano's lifetime, the terms *gentilhomme* (gentleman) and *homme d'épée* (swordsman) were synonymous. From the mid-sixteenth century to the mid-seventeenth century the fury of duelling had grown and grown. With the inexorable rise of the bourgeoisie, rich and successful tradesmen were often capable of living more nobly than the nobles, at least in terms of outward show. A new social instability had crept into French society. As the definition of a gentleman became hazier, so the duel became ever more popular and widespread. While the country was rapidly leaving its feudal past behind, the aristocracy found itself pressured by a successful and expanding bourgeoisie, consequently the old marks of nobility became suspect. As Le Bret's comment makes explicit, duelling was not just the fastest way to make oneself known, but also the only truly certain way. By the time Cyrano entered into the world of the cadets, the literature of the time was unequivocal in attributing to the duel the status of an unquestionable proof of nobility or *marque de noblesse.*

Despite ancient roots that can be traced back to gladiatorial Rome, via the age of knightly chivalry and the medieval trial by combat, the phenomenon of the duel had come to represent a thoroughly modern affirmation of individuality. The duellist, who chose to risk death, not for king and country, but for the individual issue of a personal quarrel or point of honour, showed proof of a dangerous independence that the authorities were determined to suppress at any cost. As a duellist, Cyrano was firmly on the side of the rebels. Richelieu expressed his determination to put an end to duelling while at the same time admitting the magnitude of the task: 'It is difficult to find a sure way to stop the course of this fury.'[3] In his memoirs, he reflected on the extraordinary proliferation of combats and there is a despairing poetry to his remark that, 'duels have become so commonplace that the streets have begun to serve as battlefields and, as if the day were not long enough for them to vent all their fury, the duellists continue to fight under the stars or by the light of torches that serve as deadly suns.'[4]

In the twenty years between 1588 and 1608, 7,000 nobles died in duels. There was an urgent need to put an end to this bloody insubordination. This urgency was the reason why Count Montmorency-Bouteville served as an example and ended his days on the scaffold. Montmorency-Bouteville's execution evidently did not suffice in itself to ensure the shift of public opinion away from adulation of the heroic duellist. The popular outcry at the time, and the success of *Le Cid* over a decade later, demonstrate that. Attitudes to duelling were complex and shifting; *Le Cid* was both tremendously successful and marked by controversy. Corneille's genius was in capturing the complexity of the subject.

Back in the mid-sixteenth century, the council of Trent had pronounced a condemnation of the duel, which established the excommunication, not only of the duellists themselves, but also of any prince who allowed the practice to continue unpunished within his realm. The irreligious aspect of the duel was therefore an important argument urged against it by the various reformers of the period. As, for example, in the 1617 religious text *Revelations of the Solitary Hermit* by J. Chenel de la Chapperonaye, in which the author rages against the profoundly immoral, suicidal impulse which drives duellists to their demonic encounters. 'It is the action of an atheist, since all sorts of religions condemn it. It is the action of a man in despair, possessed by the devil, hurling himself into perdition in cold blood, like the man who hangs himself and brings about his own death.'[5] Duelling was inextricably linked to blasphemy and the ruling of the council of Trent had made this explicit. When Montmorency-Bouteville was executed for duelling in 1627, it was actually as the result of his second royal death sentence.

Three years earlier, the troublesome noble had fought a duel on Easter Sunday after a drunken quarrel in a tavern. The added outrage of the date on which the duel took place had provoked the genuinely pious King Louis into pronouncing Montmorency-Bouteville's death sentence. The nobleman was, however, given sufficient warning to allow him to go into exile and in the event it was only his effigy which was strung up – and even that symbolic act was to be a fleeting gesture as the effigy was swiftly cut down again by Montmorency-Bouteville's supporters. This first offence was duly pardoned and Montmorency-Bouteville soon returned to court. The account of his crime provided by a contemporary gazette, the *Mercure français*, insists on the gravity of the offence but at the same time reveals an overwhelming fascination with the taboo subject:

> We will not relate here the subject of the quarrel that took place between Sir Bouteville de Montmorency, & the Count de Pontgibault, nor how the challenge was made, nor how they each

> sent to look for a second, nor how they took knives from the tavern to serve as daggers, nor the wicked and despicable words that it is reported one of them said as he went to fight, nor what happened in the course of their fight which took place on Easter day itself . . .

The strategy of reporting the controversial affair in this bizarre negative fashion springs from the need to avoid censorship. All Paris was clearly dying to hear the details and although forced to disappoint its public the *Mercure* was not going to go so far as to miss out altogether on such a story. When the massive outcry against Montmorency-Bouteville's second and fatal condemnation broke out, the *Mercure* even went as far as to publish a 'Reproof from Lady Bouteville to the King'. Richelieu was forced to confront the problem using subtler measures. In order to combat the enormous popular support for the doomed duellist, the cardinal shifted to a different tactic – propaganda. He published a series of pamphlets which presented duelling as an offence against God, the king and the nation itself. The pamphlets were carefully imagined and inventive. They ranged from a straight address to the nobility, *Les Paroles de la France à la noblesse française*; to a letter from a fictional Dutchman, arguing that while French duellists were slaughtering each other their enemies the Spanish were preparing to profit from the resulting chaos; to a dramatic monologue in which Montmorency-Bouteville himself addressed his fellow duellists from beyond the grave, urging them not to make the same mistake as him: 'Be wise at my expense, take advantage of my loss and renounce this unfortunate custom of duelling which a Fury has brought into France out of Hell to destroy souls and bodies and to weaken the Kingdom in the interests of its foes.'[6]

At the point when Cyrano began his duelling career in earnest among the cadets, the authorities were attempting the new tactic of clemency. In 1638 and again in 1640 royal pardons had been issued in the face of too many duels for the king to be able to punish. As Corneille points out, the dilemma facing the monarch who wished to control the murderous fury of the duellists was that, not only were they often too valuable to sacrifice, but their much vaunted indifference in the face of death meant that expecting the threat of capital punishment to dissuade them was woefully optimistic.

The Count: No threats can daunt me, I've no fear of death.
I'll weather any storms while I have breath.
I might be forced to live in misery,
But without honour life is death for me.[7]

Alternative solutions were required and during Cyrano's lifetime the authorities experimented with a system whereby, after a quarrel between two noblemen, one of the potential duellists would be put under guard in order to prevent the fight. Obviously, this arrangement relied on the relevant authorities being warned of the initial quarrel in time to intervene. This flaw in the system gave rise to a perception of this preventative measure as one only likely to be put in place with the cowardly cooperation of one of the duellists. Cyrano makes exactly that satirical point in his comedy *The Pedant Tricked* – a play, elements of whose composition he may well have been working on at this time. The duellist under guard in Cyrano's comedy is called Captain Chateaufort. He is a coward who brags about his courage but who is totally terrified by the prospect of a duel. His careful connivance with his guard '*le soin de bien garder mon Garde*' is made all too clear when he realizes that he is no longer accompanied and starts to panic at the horrifying prospect of suddenly being called upon actually to fight.

Chateaufort: Hey! Oh My God, Sirs, I have lost my guard, has none of you met with him? . . . He's a guard that the Marshals of

> France sent me in order to prevent me from fighting the bloodiest duel ever to redden the grass in the Clerks Meadow. Heavens above, what will the nobles say when they learn that I have not taken care to guard my guard?[8]

Cyrano was not alone in considering that the only way the state would successfully prevent a duel was with the cowardly connivance of one of the potential combatants. In 1650, Louis XIV introduced a pledge against duelling that the nobility were pressured to sign. The notion was very slow to take root and the vow to abstain from duelling, and to further undertake to dissuade others from the practice, remained largely ineffectual, despite the apparent reasonableness of the proposition: the idea being that if all the nobles jointly renounced the duel, then questions of honour would no longer be resolved by bloodshed. The text of the pledge emphasized the irreligious and irrational nature of the duel, as well as its illegality. Signatories were formalizing a promise: 'not to fight a duel for any conceivable cause, and to give all possible testimony of the hatred they have of the duel as of a thing that is against reason and the laws of the State and incompatible with salvation and the Christian religion.'[9] Not only did the nobles prove reluctant to sign, but the courtiers openly mocked the idea and dismissed those who had signed, as presumably infirm and therefore grateful for the excuse.

The idea that one could refuse a duel was simply not taken seriously at first, the practice having become so ingrained in the noble consciousness. The importance of demonstrating one's courage was paramount. The resolution of conflict through discussion was hardly in keeping with years of warrior tradition and an apology for an offence was considered worse than useless. Corneille had initially included lines to this purpose in the text of *Le Cid*, but had suppressed them as too provocative. They were well known throughout courtly circles nonetheless, and spread throughout fashionable Paris as a witty summary of the necessity of the duel.

> These satisfactions do not calm the soul
> Who accepts them has nothing, who makes them defames himself,
> And of all such agreements the most common effect
> Is to make two men lose their honour instead of one.[10]

The logic of this conviction that an apology fails to 'satisfy' the honour of either party, but rather dishonours both still further is unexpected but insistent. The language of duelling frequently refers to the need to remove the 'stain' of dishonour from the family name and the only effective method was to resort to violence and bloodshed. In 1606, the colourfully named English author Lodowick Bryskett wrote *A Discourse of Civill Life*, a work advertised as being, 'fit to instruct a Gentleman in the course of a virtuous life'. Bryskett explained the importance of the idea of 'honesty' to the mechanics of the duel. Essentially, he underlines the fact that it is so much more shameful to be accused of lying than it is to be insulted, that in an angry exchange any initial insulting comment is reduced to nothing by the response 'thou liest', and it is therefore the honour of the man who finds himself accused of lying that is at stake rather than the man who was initially insulted. Bryskett goes on to state 'it standeth so charged in his honor and reputation, that he can not disburden himselfe of that imputation, but by striking of him that hath so given it, or by challenging him to combat'.[11] According to the logic of the duel, any initial insult may be neutralized by an accusation of dishonesty; it was the response to an insult which provoked the duel not usually the insult or argument directly. The *démenti* or 'giving the lie' was the spark that began the conflagration. It was common practice for the demand for satisfaction to be formalized and written down in the form of a *cartel*.

In the 1640s, Cyrano penned a series of satirical letters; these were initially circulated in manuscript form to a select readership, then collected together and published in 1654. In one witty tirade, that has come to be known as 'Le Duelliste', Cyrano joked that he had no time to read anything else because he was so inundated by written requests to fight. Theoretically, this could lend support to the claims of Cyrano's enemies, who wrote (after his death) that all his duels came about as a result of his reaction to insults about the size of his nose. Such accusations are implausible but impossible to disprove since none of the *cartels* survive.

Although the duel had its origins in the judicial practice of settling disputes through trial by combat, and although many duels were fought in order to avenge private grievances (a notorious and clichéd example would be the cuckolded husbands who resorted to the duel to restore their honour) the enormous variety of motivation for the fights was naturally as diverse as human nature. Not only that, but as the practice gained in popularity the question of motivation became increasingly secondary. The duellists were fighting in order to demonstrate their courage and their nobility and the less reason they had to take up arms against one another the greater the prestige in doing so. This gives us a clue to the contradiction between the posthumous allegations of Cyrano's enemies and Le Bret's version. Cyrano's friend never gives a specific reason for any of the fights, mentioning only Cyrano's invincible reputation attracting challengers to him, and emphasizing the fact that he fought as a second and not on his own behalf. Therefore depending on who you choose to believe – and given the lack of proof it can only ever be a matter of belief – Cyrano was either vicious and morbidly sensitive, constantly giving the lie to his tormentors and fighting duels as a doomed attempt to stave off the humiliation of being constantly insulted, or he was the dashing and reckless young hero who fought for his friends and risked his life, purely for the principal of the thing. The truth presumably falls somewhere between the two.

In his play *Le Bourgeois Gentilhomme* Molière included a reference to the practice of duelling as a codification of 'true nobility' in keeping with the practice of fellow playwrights Corneille and Cyrano. The 'bourgeois gentleman' of the title is determined to act the nobleman convincingly and one of the steps he takes towards fulfilling this ambition is to engage a fencing master, although his innate cowardice wins through in the end. On creating a ballet for the court Molière was forced to negotiate the shift in attitudes to the duel which Louis XIV was attempting to institute. In *Les Fâcheux* (as in *Le coucou imaginaire, Le mariage forcé* and *Les fourberies de Scapin*) Molière links the duel to irrationality and dangerous hotheadedness. In the course of the action, the noble hero Eraste is constantly assailed by irritating interruptions as he attempts to arrange a romantic tryst with his beloved. One of these interruptions takes the form of another noble who has heard that Eraste has been called out to fight a duel and is determined to act as his second. Even when Eraste explains that he is on his way to a romantic rendezvous the second tries to insist on accompanying him. The sensible and witty hero does not wish to fight and Molière gratified his royal audience with a long speech supporting the king's authority and his anti-duelling campaigns.

> Eraste: I was a soldier before I was a courtier. I served fourteen years, and I think I may fairly refrain from such a step with propriety, not fearing that the refusal of my sword can be imputed to cowardice. A duel puts one in an awkward light, and our King is not the mere shadow of a monarch. He knows how to make the highest in the state obey him, and I think he acts like a wise Prince. When he needs my service, I have courage enough to perform it; but I have none to displease him. His commands are a supreme law to me; seek someone else to disobey him.[12]

Eraste's insistence that it is perfectly noble and brave to refuse a duel is pure propaganda and the inclusion of this speech in the play is evidence that, although the current of public opinion may have been beginning to change, there was far to go before a war hero who bravely scorns duelling would be anything more than a decidedly far-fetched work of fiction. The reality was that, unlike Eraste, most of the king's army did not make his order 'a supreme law' – at least not where duelling was concerned.

Since Le Bret's account of Cyrano's duels with the cadets gives no details of the combats themselves we have no way of knowing for certain what the causes of the fights were, nor whether lives were lost, nor if Cyrano sustained any injuries in the course of the fights. It is possible that the duels remained amongst the cadets and that the fights were therefore stopped at the point when the first blood was spilt. It is also perfectly possible that one or more of the duels in which Cyrano fought may have been a fight to the death. Throughout his biography of Cyrano, Le Bret emphasizes his friend's good humour and insists that he never fought on his own account but always as a second. The honour to be accrued from the position of second was all the greater because the second risked his life without any real personal motivation apart from friendship, thus the danger and the thrill were all the purer. The accounts that paint the clearest picture of such combats are those found in the reminiscences of some of the memorialists of the age. Roger de Rabutin, Comte de Bussy was a courtier and soldier who wrote prolifically throughout his career and whose memoirs provide several descriptions of the experience of a duel told from the point of view of the combatant.

Bussy-Rabutin was just one year older than Cyrano but his high birth guaranteed him a far more illustrious career. Like Cyrano, Bussy-Rabutin had determined early on to join the military: 'As soon as I entered into society my first and my strongest inclination was to become an honest gentleman and to achieve great military honours.' He was present at his first siege at the age of sixteen and four years later was commanding his father's infantry regiment.

On his father's death in 1645, Bussy succeeded him as lieutenant general of the king's armies in Nivernais and state counsellor. Alongside his military career, Bussy was a prolific letter writer, who also composed songs, poetry and witty bons mots to amuse his friends. His most successful work was the scandalous *Histoire Amoureuse des Gaules* (*Amorous History of the Gauls*), a hugely popular, salacious romp through all the sexual liaisons of the various prominent figures at court, the publication of which earned him a thirteen-month residence in the Bastille. Bussy's account of his duel with a Gascon called Busc is unusual, in that for once the story is being told by the losing party, and the author admits to his fear and to the panic that causes him to grab his opponent's sword by the blade in a last desperate attempt to save himself.

> On the second blow that I struck I pierced his lung; and because I had advanced close to him I tried to break, but without thinking of the curtain behind me, such that I fell over backwards. Busc who felt himself gravely injured threw himself on me; and screaming at me to beg for my life, he tried at the same time to plunge his sword into my body but I dodged the blow and the sword just scraped my ribs and entered the ground. My fear increased twofold and made me grab his sword by the blade; but in tearing it away he cut my fingers and particularly my thumb then putting his weapon to my throat he forced me to give up my own.[13]

Count de Forbin was another high-born military man who wrote his memoirs and included the stories of duels he had fought. Unlike Bussy, he does not choose to recount any defeats and the duel is presented as an essential part of his noble advancement. He describes how, on fighting his first-ever duel, he wins the approval of his uncle, who, proud of the courage he has displayed, proceeds to arrange his promotion to a higher military rank. Although

Forbin's promotion was probably a matter of course, springing as it did from his influential family connections, he presents the duel as pivotal in the decision being taken at that time. Later in the memoir, he describes a duel with Le Chevalier de Gourdon which makes for horrifying reading:

> We fought in front of the bishop's palace; I struck him in the stomach and then again in the throat where, in parrying, my sword got stuck. Finding myself without my weapon, I received a wound in the ribs, which forced me back several paces; at that moment, my sword, which had been sticking out of the cavalier's throat fell to the ground: he picked it up. I wanted to throw myself at him, but he presented me with the points of the two swords and said: 'Stop there, you are disarmed! Here, take your sword! You have murdered me but I am an honest man.' So saying he fell stone dead.[14]

The sheer violence of the phenomenon should not be underestimated, and the writers who claimed after Cyrano's death that he was disfigured by duelling scars may not have been relying entirely on their imaginations. Naturally, it was precisely this violence which attracted so many young men of the era to the duel, the extreme sport of the age. In 1645 René de Ceriziers published a book in which he analysed the essentials of military glory. He writes that courage is the single most essential quality in a great captain: 'One of the most necessary parts of those who command is courage; since courage is as much the making of a Hero as reason is the making of a man.' Despite the illegality of the duel he clearly approves wholeheartedly of the practice and contents himself with the following equivocation: 'Since I cannot name it a worthy act of courage; I will call it the most beautiful error and the most forgivable sin of youth.'[15]

Ceriziers is just one in a long line of admirers of this 'most forgivable sin'; the heroic aspect appealed not just to the reckless young men themselves and to contemporary dramatists but to generations to follow. In the nineteenth century, Alexandre Dumas, Théophile Gautier and Charles Nodier not only chose to write about swashbuckling adventurers but they aspired to emulate then. Along with fellow author Paul Féval, who contented himself with being an attentive spectator, they frequented the fencing school of Maître Augustin Grisier at number 4 rue du Faubourg Montmartre, where they undertook intensive training in the art of swordplay. Dumas even gained the reputation as an excellent duellist, although, much to his vociferous disgust, he was more often called out to duel with pistols, the more modern and infinitely less noble weapon of choice at the time. In spite of their fascination with the duel, the authors who described the swashbuckling legends of the seventeenth century recognized that the historical reality of the practice needed a little modification in order to be acceptable to their readership. Thus they tended to situate their combats in contexts where the hero's motivation for fighting was clear, and to cast the fights in the simple terms of good versus evil. Of the countless duels fought in the seventeenth century, precious few would be found to fit such a pattern. The author of an anti-duelling text of the era entitled *Notable Discourse on Duels* laments this element of thoughtlessness in the combats and the fact that the duellists were not even concerned whether they were fighting for a just cause or not. 'Today no one looks more closely [at motives]. As soon as one is called, one must fight, at any cost, whether for right or wrong.'[16] The reason for the fights was relatively unimportant and this insouciance was not in keeping with the rules of fiction, where honour and danger needed to be placed in a clear context of right and wrong.

The duellist as reckless thrill-seeker is not a model that appears in any of the story-book versions of the phenomenon, and yet it is undeniably an important element in explaining the attraction of this extraordinarily dangerous craze. In reality, when Cyrano fought his duels, right and wrong were not the issues at stake; however he was not purely motivated by the lure of the forbidden and the heady rush of dicing with death. There was an expectation among the duellists that their exploits deserved a degree of recognition. The need to 'make himself known' is the reason that Le Bret gives for Cyrano's combats. To some extent, this search for recognition is reflected in the fictional representations of the duel, and the combat is frequently shown as the catalyst which leads to the revelation of the 'true worth' of the hero, and a consequent dramatic transformation of his situation. Sadly as Cyrano was to discover, in real life, without powerful friends or the leverage of significant wealth, the recognition of one's extraordinary courage did not necessarily lead on to the transformation of one's situation.

Rostand had read enough of the real Cyrano's writing to realize that an added dimension to the caricature would save his dramatic hero from being a pathetic or petulant figure. Like Prévot, Rostand saw in Cyrano a personality infused with a determination to surpass his own limitations and those that society would attempt to impose on him. The stage Cyrano declares: 'I've decided to excel in everything' and the original is suddenly vividly present.[17] Rostand clearly saw the dramatic potential of Cyrano's duels as a priceless opportunity and gifted the great actor Coquelin with the inspired scene of a duel in verse, in which Cyrano fences and improvises a ballad at the same time; thereby simultaneously demonstrating his intellectual and physical superiority to his opponent. The repetition of the line with the promise, or rather the threat, '*à la fin de l'envoi je touche!*' is a particularly memorable device. The stage Cyrano is as good as his word and vanquishes the enemy to the admiring applause of the surrounding onlookers (and the theatrical audience). At which point, Rostand neatly worked in a graceful nod to Alexandre Dumas; a soldier steps forward out of the crowd to congratulate Cyrano, and is then revealed to be none other than the great d'Artagnan.

A demon of bravery

Once his period of training with the cadets in Paris was complete, the real Cyrano left for Mouzon and the front line of the war with Germany. The city was under siege and the young man would face the hardships of a military campaign and either confirm or disprove the opinion expressed later by Napoleon Bonaparte, the most successful French military leader of all time, that: 'Good duellists make bad soldiers.'

6

Make love not war

In Cyrano's mature work reflections on the futility of war abound. He goes to some length to develop the theory that it is ultimately more honourable to make love and create new life than to make war and destroy it. Or as he puts it, 'It is much more honest to sweat at the construction than the destruction of one's species.'[1] It seems paradoxical that the soldier who had thrown himself so wholeheartedly into the bloody violence of the duel should turn pacifist, and declare the enterprise of warfare 'a channel for every injustice' but that was the eventual result of Cyrano's time in the army. His first experience of a military engagement was at the siege of Mouzon in 1639. This was just one of the many battles that formed part of the ongoing Thirty Years War. Mouzon is not far from the French border with Luxembourg and the Germans were besieging the French inhabitants with the intention of extending their reach further into Louis XIII's kingdom.

Siege warfare was perhaps the most important element of military strategy in the seventeenth century. In his account of the fundamentals of a gentlemanly education Cardinal Richelieu included the study of fortifications as an essential subject. In another text of the period by the Italian Montecuccoli, the author felt sufficiently sure of his readership's familiarity with the art of the siege to be able to introduce the subject with an almost comic brevity: 'They must set up camp, open the trench, construct the approaches, place the cannons, force the exterior, open the counterscarp, pass the ditch with the tunnels, secure the sapper, make a breach and launch the attack.'[2] The simplicity of this list belies a messy and uncertain reality in which the outcome of any engagement was far from sure.

In the real world, the military textbook ceases to have much meaning. Instead we can turn to a fragment of autobiographical information about the siege of Mouzon to be found in Cyrano's letter 'Sur le blocus d'une ville' (On the blockade of a town). This letter, which recounts the author's experience of being under siege with his fellow officers, is only an unfinished fragment. In contrast to the majority of his published letters where Cyrano's imagination overflows with an abundance of burlesque witticisms, here inspiration was clearly absent and, although he attempts to make light of a terrible situation, the jokes fall rather flat. The letter draws a flippant parallel between the slow starvation inflicted on a besieged city and the lenten fasting of Catholic tradition. 'We have no reason at all to complain, we are in another sort of Heaven, since we neither drink nor eat; they want to bring us to Paradise through starvation; and for fear that we might take nourishment in at the ears they even forbid us words in bad taste.'[3]

The image of the commanding officers refusing the men even the sustenance of *paroles grasses* – that is coarse phrases or literally 'greasy words' – affords a brief glimpse of the undisciplined soldiers indulging in the minor rebellion of vulgarity. Cyrano demonstrates his solidarity with the men and he notes mockingly that attempting to forbid miserable, hungry soldiers from expressing themselves crudely is as pointless as hoping they can survive on the nourishment of a dirty joke. The gallows humour of the letter, and in particular the fact that it simply tails off, as if the author lacked the energy to continue, speak volumes for the demoralizing effect of the siege.

On 21 June 1639, Marshal de Châtillon arrived with reinforcements to relieve the besieged soldiers. The French army were victorious, the enemy were forced to withdraw. Supply lines could be opened once again and the men were saved from a slow death from starvation. Meanwhile, Cyrano had been wounded in one of the attacks; a musket ball had passed right through his side. The unfinished state of the letter may even be testament to this unexpected end to Cyrano's famous ability to focus and write even in the midst of military chaos. Such an injury could easily have been fatal in a time when surgical procedures were approximate at best and the importance of basic hygiene practically unknown. The wound may well have been cauterized to aid healing: a brand applied to the flesh to sear the wound, a practice which acted as a very rudimentary method of sterilization. The pain of such a procedure would have been horrific but Cyrano was fortunate enough – if the musket ball had lodged in his flesh, it is possible that he would have survived the operation to remove it, but probably not the inevitable post-operative infection.

Bussy-Rabutin, who fell gravely ill while on campaign, was a close friend of the Prince de Condé and, as such, earned the dubious privilege of being treated by the prince's personal physician. He sums up the skill of his medical attendant with admirable brevity: 'Luckily he fell ill himself and died; if not he would have killed me.' Cyrano, whose health was always poor, from the time of his first injury onwards, came up with a blasphemous version of the same joke. In his satirical letter 'Contre les médecins' (Against Doctors), he compares doctors to Christ because their deaths are mankind's salvation: 'they die as well as God for the salvation of man'.[4] The letter is a comic masterpiece, in which Cyrano goes into great detail about the horrors and indignities inflicted on him by the 'torturers' of the medical profession. It ends with a paroxysm of hilarity as the letter suddenly shifts to the present tense, when the patient, seeing his doctor approaching, screeches at him, '*Vade retro Satanas*' (Get thee behind me Satan), as if hoping to exorcize the terrible demon.

Cyrano's second military campaign saw him taking part in the siege of Arras. The recapture of Arras from the occupying Spanish forces was of critical importance for the king due to France's deepening involvement in the power struggles of the Thirty Years War. The town's strategic position close to the border with the Low Countries gave it military significance in Cyrano's time and many years later when the trenches of the First World War saw the nearby landscape soaked with blood. Towards the end of April 1640, French forces arrived at Arras. The initial difficulty facing the French troops was how even to set up camp near enough to the target without drawing devastating Spanish fire. As a result, a diversionary attack was launched on the nearby towns of Aire-sur-la-Lys and Béthune, north of Arras itself. A significant section of the Spanish garrison left Arras to deal with the situation, and the French were able to set up camp.

In June, the king himself visited the encampment to inspect his troops. However, the tables were rapidly turned on the French troops when the Spanish forces encircled their encampment and the besieging French found themselves under siege. The troops were trapped for two weeks without provisions, water was scarce and sanitary conditions appalling. Epidemics seized the weakened men and the dead and dying piled up in the trenches; no one dared to brave the Spanish fire to collect the corpses. As the heat of summer added further discomforts to the dire conditions in the encampment, battles raged, unceasing and murderous. The Spanish lines were broken on the 2nd of August and by the 9th the French were victorious, reclaiming Arras for their own.

There is some controversy as to whether Cyrano had gained

promotion into the guards of the Prince de Conti at this point, which springs largely from the evidence of Cyrano's friendship with various key figures who were Conti's men. It seems unlikely that Cyrano had changed regiments, particularly since no reference to such a change is to be found. The friendships cited as proof only really show that Cyrano knew members of this regiment, which included Le Bret's younger brother, but nothing more. The controversy is founded on an anachronism, since the prince was only eleven years old at the time when Cyrano was in the army and his company was not created until 1649.

Although we know that d'Artagnan and Cyrano both fought in the siege of Arras there is no surviving documentary evidence of an encounter between the two heroes. However, since both were serving with Gascon regiments it seems at least possible that such an encounter did take place. Paul Féval *fils*, son of the creator of the legendary Lagardère, decided that such an encounter was not just possible but inevitable. His imaginative vision of the adventures of the two heroes in his popular serial novels *D'Artagnan contre Cyrano de Bergerac* (1925) and *D'Artagnan et Cyrano réconciliés* (1928) was even accompanied by a preface in which he claimed to have discovered yet another 'lost manuscript', number 4772, from which the events of the two books are drawn. On the whole Féval follows Rostand's vision of Cyrano and relates the adventures of the courageous but eccentric poet as he befriends the dashing young *Chevalier Mystère*, the love child of Anne of Austria and the Duke of Buckingham. In *D'Artagnan et Cyrano réconciliés*, Cyrano is given a happy ending for once and is married off to the beautiful Roxane. Whether that was the sort of happy ending that the real Cyrano would have chosen for himself is another question.

The occupying Spaniards taunted the French soldiers that they would only succeed in taking the city of Arras 'when rats eat cats'. In fact the French did eventually retake Arras giving rise to bizarre celebratory engravings depicting cats in full Spanish armour defeated by giant soldier rats. In the fray Cyrano had suffered another serious injury, a sword wound to the throat. In his biography, Le Bret refers to Cyrano's war wounds as an important element in his decision to leave the army, remarking with admirable understatement that the 'inconvenience' they caused him would affect him for the rest of his life. Cyrano's time in the army had also exposed him to other less concrete but more insidious dangers. His youthful vision of the world was threatened, and there can be little doubt that it was his time in the army, which, more than anything, instilled in him the bitter cynicism and unshakeable atheism that would only sharpen with age. Theoretically, joining the army was supposed to be the pinnacle of the heroic destiny of a nobleman, and as such, the young Cyrano had probably expected to encounter inspiring examples of courage and self-sacrifice in the arena of war. The reality was infinitely more prosaic, more brutal, and years later Cyrano would still be struggling with the memories of his army years, trying to make sense of the lessons he learnt about humanity in that time. Not least of which was the truth of Montaigne's maxim that: 'there is no beast so greatly to be feared by man as man'.[5]

In 1669 a novel was published which unmasked the everyday reality of life in the armed forces during the Thirty Years War. *The Adventures of Simplicius Simplicissimus* described the day-to-day occupations of the members of the so-called 'honourable profession' in the following revealing terms;

> . . . for their entire activity consisted of hard drinking, suffering hunger and thirst, whoring and pederasty, rattling dice and gambling, overeating and overdrinking, killing and being killed, harassing and being harassed, hunting down and being hunted, being afraid and causing fear, robbing and being robbed, mugging and being mugged, inflicting misery and suffering it, beating and being beaten – in a few words, spoiling and harming, and being despoiled and harmed in turn.[6]

And after such a life the future that awaited the men was without hope of respite or improvement.

> . . . they continued eagerly in their works until after a while they finally gave up the ghost, died and croaked in battles, sieges, storms, campaigns, and even in their quarters . . . except only a few oldsters who (unless they had stashed away stolen or extorted goods) made the very best panhandlers and beggars.[7]

The hero of the novel is named Simplicius as a reference to the fact that he is a simple peasant and not a nobleman, but his name is also ironic. Simplicius's wily vagabond ways and his damning view of the armed forces as seen from the bottom up are anything but simple. As well as denouncing the rape, pillage and other outrages committed by the foot soldiers the story also satirizes the corruption and brutality of the aristocrats. In between campaigns and on the marches, moving from one battleground to another, troops were quartered on local villages (larger towns were exempted from this trial) and horrendous abuses were all too frequently the result. A proverb of the time asked how many peasants were required to support a single soldier and the reply was three: one to lend him his house, a second to lend him his wife and a third to go to hell in his stead.

In 1633, Jacques Callot published a series of eighteen engravings entitled 'Miseries and Misfortunes of War'. The engravings depict soldiers on the rampage: the devastation of an inn, the pillage of a peasant dwelling, the sacking of a church and the burning of a village. The series also shows the guilty soldiers arrested and the gory punishments meted out by their superior officers and local justice. A tree is transformed into a gibbet, the firing squad is put in place and an executioner breaks the arms and legs of a torture victim strapped to the wheel. Finally, in the seventeenth engraving the peasants are shown massacring the soldiers, and the title explains the legitimacy of their revenge: 'These unfortunates revenge themselves thus for the loss of their goods, for which they [the soldiers] are solely responsible.' This penultimate scene which shows beatings and stabbings is strikingly similar to a passage in the adventures of Simplicius in which Grimmelshausen depicts the sack of a village and the reaction of the peasants. The village is in flames having been pillaged and then set alight by soldiers, some peasants have run off, others are taken prisoner, including the village pastor who gets trampled by a horse and receives a blow to the head from the rider. While the soldiers are exercising this 'tyrannous cruelty' seemingly in the grip of madness, suddenly armed peasants emerge from the forest and Grimmelshausen compares the ensuing, ferocious battle to the effect of shaking a wasps' nest.

Although Grimmelshausen was German his satirical exposé of the reality of the Thirty Years War is equally relevant to the French army. In the public archives of the town of Artois a collection of more than 3,000 letters of complaint against the army testify to the accuracy of his fictional description and to the frequency with which such outrages were occurring.

The experiences related by English travellers in France also highlight the threat that the soldiers posed to law and order. Sir Philip Perceval's tutor wrote to him from Angers in 1677 with a tale of the criminal behaviour of French troops. 'The soldiers quartered here have been very troublesome with their robberies and abuses at night til one of them, who killed a townsman, hath been hanged, so that now they are quiet enough within the gates, but without they rob people of what they are bringing to market.'[8] Lady Fanshawe, a royalist in exile, described in her memoirs her journey from Calais to Paris to join her husband. On reaching the town of Abbeville she was informed that because of the danger of highway robbery she should take a guard of garrison soldiers with her on the next stage of her journey.

> The next morning they sent me ten troopers well armed, and when I had gone about four leagues, as we ascended a hill, says

> some of these, 'Madame, look out but fear nothing'. They rid all up to a hill and met a well mounted troop of horse, about fifty or more, which after some parly wheeled about in the woods again. When we came upon the hill I asked how it was possible so many men so well armed should turne, having so few to oppose them; at which they laugh'd and say'd 'Madame, we are all of a company and quarter in this town. The truth is our pay is short, and we are forced to help ourselves this way, but we have this rule, that if we in a party guard any company, the rest never molest them, but let them pass free.' I having past all danger, as they said, gave them a pistole each, and so left them.[9]

These eyewitness accounts help to explain the rapacious behaviour of the troops, as well as the inevitability of their choosing the soft target of the local peasants, who could not bribe their way to protection. The peasants, bringing food to market, are set upon by soldiers who face an alternative of starvation. As Lady Fanshawe's guard informs her, 'pay is short, and we are forced to help ourselves in this way'. The ordinary soldiers were left with little choice but to use their professional skills – violence and intimidation – to extract the means to live from the most vulnerable members of society.

The question of how to pay and supply the vast armies mustered to fight in the various battles of the Thirty Years War proved to be an insurmountable logistical problem for the government. From 1635 onwards, as numbers of troops swelled, many of the French army's defeats were caused by the financial burden of keeping the forces in the field. Across Europe, the same difficulties confronted leaders determined to attain military dominance at any price. In *The Voyage to the Moon*, Cyrano's hero encounters a kind and gentle lunar noblewoman who pronounces judgement on the callousness of the generals laughingly sending millions to their deaths: 'And while they send more than four million better men than they off to get their heads broken, they are in their studies laughing at the circumstances of the massacre of these poor simpletons.'[10]

Despite being far from suffering, like their subordinates, from the painful uncertainty as to where the next meal might be coming from, even the most privileged of the king's soldiers were capable of extraordinarily aberrant behaviour in wartime. Bussy-Rabutin's memoirs provide us with the story of the truly bizarre way in which certain officers chose to amuse themselves while serving under the Prince de Condé at the ill-fated siege of Lérida in Spain. Bussy had been invited to a dinner with fellow officers La Vallière, Le Bretèche, Jumeaux and Barbentane. The friends decided to dine in a ruined church by the ramparts of the town; Barbentane went off into the nearby cemetery where he prised the lid off a tomb and brought out a cadaver, which he dragged back to the group. Then with the assistance of Le Bretèche they made the corpse dance to the music of the prince's violins. Bussy-Rabutin was, according to his own account, both disgusted and terrified and insisted that they take the corpse away and return it to its coffin. The dinner continued with bawdy songs and further revelry until an officer named La Trousse arrived to take guard duty with La Vallière. Seeing the state of the men, La Trousse volunteered to leave La Vallière to stay and finish his enjoyment but the drunken La Vallière chose to accompany La Trousse in order to fill him in on operations.

As the two walked along the edge of the trench, La Vallière was shot in the head and killed instantly. The revellers were informed, but chose to carry on regardless, and Jumeaux even went as far as to hurry to the prince to ask for the government of the town, previously held by his friend La Vallière. Bussy-Rabutin, meanwhile, began to convince himself that divine retribution was responsible for this sudden death and became increasingly superstitious and scared. Rumours started to fly around the camp that the corpse was the body of a saint miraculously preserved from decay. Bussy

Rabutin made a deal with Jumeaux that whichever of the two died first would come to the other with news of the afterlife. When Jumeaux died suddenly a few days later Bussy-Rabutin was gripped with terror each night, fearing that his ghost would soon return. Bussy-Rabutin became convinced that the men who had been present at the supper were all cursed and that they would all die off one by one. He ended up running away from Spain and returning home to Burgundy. The prince eventually had to abandon the siege and the name of the town, Lérida, became synonymous with failure and many satirical rhymes were made about the defeat.

Aristocratic officers like Bussy-Rabutin and his friends rose in rank using money and influence and, at the top of the hierarchy, the supreme commander-in-chief of the French army was the king himself. Both Louis XIII and his son after him were groomed from childhood to be warrior princes who led by example. Having taken part in drilling exercises and war games from a very young age, the monarch was expected to command his troops from the front line of battle to the extent that the French king occasionally found himself in the very thick of the action. In one notorious incident at a siege of 1654 a soldier had his hand blown off by a cannon ball just metres away from the young Louis XIV. It was reported that the unfortunate casualty staggered to where his severed hand lay in the mud and 'nobly picking it up again he came to present it to the King, whom he told that he was proud to have lost the limb in his service'. This little anecdote is related by Michel de Marroles in his *History of the Kings of France*, as an example of the extremes of willing self-sacrifice to which the king's loyal subjects were prepared to go. Whether the account is accurate or not, the fact that Marroles presents it as such is sufficient evidence of the strength of devotion which was expected of the king's men. Louis's reaction is not recorded in the anecdote and one is naturally left wondering: what exactly is the correct royal etiquette for the reception of bloody severed limbs? The king visited his troops at the siege of Arras but we have no record of Cyrano's reaction to this close-up view of the head of state. The right to command was seen as a privilege of birth as much in military terms as in politics. This was partly a throwback to feudalism and partly due to the venality of offices as the ever observant (and ever critical) John Reresby noted in his *Memoirs and Travels*,

> The gentry are well bred, but no scholars, being usually taken from their studies at about fourteen, then put into the academy to learn their exercises, as fencing, dancing, music, riding the great horse, and the like, and then sent into the army, where if they purchase not some command, after a campaign or two (for the stoutest must pay as well as the rest) they return to such employments as their friends prepare for them elsewhere.[11]

Reresby also provides a further clue as to the brevity of Cyrano's military career with his parenthetical remark that 'the stoutest must pay as well as the rest'. It was not enough to gain a reputation as a demon of courage – no amount of heroics could compensate the lack of cold hard cash. As, for example, in the case of the Gascon Captain Tréville (of Musketeer fame) who served for twenty years as the acting commander of his regiment with neither the official title nor the pay commensurate to the post because the position nominally belonged to the king's favourite Luynes. Appointed when he was just fifteen, Luynes was never expected to assume any of the responsibilities of the position or do any work. Tréville was there for that and it would only take two decades of this thankless toil in the shadow of an overprivileged child before Tréville would gain his due recognition only to have the honour snatched away again when Cardinal Mazarin disbanded the regiment. After a campaign or two Cyrano was in no position to purchase a command and was faced with the alternative of time-serving, like the loyal Tréville, or cutting his losses and returning to Paris while still in possession of all his limbs. Cyrano's choice was soon made.

The estimated death toll for the Thirty Years War is 2,071,000 and this figure does not even include those on the fringes of the combat who found themselves preyed upon by their own national troops. One of the most tragic and telling testimonies to the miseries of the Thirty Years War is that provided by a few lines scrawled in a family Bible in the final year of the war: 'They say that the terrible war is over now. But there is still no sign of peace. Envy, hatred and greed are everywhere; they are all the war has taught us [. . .] We live like animals eating bark and grass. No one could ever have imagined that such things would happen to us. Many people say that there is no God.' Astonishingly, the writer ends with a frail ray of hope, evidence of the extraordinary strength and dignity that are sometimes kindled in the human heart by terrible suffering: 'But we still believe that God has not abandoned us. We must unite and help one another.'[12]

The consolation of faith would not have reassured Cyrano, he was not susceptible to the idea that the horrific scenes he witnessed as a soldier were part of some divine plan. He was all too aware of the resolutely human origins of the conflict. After all, the French were fighting on the side of the Protestant Dutch and Swedes (despite being themselves a Catholic nation) due to the political necessity of supporting resistance to their dangerously powerful Catholic rivals, Spain and the Holy Roman Empire. Any argument for the religious justification of the conflict was on decidedly shaky ground. In *The Voyage to the Moon*, Cyrano talks about the use of military music as a means to distract and betray the men, preventing them from reflecting on the importance of their lives by whipping them up into a fury of bloodlust and fear. In order to communicate his shame and disappointment in mankind, Cyrano invented an escape voyage into outer space, where he imagined the possibility of more humane civilizations. Only in this way could his criticism of the myriad failings of the human race be voiced with impunity. The lunar noblewoman, 'the prettiest of the queen's ladies-in-waiting', who had condemned the barbarity of generals sending their men to die in the wars was equally unsparing of the victims of the slaughter. She acknowledges the courage shown by the men who fight for their country, but undercuts the remark with a sarcastic reflection on the flimsiness of their motivation: 'But I am wrong to blame the valour of your brave subjects: they do well to die for their country; the affair is important, since it means the difference between being the subject of a king who wears a ruff or one who wears bands.'[13]

Elsewhere, Cyrano would express the heartfelt conviction that 'a true gentleman is neither French, nor German nor Spanish; he is a citizen of the world and his homeland is everywhere'.[14] Cyrano's insistence that sex is nobler than killing is further developed when his lunar-voyaging hero sniggeringly remarks the fact that the noblemen in the moon wear something other than a sword to symbolize their rank and honour. Eventually, having first made sure there are no ladies present, he plucks up the courage to ask whether the object hanging from the belts of the courtiers really is what he thinks it is. The response is dignified and determined: 'Know then that the sash with which this man is honoured and whereby hangs a form of medal in the shape of a virile member is the symbol of a gentleman and the mark that distinguishes a nobleman from a commoner.'[15] The space traveller is unable to contain his amusement at this and bursts out laughing. He then condescendingly reveals the superior terrestrial tradition of wearing a sword as the mark of nobility. The lunar gentleman is unperturbed and calmly explains why this is yet another proof of the moral inferiority of the terrestrial viewpoint.

> He was not moved by this but exclaimed: 'My little man, the nobles in your world are mad to parade an instrument which is the mark of a hangman, which is only forged for our destruction

> and is indeed the sworn enemy of everything that lives! And just as mad to hide a member without which we should be in the category of things that are not . . . Woe to the country where the marks of generation are ignominious and those of destruction are honourable! You call that member "the parts of shame" as if there were anything more glorious than to give life and anything more infamous than to take it away.'[16]

In Cyrano's imagination, warfare on the moon was strictly regulated in order to prevent any combat between unequally matched enemies, and preference given to the settlement of disputes by peaceful arbitration. The mature Cyrano also denounced the duel; in a spirit of humorous perversity the great duellist took pleasure in proving that all victories in single combat were, ultimately, a matter of luck. During his time with the cadets, Cyrano seems to have been forced to accept the truth of the statement, found in an anti-duelling text by the archbishop of Embrun, that: 'The most famous duellists have never been our most illustrious captains.'[17] This truism would be enshrined in the annals of military history thanks to its repetition by Napoleon. Although left with no choice but to abandon his hopes of winning glory on the battlefield, Cyrano did not immediately give up on the idea that honour may be acquired by arms. The hour of his greatest martial achievement was still to come.

7
The itch for glory

It would be anachronistic to picture the young Cyrano leaving the army in 1641 as some kind of seventeenth-century conscientious objector. His decision was essentially pragmatic and, although he abandoned the career of arms, he continued to fight duels and his disenchantment with violence and bloodshed was to be a slow and gradual process. He always retained a profound admiration for the military heroics of figures like Alexander the Great, Achilles and Hercules. When Le Bret describes this period in Cyrano's life, he does not oversimplify his friend's situation. Various factors had combined to bring Cyrano's military career to an abrupt halt and Le Bret is honest enough to include them all. Firstly, in his typically calm and understated manner, he describes the two major wounds that Cyrano had received in the thick of battle. Cyrano's health was dramatically compromised, but not to an extent that would have seen him invalided out of the army. One of the most successful and revered military leaders of Cyrano's time lost an arm, a leg, an eye and an ear in battle; Marshal Jean de Gassion was a decade older than Cyrano and a gifted military strategist. He was appointed to one of the highest military dignities in the land in 1643 when he was named a marshal of France. In his spirited defence of Cardinal Mazarin, Cyrano mentions this appointment approvingly as a proof of the cardinal's ability to recognize and reward military talent. He obviously respected and admired Gassion but not enough to want to follow in his footsteps.

Le Bret also remarks on his friend's 'small hope of consideration'.[1] This was a less tangible but considerably more significant handicap than Cyrano's injuries. After a couple of campaigns a soldier from a noble background had served his apprenticeship and it was expected that he would purchase a captaincy and start to advance in rank. It was essential to progress to higher military dignities in keeping with one's social standing. To stay as a lowly subordinate would have jarred not only with Cyrano's independent spirit but also with his strong sense of his own importance. If he had remained in the army without advancing he would have destroyed his own myth in the process. Le Bret, as the keeper of the flame, does not allow that Cyrano's 'small hope of consideration' was due to the fact that his family were neither wealthy nor influential enough to secure the next step up in his military career, because (at least on his mother's side) they were.

Instead he focuses on a less degrading obstacle to success – Cyrano's own free-spirited refusal to accept the help of an influential patron who could have ensured his advancement. This is a neat sleight of hand, concealing Cyrano's relatively humble position behind a mask of haughty independence. Such a claim would seem a ludicrous bluff were it not that Le Bret is able to back up his suggestion that Cyrano proudly refused to attach himself to a noble patron with a concrete example. Early in the 1640s, not long after leaving the army, Cyrano apparently rejected an offer of patronage from none other than Marshal de Gassion himself. Despite his obvious admiration for the military commander, the soldier-poet was not tempted to rejoin the ranks of the king's army and, when the one-legged hero died at the siege of Lens in 1647, Cyrano was not by his side.

Le Bret cites the frequency with which Cyrano was called upon by his fellow soldiers to fight in duels as another of the reasons why he wished to leave the army. Cyrano's reputation, as a skilled and courageous duellist, made him the ideal choice as a second and consequently he was apparently permanently in demand. Le Bret's insistence that Cyrano fought over a hundred duels as a second and none at all on his own account seems highly improbable, but it's not impossible. Elsewhere, Le Bret stresses his friend's great good humour and the sweetness of his disposition, although, given the vituperative nature of some of the satirical letters that Cyrano wrote, it is rather hard to believe that he was always as conciliatory as Le Bret implies. The letters he wrote on the subject reveal that Cyrano himself learned not to take his reputation as an invincible duellist too seriously. In the letter 'Against a coward', Cyrano takes his usual contrary stance and, assuming the character of a craven coward, he proceeds to outline a hilarious series of excuses for not fighting a duel. He even quotes the famous Cornelian maxim from *Le Cid* that 'Stained honour may be washed clean only with blood', purely in order to turn it to ridicule. Although the letter is written in the first person and, despite Cyrano's obvious delight in confounding expectations, the piece is, above all, a comic fiction and the persona of the coward owes a great deal to the stock theatrical buffoon the *matamore*.

In *Le Pédant Joué* Cyrano had also taken pleasure in inventing ridiculous posturing speeches for Chateaufort who is a perfect example of this type, a braggart whose excessive boasts about his courage and his powers of seduction cannot conceal his innate cowardice or his amorous failures. Cyrano's legend has suffered from the gleeful pleasure with which he imagined the ranting and humiliation of this fictional character. After his death Cyrano's enemies cast him in the role of cowardly braggart and attributed to him all the grotesqueness of his own fictional creations. Even Rostand's Cyrano is a descendant of the matamore, sharing his ranting and bluster and his humiliating rejection by a beautiful young woman. The shadow of Cyrano's swashbuckling prowess looms large and his decision to put such things behind him at a relatively young age is all but eclipsed by the flamboyance of the legend.

In late 1640 or early 1641, Cyrano enrolled himself as a student at the Collège de Lisieux. He had never completed his original degree at the Collège de Beauvais and he did not last long at this new institution either. He was strongly attracted to the newest fields of enquiry and these were not studied in the stuffy confines of the Jesuit-run colleges. One of the writers Cyrano most admired wrote that it was their excess of virtue which led to the *libertins* being marginalized. In his *Heroic Verses*, Tristan L'Hermite declared that virtue was his 'high mistress' and that this caused him to shun worldly success. In Cyrano's two-volume masterpiece *The Voyages to the Sun and the Moon*, he refers to various contemporary figures in order to pay homage to their erudition and originality, but none receives more heartfelt, unequivocal praise than Tristan. The passage in question begins with a trademark piece of verbal trickery as Tristan is denounced as 'the disgrace of his nation'. This is then revealed to be one of Cyrano's typical paradoxes because the disgrace referred to is the failure of the great and the good of France to honour such a worthy individual: 'the disgrace of his nation; since it is certainly a disgrace to the great nobles of your State to recognise in him without worshipping it, the virtue that he enshrines'.[2] Cyrano follows Tristan's lead in identifying the poet's defining characteristic as virtue. He goes on: 'He is thoroughly witty, thoroughly brave [. . .] In short I can add nothing to the praise of this great man, except to say that he is the sole poet, the sole philosopher, and the sole free man that you have.'[3]

There are certain interesting parallels between the biographies of the two authors. Tristan's real name was François but he adopted the name Tristan in order to increase his own personal prestige by highlighting his connection to an illustrious ancestor of the same name, who was grand provost at the court of Louis XI in the late Middle Ages. In his poem entitled 'La Servitude', Tristan reflects on the humiliation of dependence. The rhetorical question he poses could almost have been the inspiration for Rostand's tirade:

> *Should I go about to abase myself in a thousand, thousand different*
> *ways*
> *And lay siege to twenty houses,*
> *In order to snatch the bread that is not offered to me?*[4]

Tristan was reasonably well connected but not personally wealthy, and his life was plagued by ill health. Neither his poverty, nor his poor health was much helped by his self-confessed addictions to drinking and gambling. He was also a redoubtable duellist and had to flee from his position as a page in the court of Henri IV after killing an opponent when he was only in his early teens. He recounts his ensuing adventures in England, Poland and Spain in the semi-autobiographical novel *The Disgraced Page*.

It has been suggested that Cyrano may also have travelled to Poland and to England and that the strong friendship between the two men may have been forged in part from these common experiences. But apart from fictional references to these destinations, no proof for such a theory has yet been uncovered. Cyrano and Tristan shared a fascination with alchemy and Cyrano makes explicit reference to this fact in an aside in which the character who praises Tristan is revealed to be an escapee from Tristan's own novel *The Disgraced Page*, an ancient sage, who had so mastered the alchemical arts as to succeed in creating the philosopher's stone.

If the testimony of contemporary authors such as the Italian diplomat Primi Visconti are to be believed then a preference for study over slaughter was a far from fashionable choice. Rather it was a decision which from a worldly point of view must inevitably bring Cyrano down in the estimation of his peers. 'Indeed, in France none but military honours are held in esteem, those of literature and of all other professions are despised and a man of quality who knows how to write is considered vile.'[5] Still more explicitly, Guez de Balzac, in a letter of 1637, ridicules the very idea that anyone should be prepared to sink so low. 'Is it possible that a man . . . who has not received a commandment from the King on pain of death to go to his books could wish to abandon the rank of honest gentleman that he holds in the world in order to go and take up that of ridiculous and impertinent child amidst teachers and schoolboys?'[6] Balzac's mockery helps to explain why Théophile de Viau, Tristan and Cyrano all wrote about being poor and disregarded. Choosing to be a poet, who wrote, not for the delight of the king and his courtiers or for a wealthy patron, but simply to be truc to himself, was choosing to fail in worldly terms.

And yet, in the same year as he entered the Collège de Lisieux, Cyrano also entered into two contracts, which reveal that he had not entirely abandoned all ideas of mixing in fashionable society. Papers survive which reveal that, on 8 October 1641, Cyrano entered into a contract with Pierre Moussard, a fencing master with a studio on rue Saint Jacques. The agreement was that Moussard would provide regular lessons for the period of two years for the price of 10 livres a month. On the 23rd of the same month Cyrano also entered into an identical arrangement with one David Dupron, a dancing master based in the same street. This biographical fragment recalls Molière's play in which the social-climbing bourgeois gentleman also engages himself dancing and fencing masters, in order to ape the accomplishments of the nobility. Sadly, no further trace of Cyrano's lessons survive, so we have no way of knowing whether Maître Dupron considered him a miracle of grace or a clodhopping idiot. Maître Moussard on the other hand must have been proud to call Cyrano his pupil, since he carried off a swashbuckling feat of such bravado as to capture the attention even of the great Gassion himself: the duel with one hundred men.

Le Bret gives the names of at least three eye witnesses to Cyrano's most momentous exploit. He describes how Monsieur de Bourgogne, who was the *maître de camp* of the Prince de Conti's infantry regiment, had been responsible for informing Marshal de Gassion and further notes that two other soldiers, Monsieur de Cavais and Monsieur de Cuigy, were also witnesses to the scene. Le Bret's version of events briefly states that the men felled by Cyrano deserved their fate and that 'two of them paid with their lives and seven others with serious injuries for their malicious plot'. Le Bret readily admits that the story is unconvincing and that it would be dismissed as pure fiction, were it not that the scene was witnessed by these 'several persons of quality', who made it their business to spread the word widely enough to eliminate the possibility of doubt. Le Bret refers to the assailants as intending to 'insult' one of Cyrano's friends, and this may be a clue as to the true nature of this extraordinary ambush in broad daylight at the de Nesle gate. It seems most probable that the men were lackeys, armed with a motley selection of swords, knives and clubs, paid to administer a *bastonnade* (a severe beating with clubs) perhaps to silence one of Cyrano's controversial circle once and for all. The bastonnade was a fate traditionally reserved for poets and writers, who, by virtue of their profession, were considered to have descended too far below the rank of the nobility to merit an exchange of swordplay, and the codes of duelling strictly stated that a duel could only be fought between combatants of equal rank. Hence the bastonnade was the fate reserved for those who were not important enough to merit a true duel. The very fact of administering such a beating was a terrible insult because it implied that the subject was far beneath the dignity of their attacker.

Who ordered this attack and whether the intended victim was Lignières, another poet friend, or even Cyrano himself, remains a mystery – Rostand's identification of the Duc de Guise as the culprit has no more basis in historical fact than his vision of Lignières as the intended victim. Le Bret's reference to 'a friend' as the target of this attack is very vague; no doubt he wanted to gloss over the question of what the person singled out for this excessive punishment had done to merit the 'insult' of an armed ambush. Here we find ourselves in territory that is dark and difficult to negotiate, with very good reason. Le Bret's biography bears the traces of the rigorous censorship that was the norm at the time and, as we will see later, there are still murkier aspects of Cyrano's tragic destiny that he tried to talk about, only to be rapidly silenced.

Considering the circles in which Cyrano moved, and his close association with the thought-crime of libertinism, there can have been no shortage of threatening presences desperate to see him and his like taught a violent lesson. If Le Bret's account passes over this last paroxysm of Cyrano's passion for physical combat rather quickly, that may point to the fact that the incident was still dangerous to discuss even at a distance of some twelve or thirteen years. Le Bret places the events of the fight with one hundred men at the period in Cyrano's life when he had left the army in order to devote himself full time to study. As he puts it, Cyrano 'had abandoned Mars in order to devote himself to Minerva'. Cyrano soon strayed out of the realms of straightforward martial devotion to the monarch and the state and was to become deeply engaged in a programme of study that was radical in the extreme. It is entirely possible that, having already begun to exercise his considerable talents as a satirist, Cyrano had himself offended someone highly placed and wealthy enough to command a crushing retribution.

We have a few shreds of evidence regarding Cyrano's activities in the years 1640–2, such as the contracts he entered into with Dupron and Moussard and these make it seem likely that the incident took place in 1642–3, but without further proof any date is necessarily purely speculative. Le Bret's unfailing loyalty to Cyrano saw him tell the story in such a way as to minimize the question of why the ambush happened in the first place and to focus attention instead on Cyrano's skill and daring, but it may well have been an early, unsuccessful attempt to silence the turbulent poet or intimidate him into submission and greater circumspection. The attack (just like all the beatings Cyrano had received in the course of his schooling) had the exact opposite result, confirming Cyrano in a lifelong determination to resist intimidation and to defy authority at any cost.

Despite Le Bret's unassuming tone, the story of the duel with one hundred men smacks of the publicity stunt. There is an element of theatricality to the tale, which suggests that Cyrano knew all too well the importance of the spectacle that he was engineering. He made sure to have witnesses and he made sure to fight alone against overwhelming odds. Cyrano had turned his back on a military career but he railed against the exclusion from the ranks of honourable gentlemen supposedly implicit in such a step. The climate of popular opinion at the time saw intellectual engagement as suspect, set against the unthinking loyalty and unquestioning obedience that characterized the greatest 'honour' of the military ideal. Cyrano determined to stand up for the honour of the poet, the courage of the intellectual. The bastonnade, an inglorious ambush by mercenary thugs, was a powerful symbol of a poet's demotion from the ranks of polite society, marking him out as it did as one undeserving of the gentlemanly ritual of the duel. Cyrano refused to play by the rules and transformed what should have been a potentially deadly rite of humiliation and defeat into a flamboyant life-affirming triumph.

Perhaps more than any other element of his biography, the story of the duel with one hundred men sealed Cyrano's posthumous reputation as a reckless, hot-headed, dare-devil. Here again we see the paradox of Cyrano's apotheosis from man to legend: what was in truth an act of considered rebellion against the status quo became characterized as little more than an aggressive whim. In Rostand's play, Cyrano's infamous duel with one hundred men takes place at night and is introduced with a lyrical description of Paris by moonlight whose air of mystery seems entirely appropriate to an encounter that Le Bret terms a 'superhuman combat'.

> *Ah! Paris, swimming through nocturnal mist,*
> *The rooftops draped in azure, shyly kissed*
> *By an uncertain moon – proscenium*
> *All dressed and ready for the scene to come,*
> *Or like a magic mirror, breathes the Seine,*
> *Trembling, compact of myth and mystery –*
> *You're going to see now what you're going to see.*[7]

Despite the closing promise 'You're going to see now what you're going to see', the original audience of 1897 did not in fact witness the fight itself as the first act ends just after this speech. Later film versions, like that starring Gérard Depardieu, have since taken on the challenge of choreographing the extraordinary swordplay required to re-enact a battle featuring one man against a hundred opponents. Much is made of the element of surprise and the fear induced in Cyrano's antagonists by his sudden appearance out of the darkness, but in Le Bret's account of the fight the scene actually takes place in broad daylight. The duel with one hundred men has become an integral part of the myth of Cyrano and it doesn't much matter whether there is an element of exaggeration in the telling. Of course it is unlikely there were really as many as one hundred assailants lying in wait for Cyrano, but Le Bret lists two deaths and seven seriously wounded which puts the lowest possible figure at nine against one. If we accept that at least some others must have escaped unhurt, having run away at the first sign that things were not going as expected, the odds lengthen still further. Any way you look at it, it was an impressive feat of skill and daring.

It was perhaps the fact of having pulled off such a Herculean escapade that gave Cyrano the confidence to poke fun at his own redoubtable reputation. In a letter entitled 'Le Duelliste' Cyrano expresses the same idea that Le Bret would touch on in his biography, jokingly referring to the fact that his reputation attracted constant calls for him to fight. 'I sometimes imagine that I have become a porcupine, seeing that no one can approach me without pricking himself.'[8] Cyrano's comic vision of himself as a porcupine stems from a play on the word 'piquer' which can mean both anger and prick. In depicting himself as the hapless porcupine who does not set out to quarrel but who inadvertently spikes anyone who comes near, Cyrano also neatly characterized himself as the only true gentleman amid a crowd of hotheads who unlike the porcupine-hero have failed to recognize the truth of La Rochefoucauld's maxim: *Le vrai honnête homme est celui qui ne se pique de rien* (The true gentleman never allows himself to be angered). Underneath the laughter there is also a melancholy echo of the picture Cyrano had drawn of the lost soul of Montmorency-Bouteville, lamenting his isolation; a human porcupine was necessarily also 'a man who carried solitude with him'.

An air of injured innocence and apparent indifference to the world was a favourite comic stance of Cyrano's in his satirical letters and in the 'Lettre contre un faux brave' (Against a cowardly braggart) he neatly combines menace and mockery, as he remonstrates with his 'dear friend' for dishonestly bragging that the great Cyrano intends to kill him: 'It has been reported to me from various sources that you have been bragging that I planned to murder you. Alas! My dear friend, do you think me so crazy as to attempt the impossible? Ha! For pity's sake, where can one strike a man in order to kill him instantly when he has neither a heart nor a brain?'[9]

Elsewhere, he creates a witty play on words, inspired by the constant requests for him to fight as a second: 'Really you would be very wrong to call me now the first of men; because I protest that for over a month now I have been everybody's second.'[10] The unwritten double meaning to this particular paradox is that the modesty of the protest belies a cunning bit of self-promotion, because in terms of honour the 'second' is actually 'first'. By far the most irreverent of all Cyrano's duelling jokes is the one ending the letter 'The Duellist'. He begs Le Bret to return to Paris to exercise his calming influence and return Cyrano to philosophical mood before the 'itch for glory' pushes him to fatal extremes: 'I am afraid that this itch for glory may invite me to carry my name as far as Heaven itself. That is why I beg you to come back soon, because it would anger terribly me if on your return instead of finding me in my study you were to find me in a church . . .'[11] Cyrano's anger, at being in church for his own funeral, rather than at his books in his study, is obvious and comically incongruous, but the lines also contain a typical libertine double meaning. He also implies that he would be furious should his friend find him worshipping or praying in church instead of studying or writing.

Legend has it that Cyrano's fight with the crowd of hired assassins was undertaken in defence of his friend Lignières, thereby lending greater substance to the paradoxical claim made in Cyrano's letter on duelling: 'In truth, it is a very great consolation to me to be hated because I am loved; to find enemies everywhere because I have friends everywhere and to see that my unhappiness stems from my good fortune.'[12] Le Bret's biography does not confirm this theory; Lignières is briefly referred to as someone who was a good friend of Cyrano's, but not in the context of the fight at the de Nesle gate.

Émile Magne, the academic who had attacked Rostand so vociferously on the subject of the anachronisms and inaccuracies to be found in his play, wrote an entire book devoted to the subject of

Cyrano's friendship with the Chevalier de Lignières. The book is surprisingly playful and presents Magne's own version of events drawn from his wide reading. Magne follows Rostand in attributing the fight with one hundred men to a defence of Lignières but without providing any additional evidence. Rather surprisingly, given his fury at Rostand for making such a caricature of Cyrano he introduces the idea that the friendship between the two men was in part based on the length of their noses. He quotes some lines of Lignières's as decisive proof of this affinity.

> *When they laugh at my nose, I never get angry*
> *I hold that large noses are not without their charms*
> *And that a big nose never made a face less attractive.*[13]

Strangely Magne is also guilty of putting the words of one of Cyrano's comic creations into the mouth of his hero. At the moment when he is poised to begin his Herculean attack, Magne's Cyrano suddenly launches into an absurd overblown series of boasts, taken directly from one of the satirical letters. Magne apparently didn't consider the spectacular inappropriateness of giving his hero lines which the real Cyrano penned revelling in the stupidity of their bombast and bluff. Cyrano becomes the victim of his own success and is made the target of his own comic buffoonery. Cyrano's fictions have sufficient life that they often vie with and overcome the truth. It is Cyrano's propensity to construct his own myth that makes this process inevitable; he constantly tempts his readers to try to reach the truth behind the fiction. Every book, play, film, opera, poem or piece of music ever written about Cyrano (this one included) inevitably has its roots in this skilled manipulation of his own image in which the original so delighted.

Edmond Rostand took the idea of this free-spirited, almost self-destructively independent character and spun from it one of the finest speeches of his playwriting career. In the second act of the play, a penniless Cyrano refuses an offer of patronage from the Duc de Guise, determined to retain his liberty at any cost. When Le Bret accuses him of taking an exaggerated stance, he replies;

> *Well then yes, I exaggerate! . . .*
> *But for the principle of the thing and as an example*
> *I think that it's good to exaggerate.*

Rostand then proceeds to outline this 'principle' and 'example' in a long speech which is known as *Le tirade de Non Merci*. The tirade is one of the most superb moments of the whole play. It is very cleverly constructed: Cyrano begins by asking 'So what should I do?' and then makes a series of suggestions of suitably cringing, self-serving behaviour. These are sarcastically framed as questions and Cyrano answers himself with a sardonic rejection of such servility, always repeating the same simple response: *Non, merci.*

> Cyrano: *What would you have me do?*
> *Seek out a powerful protector, pursue*
> *A potent patron? Cling like a leeching vine*
> *To a tree?* Crawl *my way up? Fawn, whine*
> *For all that sticky candy called success?*
> *No, thank you. Be a sycophant and dress*
> *In sickly rhymes a prayer to a moneylender?*
> *Play the buffoon, desperate to engender*
> *A smirk on a refrigerated jowl?*
> *No, thank you. Slake my morning mouth with foul*
> *Lees and leavings, breakfast off a toad?*
> *Wriggle and grovel on the dirty road*
> *To advancement and wear the skin of my belly through?*
> *Get grimy calluses on my kneecaps? Do*
> *A daily dozen to soften up my spine?*
> *No, thank you . . .*[14]

The use of repetition and the increasing vehemence of the speech allow the actor to build to a crescendo and then suddenly switch registers to end with an idealized vision of the alternative destiny which Cyrano desires for himself and his fellow freethinkers.

> *No, no, no,*
> *Thank you, no. No, thank you. But to go*
> *Free of the filthy world, to sing, to be*
> *Blessed with a voice vibrating virility,*
> *Blessed with an eye equipped for looking at*
> *Things as they really are, cocking my hat*
> *Where I please, at a word, at a deed, at a yes or no,*
> *Fighting or writing; this is the true life. So*
> *I go along any road under my moon,*
> *Careless of glory, indifferent to the boon*
> *Or bane of fortune, without hope, without fear,*
> *Writing only the words down that I hear*
> Here – *and saying, with a sort of modesty,*
> *'My heart, be satisfied with what you see*
> *And smell and taste in your own garden – weeds,*
> *As much as fruit and flowers.' [. . .]*
> *I myself am a tree,*
> *Not high perhaps, not beautiful, but free –*
> *My flesh deciduous, but the enduring bone*
> *Of spirit, tough, indifferent, and alone!*[15]

The passionate force of this outburst and the powerful images in which Rostand cloaks Cyrano's 'exaggeration' serve to elevate the 'principle' above the mundane level of everyday reality. This is Rostand's dream of what a poet should be and naturally has only the faintest corresponding echo in real life. In reality neither Cyrano nor Rostand could ever have been said to have been totally

Careless of glory, indifferent to the boon
Or bane of fortune.

After all, Rostand was not starving in a garret when he wrote these lines, he was the pampered darling of French high society, and the real Cyrano was not above penning a lucrative defence of Cardinal Mazarin, nor of eventually accepting the intervention of a patron in order to see his works make it into print.

The reality of Cyrano's writing career may have been more prosaic and less exalted than Rostand's dream of it, but the underlying principle remains the same. Le Bret makes this explicit, when he reiterates his remarks about Cyrano's reluctance to accept help for fear of compromising his artistic freedom. Le Bret explains that the notion of personal freedom was so essential to his friend's nature that even conformity to accepted opinion seemed a constraint to Cyrano:

> He did not limit his hatred of subjection to that which a great nobleman to whom one might attach oneself would demand; he extended it still further, and even as far as any thing that seemed to him to constrain thought itself and his opinions in which he wished to remain as free as in his most indifferent actions.[16]

This little passage provides a neat summary of the literary movement to which Cyrano's works have been allied. He is known as one of the *libertins* or the freethinkers. At the time their intellectual nonconformity was viewed with deep suspicion and the freethinkers were often marginal, their place in society precarious at best, criminal at worst. In 1623, the Jesuit priest Father Garasse published a lengthy and virulent attack on the freethinkers, entitled *La Doctrine Curieuse des Beaux Esprits de ce temps* (The Curious Doctrine of the fine wits of our age). The title was darkly sarcastic; Garasse considered the provocative young wits of his age as agents of the Antichrist. 'The devil instructs and trains certain wicked minds, who are more damned than devils incarnate [. . .] When a mind abandons itself to evildoing it is like an unstoppable gangrene one must cut, sever and burn otherwise the affair is desperate.'[17]

The writer against whom Garasse's most vitriolic outbursts were directed was one of Cyrano's most important influences, the satirical poet Théophile de Viau. Garasse had not succeeded in seeing Théophile burned at the stake, but the poet perished in exile in 1625, his health having been fatally undermined by a long period of imprisonment. Garasse's work had precipitated his downfall and it was only due to the intervention of Théophile's influential supporters that he managed to escape the death sentence that had been pronounced on him at his trial. Théophile's work was an important model for Cyrano's own forays into the world of letters and it was often outrageously blasphemous and offensive. He deliberately courted controversy with his obscene and irreverent writing and there is no question that his influence was very significant in creating a new way of thinking about what it meant to be a writer. Théophile and the libertins who followed him considered their intellectual and artistic freedom as paramount, and this was a dangerous precedent to set. In his 'Ode' Théophile painted a vivid (self-)portrait of the libertin:

He never envies others,
When all those happier than him
Mock his misery
Laughter is his only retort.
[. . .]
The sparkle of golden rooms,
Where princes are worshipped,
Appeal less to him than the fresh face
Of the countryside or the clouds.
[. . .]

He has never pretended to
Either fortune or poverty;
He is neither servant nor master
He is nought but what he would be.[18]

In our time the word *libertine* has become synonomous with immorality and sexual licence but, as Théophile's lines reveal, the original sense of the word was that of freedom to be true to oneself, to be 'neither servant nor master'. In the eighteenth century the figure of the libertine was typified by that amoral, lascivious rake the Vicomte de Valmont, the charismatic anti-hero of Choderlos de Laclos's scandalous novel *Les Liaisons Dangereuses*. This shift in meaning was in part due to scare-mongering works like Garasse's and was also influenced by Molière's popular comedy *Dom Juan*, in which the eponymous hero is an exaggerated burlesque caricature of a libertin. Molière's Dom Juan is an unrepentant atheist and a serial womanizer and it has been suggested that the character was modelled in part on that of the real Cyrano. Dom Juan's epitaph is pronounced by his impudent manservant Sganarelle who declares that his master's death is a cause of rejoicing for the whole world except him, but he mourns his master's death purely for the sake of his lost wages:

> Sganarelle: Alas! My wages! My wages! Everyone is satisfied by his death. Offended heaven, violated laws, maids seduced, families dishonoured, parents outraged, wives ruined, husbands driven to despair, all are satisfied. I alone am unhappy. My wages, my wages, my wages![19]

Molière took the idea of the libertine to its extreme for comic effect, but the reality was that, in Cyrano's time, the true freethinkers were not necessarily hedonistic pleasure-seekers – they were intellectual rebels. This is why Le Bret stresses the importance of Cyrano's intellectual enthusiasm as the deciding factor in his decision to leave the army: 'And finally, the great love that he had for study made him renounce entirely the career of war, which demands all of a man and renders him as much an enemy of literature as literature makes him the friend of peace.'[20] Cyrano was a 'friend of peace' then, but no pacifist. If he were also a womanizer, like Dom Juan (or any other kind of hedonist), Le Bret would have been the last to say so. Ever the loyal defender of his friend's choices, Le Bret was as open about Cyrano's passion for study as he was reticent about other passions that may have flamed his blood.

8

Far from having lost my heart

On 14 July 1642, Cyrano's family were assembled to attend the wedding of his cousin Marie de Cyrano. Marie married a man named Honoré Morel and it is thanks to Baron Frédy de Coubertin, a descendant of their union, that we have a description of the Cyrano coat of arms. It was azure blue and featured a silver chevron and two gold stars, as well as a rampant lion with a brilliant red tongue. Cyrano may have made liberal use of this coat of arms to further bolster his pretensions to nobility. While his cousin Marie was publicly celebrating her summer wedding surrounded by family and friends, Cyrano's own romantic involvements remained a closely guarded secret. It is rather ironic that the stage Cyrano should protest (untruthfully) that the passionate love letters, which he provides for Christian to send to Roxane, are nothing more than exercises of style, written on a whim and with no genuine feeling behind them: 'the more eloquent for being insincere', since this is exactly how the critics interpret the love letters of the real Cyrano.[1] Jacques Prévot states baldly 'woman is absent from them' alleging that: 'Cyrano tells nothing of his heart; literary creation here [. . .] rests on no power of real emotion, no nostalgia, it

is nourished by no passion, present or past, it expresses no experiences and does not spring from any spontaneity.'[2]

Whether one accepts Prévot's sweeping dismissal of Cyrano's letters or not, his magisterial pronouncement usefully underlines the fact that any interrogation of Cyrano's published love letters for details of his private life is a futile exercise. The title phrase of this chapter, a typical equivocation from one of Cyrano's love letters, echoes the question asked by so many curious admirers of the great swordsman – did the real Cyrano ever lose his heart? The fact is that such a question must remain unanswered. In the absence of any concrete proof, critics and historians may speculate about Cyrano's feelings and the intimate details of his love life, but the truth will remain as mysterious as Cyrano intended. Le Bret waxes lyrical about Cyrano's many friendships but barely mentions his love life. He restricts himself to a phrase whose very discretion has only served to inflame further curiosity. Le Bret states, somewhat enigmatically, that Cyrano showed 'so great a reticence towards the fair sex that one could say that he never overstepped the bounds of the respect owed to them.'[3] Recent critics have seen in this phrase a covert avowal of Cyrano's homosexuality, particularly when allied to the mysterious hint of a 'dangerous tendency' in Cyrano's behaviour in late adolescence.

Aside from the interpretation of certain homoerotic passages in his work, the most conclusive evidence offered to support the idea is Cyrano's close connection to two men who were almost certainly lovers and his virulent dispute with one of them, which has been construed as the result of a tortured love affair. The two men, identified as forming this unhappy gay love triangle with Cyrano, were the poet Dassoucy (who was repeatedly prosecuted and imprisoned for his homosexuality) and a young man named Chapelle. Cyrano's association with them probably dates from the early 1640s, when he had left the army and was studying at the Collège de Lisieux and taking those dancing and fencing lessons.

Claude-Emmanuel Lhuillier de la Chapelle, usually known as Chapelle, was born in 1626. Seven years younger than Cyrano, he was the bastard child of a young noblewoman named Marie Chanut. Marie was the sister of the French ambassador to Sweden and having been seduced and abandoned by Lhuillier she married one Hector Musnier, who was perhaps not altogether thrilled by her shady history, although he may well have agreed to take Marie as his wife precisely because her notorious connection with Lhuillier enabled him to demand an inflated dowry. Such payments went a long way towards reconciling a man to a certain moral flexibility in his bride. Perhaps unsurprisingly, the marriage was not a success and Hector and Marie seem to have separated after a short time.

Chapelle was extremely fortunate to be his father's only son, ordinarily the fate of a bastard son supplanted by a legitimate heir was not a happy one – that familiar conflict is played out in Shakespeare's *King Lear* between the half-brothers Edgar, the legitimate and dutiful son, and Edmund, the intelligent and manipulative schemer who turns out to be an evil bastard. As his father's legitimate heir, Chapelle had access to a world of privilege and ease. In 1642 Lhuillier senior took steps to have his child legitimized. He had not only introduced his son to his favoured brothel to complete his education, but rather more helpfully had also taken the trouble to secure the philosopher and mathematician Pierre Gassendi, one of the greatest minds of the age, as a tutor for him. Lhuillier had first been introduced to Gassendi in 1628 by a mutual friend and the two men had embarked on a lengthy tour of Holland together in December of the same year.

Born 22 January 1592, Gassendi was nearly fifty years old when Cyrano first came into his orbit. He was a great philosopher and an enthusiastic proponent of experimental science. His contribution to science is commemorated by the fact that there is a crater on the moon named after him. Gassendi was a sincere Christian but he centred his teaching around the scepticism of the classical philosopher Epicurus. He was not a radical but a deeply modest individual and a natural teacher. He was to play a pivotal role in Cyrano's career.

Cyrano seems to have been a student of Gassendi in the period 1641–3. Writing in 1707, an early biographer of Molière describes Cyrano infiltrating the circle of like-minded young friends that Chapelle had gathered around him to profit from Gassendi's teaching. According to Grimarest (who got most of his information from Molière's daughter and his protégé, a young actor named Baron) the group included both Molière and Cyrano, but the biographer alleges that Cyrano was accepted only with 'reluctance' due to his 'turbulent spirit'. He does acknowledge that Cyrano was apparently gifted with an excellent memory and was clearly 'very eager for knowledge'. His vision of how the group's initially unwelcoming attitude to Cyrano was overcome takes the form of a rhetorical question: 'how to be rid of a young man as ingratiating, as lively, as Gascon as Cyrano?'[4] This is the second mention he makes of Cyrano's supposed Gascon origins; the great swordsman had apparently early established, not just his reputation for flamboyant vivacity and wit, but his fictional background as well. A later version of the same story, as retold by Father Niceron, sees an interesting variant creeping in. Where Grimarest had Cyrano being reluctantly accepted into a group, where his excitable temperament was at odds with the studious atmosphere, Niceron has Cyrano effecting his entry sword in hand and intimidating the students and their master with his threats. This is a good example of the way that exaggeration was to blacken Cyrano's reputation and set his story off down the path of caricature.

Cyrano's later work reveals that however turbulent he may have been, he was certainly also an enthusiastic and talented student. He was passionate about communicating and exploring the ideas of the new philosophy and he is careful to cite Gassendi by name and note the importance of the great man's work. Cyrano never completed his studies at the Collège de Lisieux, his name does not figure on the list of those taking their degrees and it seems probable that, having found a richer and far more modern curriculum being taught by Gassendi, he soon abandoned the more traditional educational model as a result. It was to Chapelle, as much as to Gassendi himself, that Cyrano owed the favour of his acceptance into this erudite company and, according to the bitter comments made in later life by an aged Dassoucy, he was also beholden to Chapelle for lodging, food and drink and probably for more besides.

In his semi-autobiographical work *The Adventures of M. Dassoucy*, the author describes being introduced to the sixteen-year-old Chapelle by Cyrano and talks about having shared Chapelle's bed. Dassoucy's version of events is naturally clouded by the fact that he could not write openly about homosexual relationships but he strongly implies that Cyrano and Chapelle were lovers. The simple fact is that, without clearer evidence, the exact details of the enmity that later erupted between Cyrano and Dassoucy will remain a matter of speculation. Literary quarrel or lovers' tiff? Romantic or intellectual rivalry? Either is possible and, although Cyrano's outpouring of angry vitriol against his former friend has been read as, either the excoriating fury of a betrayed lover, or the righteous anger of a plagiarized author, perhaps the most likely answer is that it was a little of both. The quarrel is one to which we will return, but at this stage in the early 1640s, whatever romantic entanglements there may have been between the three men, they seem to have been frequent companions and good friends, and to have remained so for the best part of the decade.

The love letters are the works for which the fictional Cyrano is best known and a vitally important plot device in Rostand's play. And yet, although the real Cyrano was not above using his literary talent to engage in passionate and playful games of seduction, he was always more interested in subversion than sentiment and was not a man to concentrate his energies solely on the pursuit of romance, or to spill his deepest feelings on to the page for public consumption. The very elusiveness of Cyrano's secret emotions has stimulated legions of later authors to proclaim their own inventions as the key to the mystery.

In 1927 Louis-Raymond Lefèvre published a *Life of Cyrano de Bergerac* in which he dedicated a chapter to revealing the secrets of Cyrano's love life. He claims to have been scrupulously exact in his research but admits to having 'taken the liberty' in the absence of any documentary evidence to the contrary, of supposing that all Cyrano's love letters were addressed to one woman. Lefèvre weaves together various details from the letters such as the encounter at a fishing party and the gift of bracelets woven from the beloved's hair and from these disparate elements he constructs a vivid and unhappy tale. Lefèvre's Cyrano is clearly a descendant of Rostand's creation sharing the stage Cyrano's romantic soul. He has waited in vain for an encounter with the perfectly beautiful and noble creature who will live up to his soaring ideals: 'a woman worthy of his spirit, and capable of enjoying not just sensual pleasures but the refined passion which the "*précieuses*" had celebrated. He sighed in anticipation as he waited for fate to bring him this dream woman.'[5] Rather cruelly fate (or rather L.-R. Lefèvre) sends Cyrano, not his soulmate, but a red-haired temptress named Alexie, who is the polar opposite of the virtuous and idealistic Roxane. The avaricious Alexie nearly bankrupts her naive admirer, mercilessly exploiting his generosity and then, when he can no longer continue paying her many debts, she heartlessly casts him aside. The day after their split the desolate Cyrano wakes up to the realization that his dream woman has infected him with the pox. Whatever the reality behind its creation, Cyrano's letter 'For a red-haired lady', is one of the gems of his early work. Thanks to its combination of playfulness and sensuality, it remains one of the most effective and touching of all the published love letters. Reading the closing lines one can scarcely blame Lefèvre for his extravagant flights of fancy:

> Therefore, since we must all become slaves to beauty, would it not be better to lose our freedom in chains of gold, than chains of hemp, or iron? For myself all that I desire, o my beautiful M . . ., is that in wandering at liberty amongst these little labyrinths of gold that you have for hair, I should soon lose myself there; and all that I wish for is never to recover my freedom once lost, if you would but promise me that my life will not last longer than my servitude; and that you will not be angry if I declare myself, until death,
>
> Madame,
>
> Your I know not what?[6]

Cyrano's love letters may conceal as much as they reveal but there are undeniably moments in them that do seem to suggest the inspiration of genuine feeling, especially in the letters that were not published during his lifetime. The shortest of all the unpublished letters describes the writer's desperation after a day's separation from his beloved with an anguished simplicity that is worlds away from the studied imagery and convoluted witticisms to be found elsewhere. This little unsigned note is also the only letter which uses the familiar 'tu' form of address; this was not common in seventeenth-century correspondence. Even in letters between spouses it is more usual to find the 'vous' form, and so the note has an additional urgency and tenderness. The note is also unusual because it bears no signature and no formal opening; the addressee is indicated only by the initial M. The letter 'For a red-haired lady' is also addressed to the mysterious M.

As a writer, Cyrano always revelled in the possibilities of double meaning and paradox and seems to have found the love letter a particularly rich field for his inventive, playful wit. Love letter IV opens with declaration, 'Far from having lost my heart when I rendered you the homage of my freedom, on the contrary, I find that, since that day, my heart has grown much larger.'[7] He confounds his reader's expectation by announcing the exact opposite of a traditional lover's plaint. It is vital to recognize that the 'love letters' written by the real Cyrano are not private documents. They were written for the amusement of a select public and circulated in manuscript copies. They first appeared collected together in print in 1654 when the Duc d'Arpajon arranged for the editor Charles de Sercy to publish a selection of Cyrano's works under the title *Oeuvres Diverses*. Other similar collections of love letters also appeared around the same time, such as the *Lettres de Babet* which were promoted as the authentic correspondence between Babet and her suitor, but which are clearly a fictional construction with playful set pieces and a carefully constructed plot. Another collection, the *Lettres Portugaises*, were ostensibly translated from the original Portuguese and consist of the increasingly desperate pleas of a young Portuguese woman named Mariane who had been seduced and abandoned by a French knight. Critics agree that there may well have been a genuine relationship behind these letters, convincing historical counterparts for the real Mariane and her knight having been identified in Mariana Alcoforada and the Comte de Chamilly. But the published version is a literary piece, a fictional work by the letters' 'translator' the Comte de Guilleragues.

The notable exception to the rule that love letters which made it into the public domain did so because their composition owed more to art than to emotion was the work of Marie-Catherine Desjardins whose *Lettres et billets galants* were published in 1667 despite her attempts to prevent their disclosure. Marie-Catherine was something of a literary celebrity, a successful authoress celebrated for her wit. The letters had been written to her lover Antoine Boësset, Sieur de Villedieu and they reveal the painful (for her at least) disintegration of the relationship. It seems that these letters became well known because the loathsome Villedieu, in spite of his growing indifference and infidelity, was encouraging Marie-Catherine to write to him in order to have the cachet of showing off her letters to his friends and acquaintances. Marie-Catherine seems to have struggled with her growing awareness of Villedieu's true character and the strength of her infatuation with him. In spite of significant periods of cohabitation, two signed promises of marriage and once having made it as far as the altar, where an ecclesiastical technicality prevented the ceremony from going ahead as planned, Villedieu and Marie-Catherine never married.

He eventually succeeded in persuading her to formally renounce her two signed marriage promises in order to let him marry someone else. Marie-Catherine seems to have accepted this final humiliation thanks to reassurances from Villedieu that she would remain his mistress and his one true love. It would have been perfectly credible to her that Villedieu's marriage was not a matter of the heart. But sadly the worst was yet to come. Just a few months after Villedieu's wedding France declared war on Spain and Villedieu, who was the captain of a regiment, found himself urgently needing to raise money. He borrowed from his brother and secured the rest by selling Marie-Catherine's love letters to the printer Barbin.

At first Marie-Catherine refused to believe that Villedieu would stoop so low and convinced herself that a thief must have been responsible for bringing her inmost thoughts and sufferings into the public domain. She asked friends to institute an investigation and to start legal proceedings against the thief, but her instructions included a proviso to protect Villedieu if he turned out to be the guilty party: 'If you can not defend me except by ruining him entirely, do not defend me at all I beg you.'[8] It is fairly clear that she knew what the truth of the situation would be and although her intermediaries succeeded in gettting her name removed from the letters they were unable to stop the publication. Just three months later Villedieu was killed on the battlefield at Lille. After his death his official widow quickly remarried and Marie-Catherine was thus free to continue calling herself Mme de Villedieu. Which she did for another decade until she finally married and started a family.

Marie-Catherine's letters ended up in the public domain in spite of her ardent desire to suppress them and their sincerity is further underlined by the circumstances of their publication. In contrast, Cyrano's letters do not form a coherent whole, nor can they be read as part of a recognizable dynamic of courtship or betrayal and their appearance in print was controlled and supervised by their author. Contradictory though it may seem after dismissing the letters as a source of information about Cyrano's life, it has recently been argued that a manuscript copy of one of Cyrano's letters holds the key to his disputed sexuality. Scholars have unearthed a version of the letter which is addressed to 'Monsieur', rather than 'Madame' as in all the other versions. This particular letter is one of the most irreverent and salacious that Cyrano ever penned and Jacques Prévot, working on the hint given by a reference to Saint Denis, identifies a possible masculine recipient in Charles de Marguetel de Saint Denis, seigneur de Saint-Evremond, a libertine five years Cyrano's senior. Charles de Saint-Evremond was a lifelong friend of the fabulously free-spirited courtesan Ninon de Lenclos and a writer who pleaded for religious toleration and temperate hedonism. A man after Cyrano's own heart, perhaps literally. The distinguished Cyrano critic Madeleine Alcover also points out that the dancing and fencing lessons which Cyrano undertook may also point to his homosexuality. She compares the premises of these all-male establishments to ancient Greek gymnasia. Whatever Cyrano's sexuality, it is unlikely that this was his primary reason for undertaking the lessons, and Alcover herself has unearthed documentary evidence that Cyrano may have felt a need to refresh his sword arm.

Four months before signing the contract with Masters Dupron

and Moussard, Cyrano and a young friend, named Louis Prévost de Dimier, had been involved in a fight with a student from another college. The manuscript of the agreement, reached to settle the matter, reveals certain details which reflect rather badly on our young hero. In a notarized document, dated 18 June 1641, Cyrano's mother signed her agreement to pay 15 livres in damages to the student named Le Heurteur, who had been assaulted by her son and his 'accomplice', as well as 15 livres to the surgeon, who treated Le Heurteur, and an unspecified amount to the college authorities to guarantee that the matter would go no further. She also testified that her son's épée and his friend's cloak had been returned to them at the same time. This is an important detail in a legal case of the time since both were valuable possessions, cloaks in particular were often the object of street robberies. The tumultuous chain of events that led to the two young men attacking another and then fleeing the scene leaving their possessions behind them is probably best left to the imagination. This is not an episode that Le Bret saw fit to include in his biography and it is a little difficult to reconcile the role of invincible duellist which Cyrano fashioned for himself, with this aperçu into the humiliation of an unruly student, who not only apparently breaks the code of the duel by fighting two against one, but also loses his sword in the brawl and ends up called to order by the college authorities and bailed out by his own mother. Here is the reverse image of the duel with one hundred men and a weaker, more human side to the legendary figure.

In Rostand's play the true motivation for Cyrano's Herculean battle is that his extraordinary courage has been further bolstered by an unexpected ray of hope in his love for Roxane. Having been informed by her maid that she wishes to see him in private, the next day he cannot control his excitement and leaps at the chance to dissipate his energies in a feat of extraordinary bravery. He drags the reluctant Lignières to his feet and insists on escorting him home himself in order to confront the armed ambush at the de

Nesle gate. Above all else, Rostand's play is a love story. The heart of the plot is Cyrano's doomed passion for his beautiful cousin Madeleine Robin, known as Roxane.

The real Madeleine was born on 24 August 1609, making her a decade older than Cyrano. Her actual surname was Robineau and she was a distant cousin of Cyrano's on his mother's side of the family. Their maternal grandmothers were cousins, both named Catherine. The lowliness of Cyrano's origins has been rather exaggerated; as we have seen, his mother's side of the family were wealthy financiers. The real-life Roxane married Christophe de Champagne, Baron de Neuvillette on 20 February 1635. In keeping with her riches and position her husband was a nobleman, but the match also seems to have had an important romantic element.

Sadly, a few years later, the unfortunate baron was killed at the siege of Arras, just as in the play, leaving a devastated and heartbroken widow to mourn his loss. On losing her husband, Rostand's Roxane retires from the world to live in a convent and spend the rest of her life mourning the death of a man whom she had never really got to know, having only just married him in a hurriedly improvised ceremony when he is sent off to fight. The real Madeleine, who had been married for five years when she lost her husband, reacted even more dramatically. When the news came, she had only recently lost her mother and she was heavily pregnant; she soon suffered a third bereavement as the child was stillborn. She must have felt terribly alone. On hearing of her husband's death in battle, she became obsessed with the fact that he had not had the chance to make a final confession and was thus condemned to the sufferings of purgatory. As the ghost of Hamlet's father eloquently puts it:

> *Cut off even in the blossoms of my sin,*
> *Unhouseled, dis-appointed, unaneled,*

No reck'ning made, but sent to my account
With all my imperfections on my head.
O horrible, O horrible, most horrible!

It was not in Madeleine's power to release her husband's spirit from the horrors of purgatory by avenging his murder as the ghost begs Hamlet to do, but in her desperation, tormented by visions of his suffering, she beseeched her confessor whether it might not be possible for her to ransom her husband's soul with her own. She declared herself ready to go to hell in his stead if only his soul could be guaranteed eternal life in Paradise. Madeleine's spiritual advisor assured her that such a pact was impossible and that all she could do was to devote the rest of her life to piety and good works and pray regularly for the soul of her departed husband. This was exactly what the distraught widow decided to do but rather than entering a convent she dedicated her time to visiting the condemned prisoners in the hideous, stinking cells of the Conciergerie prison. She would bring food and drink to the doomed criminals, pleading with the lost souls to confess their sins and repent before it was too late. She would even accompany them to the foot of the scaffold, determined not to abandon her self-appointed mission until all hope was definitively lost.

Madeleine's piety impressed one Father Cyprien de la Nativité so much that on her death in 1660, he published a biography entitled *Compendium of the virtues and the writings of Madame the Baroness of Neuvillette recently deceased in the city of Paris*. In her youth Madeleine had been a beautiful girl dedicated to luxury and pleasure. Before losing her husband she was high-spirited, witty and slightly spoilt. Father Cyprien notes that she was not just lovely to look at but also intelligent, possessed of a 'brilliant mind'. He also admits that Madeleine lost her looks relatively young, suggesting that her over-indulgence in the finer things of life had rapidly transformed her into a considerably less attractive figure. He reveals that in her later years it was no longer obvious that she had once been a beauty. He notes that even so she retained a certain something which singled her out among her sex as someone out of the ordinary. There was no tragic love affair between Cyrano and his cousin, but they were united in possessing equally headstrong and individualistic characters. In their very different ways both found themselves attracting the attention of their peers and standing out from the crowd in their determination to follow their own conception of what was right, rather than what society expected.

Madeleine's determination to make a difference in the lives of those around her is tremendously admirable, all the more so in an age when it took uncommon courage for a woman to act for herself and attempt to retain some degree of autonomy. Madeleine's spiritual advisor had expected her to confine herself to a convent, praying quietly and allowing him to take care of administering her fortune for the benefit of selected good causes. Her wilful independence and personal ministrations to dying criminals were considered vaguely scandalous. Madeleine's biographer notes the hostility of her neighbours, who dismissed her as 'insane and laughable', irritated perhaps by her habit of borrowing money in order to make charitable donations. Even her friends were to dismiss her fervour as 'madness' and 'hypochondria', as Madeleine took to wearing a hair shirt and a *cilice*, the spiked belt that cuts into the skin, in order to mortify the flesh and purify the soul.

The possibilities for women in Cyrano's day were strictly limited and those who stood out against the overwhelming pressure to conform were all the more notable. The celebrated courtesan Ninon de Lenclos reacted to the constraints and unfairness of a woman's lot by deciding that the rules simply did not apply to her. She famously declared: 'men enjoy thousands of freedoms that women do not taste. Therefore I will be a man.'[9] Ninon's extraordinary career and those of the two peasant women who went to war disguised as men and calling themselves Antoine de

L'Espérance and Pierre de la Jeunesse, were the startling exceptions to a general rule of obedience, repression and an oppressive lack of freedom. Witness the heartfelt cry of Montaigne's adopted daughter Mlle de Gournay in her 1622 work *Égalité des hommes et des femmes*: 'Blessed are you, reader, if you are not of that sex to whom all property is forbidden, depriving them of freedom,[. . .] in order to allow for their sole felicity for their only sovereign virtues: ignorance, servitude and the ability to play the fool if that game should appeal.'[10]

Her frustration is understandable; not only were women forced into dependence and subordination but misogyny was rife. In Cyrano's lifetime, books were published with titles like *The Purgatory of Married Men*, *The Foolish Antics of the Women of Today* and the bestselling *Alphabet of the Imperfection and Malice of Women* that went through twelve sell-out editions in thirty years. Young girls received no formal education of the sort available to their brothers. The century did see the beginning of a big shift in popular literacy as basic schooling was slowly extended to include female children, and the expansion of parish schools meant that even the poorest families increasingly had access (at least theoretically) to the basics of reading and writing. But further education was not an option for girls, however intelligent, and the best they could hope for, aside from initiation into domestic management, was to be sent to a convent for purely religious instruction. Despite this distinct lack of opportunity, many seventeenth-century young women contrived to become cultured, intellectual beings in their own right. Just at the point when many boys were gratefully closing their books on leaving school behind, the girls leaving their convents were opening them with equal eagerness.

Cyrano never married and an air of mystery surrounds his relations with the fairer sex. He was probably gay, rather than simply biding his time, waiting to meet the right woman, as his nineteenth-century biographers have suggested. We will return to

Cyrano's emotional entanglements later, but for now suffice to say that homosexuality would not necessarily have been a bar to a shrewd matrimonial alliance, as the marriages of the flamboyantly gay King Henri III, or that in Cyrano's own lifetime of the Prince de Condé demonstrated. In Cyrano's era, marriage as an institution was seldom regarded as the sanctification of a romantic or sexual liaison, it was essentially a dynastic and financial arrangement. The total lack of cupidity in Cyrano's nature may therefore partly explain his failure to secure himself an advantageous alliance with the aid of those rich maternal relations. In the seventeenth century, women were all too often considered as little more than a useful commodity to be shrewdly traded. The author of the *Entretiens spirituels* revealingly advises that in marriage, as in any contract, the choice of partner should be considered most carefully, with as much assiduous attention to detail as for 'the purchase of a horse, a house or an annuity'.[11] The celebrated Mlle de Scudéry expressed a decidedly pessimistic view of the married state which is perhaps unsurprising in an era when a woman's own views on her future marriage were the last to be consulted. 'One marries in order to hate. It is for that reason that no true lover should ever speak of marriage, because to be a lover is to want to be loved and to want to be a husband is to want to be hated.'[12] This attitude is echoed by one of the characters in the novel *La Prétieuse* by the Abbé de Pure. 'I was an innocent victim sacrificed to unknown motives and to the obscure interests of the family, but sacrificed like a slave bound and gagged [. . .] I was entombed or rather I was buried alive in my shroud in Evandre's son's bed.'[13]

In certain instances the metaphor of the reluctant bride delivered bound and gagged as a slave to her husband's family took on a horrifying reality. It was not uncommon for heiresses, as young as ten or eleven, to be kidnapped and married against their will and even against that of their own family. In his memoirs, Cyrano's contemporary Bussy-Rabutin claims to have been tricked into kidnapping a young, recently widowed heiress, having been wrongly assured that she was willing to marry him. Luckily for the young woman, Bussy was not an entirely unscrupulous fortune hunter and, as he attempted to extricate himself from this messy situation, the incident veered into the realms of farce rather than those of tragedy. Bussy found himself pursued on and off in the courts for compensation in the lengthy legal battle which followed. The heiress's outraged family refused to give in to the pressure exerted by Bussy's protector the Prince de Condé. Condé was a great general who famously had numerous camp followers; Bussy was one of the few straight men to form part of his inner circle. Widowhood could prove a boon, greatly increasing a woman's personal freedom and it seems that Bussy's heiress, Mme de Miramion, was far from keen to abandon the state. Instead, she chose, like Madeleine, to devote the rest of her life and fortune to good works. She founded a refuge for fallen women. Charitable works of this sort were the one sphere of activity in which women could exercise some degree of autonomy, although as Madeleine's example demonstrates even such selfless activity was deemed irrational and suspicious.

Rostand's Roxane is described as one of the *précieuses*, and Christian is all the more intimidated by her on discovering that she belongs to this fashionable group of female intellectuals, whose objections to the manifold inconveniences of the married state were well known. These objections were undoubtedly well founded in a justifiable dissatisfaction. They were not expressed as such, but rather as the celebration of a platonic alternative, a sort of chivalric ideal of loving friendship. In fact, Rostand's identification of Madeleine Robineau as one of the précieuses was probably based on a case of mistaken identity. The woman who featured, as the beautiful Roxane, in the pages of the *Dictionnaire Précieuses*, was actually Marie Robineau, no relation.

The real women who dedicated themselves to the précieuse ideal of cultivated refinement were soon overshadowed by their exaggerated fictional counterparts. Their excessive linguistic refinements and their fascination with gallantry and with lengthy, highly idealized romantic novels made these witty and cultivated women an easy target for ridicule. Never one to miss the opportunity for a good laugh, Molière penned *Les Précieuses ridicules* which premièred in 1659. This satire, aimed squarely at the pretensions of the female salon wits, caused a scandal on its first appearance and Molière attempted to mollify the important female members of his courtly audience, who considered themselves personally targeted by the play, by specifying that his heroines were only ignorant provincials, aping the nobility and making fools of themselves in the process. After the tremendous popular success of *Les Précieuses ridicules*, Molière went on to target female intellectuals more directly in *Les Femmes Savantes* (1672). In this play, one of the characters betrays the hypocrisy of the male response to female learning. Essentially he says that it is all right for women to be intelligent and knowledgeable as long as they hide it well:

> *In short, if she must study I don't want her to show it,*
> *She should have knowledge without wanting everyone to know it.*[14]

The writer Guez de Balzac was even less polite than Molière, declaring robustly: 'I would as lief endure a woman with a beard as one of these women who try to be savante.'[15]

Cyrano moved in more enlightened circles; his good friend the mathematician Jacques Rouhault gave weekly lectures on physics to the nobility at which the front row was always reserved for ladies. Cyrano's lifetime saw growing numbers of learned women making up for the deficiencies of their early instruction with wide reading. This trend was made possible by the increasing numbers of savants, like Descartes, choosing to publish in the vernacular rather than in Latin. Cyrano's mentor Gassendi, on the other hand, was one of those who stuck to the old scholarly tradition and who published all his scientific writings in Latin. This has been suggested as one of the reasons that his importance and the modernity of many of his ideas were long overlooked.

Towards the end of the century, another author, Bernard de Bovier la Fontenelle, published a vernacular discussion of the new ideas in astronomy, framed as a series of conversations between the author and an intelligent and well-informed young woman. In the preface to his book, *On the Plurality of Worlds* (1686), he explained that he hoped that the example of the young woman in his work would inspire and 'encourage' other young women to an appreciation of his subject matter and to the recognition that following the ideas of the new science required no greater effort than following the plot of the popular romantic novel *La Princesse de Clèves*.* From the testimony of Madame de Sévigné it seems that women were indeed increasingly at the forefront in the enthusiastic reception of new ideas. On 17 December 1664 she noted how the enthusiasm of her female friends ultimately convinced even blasé courtiers like d'Artagnan to show an interest in the appearance of a notable astronomical phenomenon. 'For four days now a comet has appeared. At first it was only talked about by women and no one cared, but now everyone has seen it. M. d'Artagnan stayed up last night to see it much to his satisfaction.'[16]

In Cyrano's lifetime things were changing for female intellectuals, but slowly. Cyrano played with the still scandalous notion of an intelligent and well-informed female when he cast the prettiest and sweetest woman in the court of the moon as an acute social commentator. This is a deliberate equivocation allowing for a double reading: Cyrano puts his most telling criticisms of the futility of war into the mouth of this charming and gentle lunar noblewoman and, in doing so, he neatly evades criticism. His

* Fittingly, the first English translation of this text published in 1688, was the work of Aphra Behn, one of the first women to make a living from her pen.

provocative dismissal of soldiers and generals alike can be overlooked as laughable and harmless, coming from the mouth of a beautiful young woman, whose words no one on earth would take seriously. This was a clever tactic, because a reader, who was sufficiently forward thinking to accept that a woman might have an intelligent and pertinent point to make, would consequently also be one unlikely to object to the radical opinions she expresses, and vice versa. The real Cyrano openly ridiculed the exaggerated gallantry that the précieuses so admired and which Rostand's Roxane demands of her hybrid lover.

In the *Voyage to the Sun*, Cyrano's hero meets a woman who is a native of 'the Republic of Truth'. She has come to live in 'the Nation of Lovers' and her literal interpretations of the traditional overly refined and metaphorical language used by her suitors (a pastiche of the literary style affected by the précieuses) highlight their inanity. She is so disturbed and terrified by the protestations of her lovers, that they 'cry seas and floods of tears for her sake' and that her 'merest glance can cause a mortal wound', that she determines to commit suicide. The most absurd and vehement of her admirers, known only as *Le Jaloux* (the jealous one), persuades the unfortunate young woman to this extreme course of action and assures her that her best escape route from the world will be to tear out her own heart to use as a vessel to carry her away. He declares that she need not fear that it can hold her, since it can hold so many others, nor that it will sink since it is so light, and that the 'favourable wind of his sighs will carry [her] safe to port in spite of the tempest of his rivals'. Fortunately, the young woman is interrupted by another of her admirers as she is attempting to cut out her own heart. The rival saves the young woman and the jealous lover is brought to justice for his crime: '. . . condemned to banishment for life and to end his days as a slave in the territories of the Republic of Truth with a prohibition to all his descendants down to the fourth generation to set foot in the Province of the Lovers;

moreover, he was enjoined never to use hyperboles on pain of death.'[17]

Cyrano's satisfaction with a world where a man could be banned from using hyperbole, on pain of death, is evident, and perhaps reveals a further gap between the fictional Cyrano and his historical counterpart. The stage Cyrano masterminds an elaborate poetic deception that wins him the heart (if not the hand) of his beloved mistress – the real Cyrano was above all a proud citizen of the Republic of Truth. He questioned the honesty of lovers' eloquence and wrote a series of love letters which were more satirical than sentimental and seem designed to mock the very protestations they contain. The real Cyrano was particularly alert to the rich source of comedy provided by the convoluted sexual politics of his time. Fans of the fictional Cyrano may be disappointed to learn that there is no corresponding tragic love story to be told about the real Cyrano. Perhaps they may also allow that his outspoken defence of individuality, passion and personal freedom, his devotion to ideals of sincerity and loyalty are a more important legacy than any gossipy account of his love life could ever be.

9

Paternoster of the wolf

Cyrano's family background was one of religious conformity and even devotion. By the time Cyrano returned from the war, his older brother Denis had entered the priesthood. This is rather unusual because Denis was the eldest son. He stood to inherit his father's entire estate and would therefore normally have been expected to make a good marriage and carry on the family name. Cyrano's sister Catherine also chose religion rather than marriage and a family. She had entered the Parisian convent of the Daughters of the Cross, in rue de Charonne, in 1637. In 1641, the year of Cyrano's return to Paris, she made her final vows and changed her name to Sister Hyacinthe. Her parents had to pay for her board and lodging during her probationary year and then provide her with a dowry which represented a significant investment. Abel's will reveals that he also owned several expensive works of religious art.

Cyrano's unorthodox opinions were clearly not just a reaction against mainstream society but also a more personal rebellion against a more than usually devout family. Although the real Cyrano may have been somewhat reticent about revealing the details of his private, emotional life, when it came to his intellectual convictions he was determinedly outspoken and never more so than when his opinions went against the norm. He was not afraid to confront the very darkest aspects of the society in which he lived. Having abandoned his military career for the intellectual life, Cyrano seems to have quickly discovered that his boundless imagination and dark wit were best suited to satire. His writing career encompassed a range of styles and over a period of a decade he was to produce two plays (a tragedy and a comedy), some verse (of which the surviving examples are mainly those written in praise of his writer friends and published in their works), various letters and a two-volume science fiction novel. We will come to the story of how his works finally made it into print later. At this stage in his career, Cyrano seems to have settled quietly in Paris and lived a fairly simple life. He had a private income from his family that was not large enough to allow him any great extravagances, but enough money to live off and so he was able to devote all his time to studying the subjects that interested him. He does not seem to have actively pursued commercial publication at this stage and so he also had total freedom to write about whatever he chose.

Often he chose the most controversial and difficult subjects possible. His determination to provoke is constantly in evidence. Even in the love letters he maintained a deliberately irreverent and occasionally downright blasphemous levity. Certain details are not without unexpected significance; the mysterious red-haired 'M' who features in the letter already mentioned is not purely a romantic figure. It is no accident that the letter focuses on the glory of the beloved's flaming red hair; at the time red hair was linked to witchcraft and devilry and was considered as something of a curse. Cyrano begins his letter by stating his intention to defy such superstitious nonsense and to admire M's hair 'like a man of sense'. In Cyrano's lifetime, belief in the Devil was as fundamental a part of Catholic orthodoxy as belief in God. As a result, belief in witchcraft and demonic possession as tangible works of the Devil was considered a firm proof of piety. A strong link had been forged between freethinking and sorcery; the refusal to believe in the terrifying hysteria of the witch-hunt was considered tantamount to denying the existence of God. The English philosopher Joseph Glanvill makes this explicit in his book *Philosophical Considerations touching Witches and Witchcraft*: 'Those that dare not bluntly say, "There is no God" content themselves (for a fair step and introduction) to deny that there are spirits and witches.'[1] Glanvill prided himself on being a deeply rational man and was an enthusiastic founding member of the Royal Society of London for the Improvement of Natural Knowledge; he would not have dreamt of putting forward a proposition such as the existence of witches and demons without strong evidence. Thus he assembled a series of thirty-five detailed accounts of incidents of demonic possession, haunting and sorcery which, when advertised as 'Proof of Apparitions, Spirits and Witches from a choice collection of modern Relations', went a long way to assuring the book's popular success.

Cyrano de Bergerac, on the other hand, remained magnificently scornful of the whole phenomenon. He dedicated two of his published letters to the subject, ostensibly writing the cases for and against the existence of witches. In fact both letters argue forcibly against. In the seventeenth century, to suggest, as Cyrano did, that witchcraft was nothing more than a pitiful mass of peasant superstition and popular credulity was to court serious controversy. Serious scientific thinkers such as Francis Bacon, René Descartes and Johannes Kepler all accepted witchcraft as an obvious part of life – why then was Cyrano so determined to swim against the tide?

The letter 'Against Witches' contains the most passionate, spontaneous outpouring of Cyrano's particular brand of individualistic idealism to be found anywhere in his works:

> No, I do not remotely believe in Witches, even though many great Persons have not been of my opinion, and I defer to no one's authority, unless accompanied by reason . . . Neither the name of Aristotle, more learned than me, nor that of Plato, nor that of Socrates persuade me one jot, if my judgement is not convinced by the reason of what they say. Reason alone is my queen . . .

For Cyrano, as the product of a profoundly conformist background, there was more at stake in a consideration of the subject of witchcraft than the supposed crimes committed by some toothless crone in a remote, forgotten village. He chose the subject to be a test case for his challenge to the supremacy of dogma over deduction, of belief over reason. Cyrano's letters on witchcraft also reveal his fascination with the sheer imaginative scope provided by the supernatural. In the letter 'For Witches', he recounts a series of delirious visions culminating in a dramatic encounter with an aged sorcerer. With typical perversity, this damnable subject matter inspired Cyrano to passages of breathtaking lyrical beauty. Cyrano opens the letter by setting the scene; he observes with careful precision the way the natural world offers eerie presages of the strange adventure to follow:

> I saw the stars shimmering in the sky with a sparkling fire; the moon was full, but much paler than normal: there were three eclipses and three times the moon seemed to hurtle down out of her sphere; the winds were paralysed, the fountains were silent, birds forgot their song, fish seemed encased in glass; not an animal moved except for the small movement of their trembling; the horror of a terrifying silence reigned throughout and everywhere Nature seemed to be in suspense awaiting some great adventure.[2]

Despite entitling the letter 'For Witches', Cyrano was actually intent, not on proving the existence of witches, but on parodying 'the dark and ridiculous imaginings' of traditional accounts of demons and sorcerers. The scene takes place at midnight by the light of a full moon; Cyrano describes being abducted and flown to the middle of a wood on an enchanted broomstick. These were familiar elements in accounts of witchcraft given by those accused and facing the stake. The mysterious sorcerer that Cyrano encounters in the dark wood also behaves in a way which Cyrano's readership would have recognized from the popular printed accounts of famous cases of demonic possession; at one point the old man falls to the ground and contorts his body into strange shapes and throughout the mysterious ceremony that he performs to summon a demon he issues strange cries and invocations. Contortions, fits and speaking in tongues were considered clear symptoms of demonic possession. Occasionally, the more sceptical observers present at public exorcisms noted that the demons possessing the victims seemed to have a surprisingly shaky grasp of Latin and no knowledge at all of Greek.

Cyrano's magician betrays no such weaknesses. Sporting a flowing beard and long white robes with a half-dead bat pinned over his heart, he performs a complex and mysterious ceremony. Still more impressively, his performance of these arcane rites is accompanied by whirlwinds, blood-red hail, thunderstorms and a rain of fire. Natural special effects of this sort were far from a consistent feature of the cases of demonic possession with which Cyrano's audience would have been so familiar. They add enormously to the theatricality and dreamlike atmosphere that Cyrano required to make his point about the difference between reality and 'ridiculous imaginings'. The magic ceremony which the old man then performs before Cyrano's very eyes involves the evisceration of a fox, a mole and a screech owl. The old man devours their hearts and mixes up a concoction of their blood with fresh dew. He spouts bizarre incantations and draws various mystic circles on the ground.

These latter, less noxious aspects of his practice recall the magical antics of another old man who appears performing a mysterious secret ceremony. The opening of Charles Sorel's 1623 novel *The Comical History of Francion* features the conjurations of the character Valentin. Unlike the terrifying sorcerer Agrippa who features in Cyrano's letter, Valentin turns out to be just a harmless old fool whom the hero Francion has tricked into performing an elaborate series of 'conjurations' in order to summon up a demon to cure his impotence. Francion takes full advantage of the old man's credulity, sending his valet to perform the role of the demon and tie the terrified old man to a tree, leaving Francion free to set off for his prearranged rendezvous for a night of passion with Valentin's beautiful (and frustrated) young wife, Laurette. Like Cyrano, Sorel was a sceptic and a libertin and he makes a vivid point about the possibility that 'magic' is all too often little more than the means for an unscrupulous swindler to take advantage of a gullible mark. Ben Jonson explored the same idea in his 1610 play *The Alchemist*.

Cyrano's Agrippa, on the other hand, is apparently no confidence trickster but the genuine article. Born in Cologne in 1486, Henry Cornelius Agrippa von Nettesheim was reputed (largely due to his own exorbitant claims) to be a fearsome sorcerer. Despite his claims to have discovered the philosopher's stone, the real Agrippa died a pauper's death in 1535. Cyrano's tall tale in the letter 'For Witches' playfully resurrects him and in doing so vindicates the old man's claim to have discovered the elixir of eternal life. At the climax of their encounter Agrippa addresses a long speech to Cyrano in which he describes in loving detail the scope of his magic powers and the evil uses to which he puts them.

According to his own account this all-powerful magician can start wars, influence the harvests, drown unwary travellers, make fairies dance in the moonlight, inspire gamblers to search under the gibbet for a lucky four-leafed clover. He describes how he liberates spirits from their graves at midnight and sends them, garbed in the obligatory sheet that no self-respecting phantom would be without, to demand that their heirs fulfil their dying wishes. He also explains that he is responsible for causing demons to haunt abandoned castles, lurking in readiness to slit the throat of any unwary peasant who might attempt to seek shelter there, guarding the secret of the treasure buried in the ruins. He claims to have taught shepherds to recite 'the Paternoster of the wolf'. It was common in contemporary witch trials for the accused to describe the demonic ceremonies of the 'sabbath' as reversed or perverted versions of traditional elements of Catholic worship. Hence the 'Paternoster of the wolf' is an unholy counterpart to the Lord's prayer. This is just one example of the ways in which demonology was dependent on orthodoxy for its very existence.

Cyrano's sorcerer also claims to be able to bestow the magical mandragore or 'hand of glory' on any pauper he should wish to enrich. He prompts thieves to burn candles made of the fat of a hanged man in order to enchant unwitting householders to sleep soundly while they are burgled. He knows the secret of enchanted coins which will keep flying back to the owner's pocket every time they are used in payment for something and of magic rings which can transport a person across the country in a single day. He claims responsibility for the appearance of poltergeists and for showing old women how to cure fevers with only words. He explains that he teaches other sorcerers how to turn themselves into werewolves, forcing them to eat any children they should encounter once they are transformed and then abandoning them when some brave soul cuts off their wolf's paw which then mysteriously turns into a human hand, leading to them being recognized and brought to justice. He also claims to be able to cure werewolves with a pitchfork wound between the eyes. He sends a tall dark man to trick fools into signing away their souls in a pact with the Devil. He blinds people crossing witches on their way to the Sabbath into seeing nothing but a group of cats. He orchestrates the obscene ceremonies of the witches' Sabbath. He sends incubi to the beds of lustful women and succubi to the beds of lecherous men. He teaches sadistic subjects how to make wax voodoo images of an enemy and then to inflict harm on them by sticking pins into the model or throwing it in the fire. He prevents butter from forming in the churn. He instructs vengeful peasants to put a knot of hair or a toad under the sheepfold belonging to the farmer they wish to ruin, with the result that all the sheep who cross over the hidden talisman inevitably fall down dead. He imparts the secret of the much dreaded curse which caused impotence to strike a man on his wedding night. He can conjure up money which once spent reveals itself to be nothing more than a handful of enchanted leaves. He knows the secrets of ghosts, magic mirrors, charms and talismans of every sort.

This extraordinary and exhausting list of achievements represents nothing less than a catalogue of popular superstitions current in Cyrano's time. The average peasant (or even educated man of science like Joseph Glanvill) would see nothing to contradict in any of the individual elements of this list, but by putting them all together and attributing them all to one great sorcerer, Cyrano highlights the implausibility and ridiculousness of these superstitions. Separately, each claim has a certain eerie power but heaped together in this way their improbability is manifest. As a true son of the scientific revolution, Cyrano is assembling the evidence in order to consider the likelihood or possibility of witchcraft. As Glanvill's work demonstrates, both those who believed and those who doubted the existence of witches felt that their cause would be best served by careful study of all the evidence. It was essential, therefore, to ascertain what could be reasonably accepted as 'evidence'. In the letter 'Against Witches' Cyrano points out that hearsay ought not to be admissible and that just because superstitious peasants recount stories of ghouls and goblins that should not influence the rigorous standard of 'proof'. His response to tales of moonlit flights through the air and other superhuman feats of witchcraft is short and to the point: 'one should not believe

Jean-Benoît Constant Coquelin was the first stage Cyrano. Rostand's play was dedicated to him with the words: 'I had intended to dedicate this poem to the spirit of Cyrano. But since his soul has passed into you, Coquelin, I dedicate it to you.'

Edmond Rostand trained as a lawyer but chose to become a writer instead. In order to fulfil his ambition to 'give lessons of the soul', he deliberately turned away from the historical Cyrano towards the creation of a romantic legend.

The flamboyant actress and theatre owner Sarah Bernhardt was instrumental in orchestrating crucial publicity for Rostand's sell-out play *Cyrano de Bergerac.*

Jean Paul Rappeneau's lavish film version of *Cyrano de Bergerac* (1990) starred Gérard Depardieu as Cyrano and Anne Brochet as Roxane. It was rumoured at the time that Depardieu even went so far as to sleep in his false nose to get into character for the multi-award-winning film.

The real Cyrano was proud of his large nose and posed for this soulful portrait by his friend the engraver Zachary Heince (c.1654).

This eighteenth-century version of Cyrano's portrait features a caption stating that he was born in Gascony. Cyrano had successfully hidden his true Parisian roots.

This portrait of the real Cyrano also includes his family coat of arms, but the family were later prosecuted for pretending to a level of nobility that was no longer theirs by right.

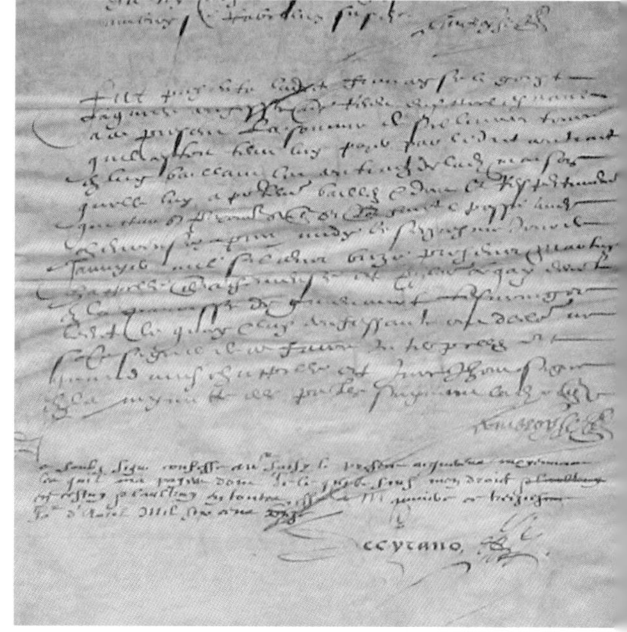

Henri Le Bret, Cyrano's loyal best friend, fought alongside him in the Cadets. They had been friends since childhood and, after Cyrano's death, Le Bret became Cyrano's first biographer and supervised his works through the presses.

The title deeds to the property from which Cyrano took the name Bergerac for himself. The signature is that of Cyrano's grandfather, Savinien; the man he was named after and whose dynamism he inherited.

LES TROIS MOUSQUETAIRES. — Un mousquetaire, placé sur le degré supérieur, l'épée nue à la main, empêchait, ou, du moins, s'efforçait d'empêcher les trois autres de monter. Ces trois autres s'escrimaient contre lui de leurs épées fort agiles. (Page 34.)

The Three Musketeers all had their real life counterparts but their transformation into literary legend was partly dependent on a hoax memoir.

Apres plusieurs degast par les soldats commis
A la fin les Paisans, quils ont pour ennemis
Les guettent à lescart et par vne surprise
Les ayant mis à mort les mettent en chem

CHARLES, COMTE D'ARTAGNAN
Capitaine Lieutenant de la premiére
Compagnie des Mousquetaires du Roi

D'artagnan also existed in real life and fought alongside Cyrano at the siege of Arras in 1640.

Tristan L'Hermite, whom Cyrano greatly admired and described as 'the only free man' in France.

From 'The Miseries and Misfortunes of War' series of engravings by Jacques Callot.

Printed for Henry Rhodes, next the swan Tavern. in
Fleet. street
F. H. Van. Hove. sculp:

Illustration from an English edition (1687) of Cyrano's deliriously funny and inventive space travel satire.

)pposite page: Cyrano tried hard to counteract popular ıperstition about witches. This was a controversial osition to take at a time when refusal to believe in the ·rrifying hysteria of the witch-hunt was considered ıntamount to denying the existence of God.

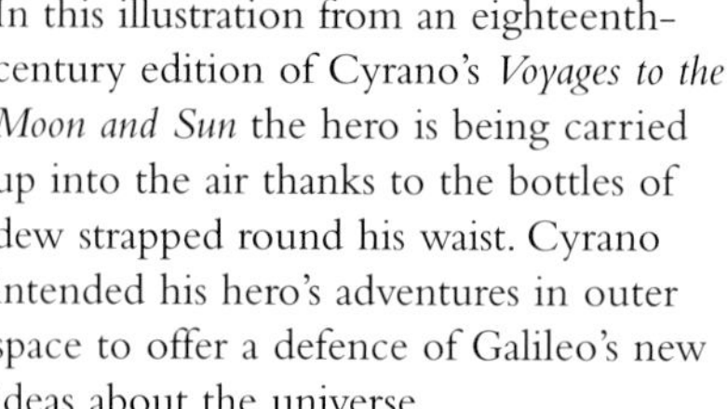

In this illustration from an eighteenth-century edition of Cyrano's *Voyages to the Moon and Sun* the hero is being carried up into the air thanks to the bottles of dew strapped round his waist. Cyrano intended his hero's adventures in outer space to offer a defence of Galileo's new ideas about the universe.

Cyrano's satirical science-fiction flight of fantasy was his masterpiece. In this illustration his hero/alter-ego 'Dyrcona' is on trial in the Republic of the Birds for the crime of being human. Original engraving hand-coloured by Fabien Gaillard.

The fat actor Montfleury, with whom Cyrano quarrelled and wrote a scurrilous attack, lambasting him for his size and his lack of wit.

Robert Parker danced the title role in the ballet of *Cyrano de Bergerac.*

Mauro Corda's new statue of Cyrano in Bergerac town centre gazes up to the heavens, in recognition of the original Cyrano's preoccupation with outer space.

Varoqueaux's statue of Cyrano in the town of Bergerac is quite badly damaged and keeps having its nose stolen.

"Bringing crowds to the Carlton, Haymarket and drawing them from all classes."
KINE WEEKLY
JOSÉ FERRER
1951 ACADEMY AWARD WINNER
IN
STANLEY KRAMER'S Production
'Londoners are crowding to enjoy the fiery acting of 'Cyrano de Bergerac' – and to pay the unusual tribute of applause at the end of each performance.'
Cyrano
de Bergerac
CO-STARRING
MALA POWERS
WITH
WILLIAM PRINCE · MORRIS CARNOVSKY
RALPH CLANTON · LLOYD CORRIGAN
VIRGINIA FARMER
Produced by STANLEY KRAMER · Directed by MICHAEL GORDON
UNITED ARTISTS

George Clooney's uncle, José Ferrer, starred as Cyrano de Bergerac on stage and on film. He won an Oscar and a Tony for the same role – a rare distinction.

Below: Steve Martin's romantic comedy *Roxanne* (1987) was inspired by the play *Cyrano de Bergerac.* Like Rostand before him, Martin included a joke in his script that was originally penned by the real Cyrano centuries before: 'Your nose was on time but you were fifteen minutes late'.

Louis Gallet's serialisation of Cyrano de Bergerac acknowledged the hero's provocative nature. His version was entitled *Captain Satan*.

Cyrano's adventures have been retold in myriad different forms, even as a comic book.

Dan Robert
Ce buste a été réalisé en 1998 par Dan ROBERT, artiste Sannoisien
et inauguré le 29 avril 2000 par Yanick PATERNOTTE,
Maire de SANNOIS.

In 1655, Cyrano died at the house of his cousin Pierre in Sannois, he was only 36 years old. Today, the small Parisian suburb is proud of its connection to the real Cyrano. This bronze bust is to be found in 'Place Cyrano'.

anything of a man but that which is human'.[3] No doubt his sister and brother would have been utterly horrified by such an assertion, since it not only casts doubt on the antics of demons and witches but also on all the saintly miracles, which were the object of devout Catholic worship.

Elsewhere, Cyrano states baldly that he does not believe in miracles, but is convinced that there is always a natural explanation for apparently supernatural events. This helps to explain something that to modern eyes can seem contradictory: the fact that it was his insistence on reason, doubt and scepticism which marked Cyrano out to his contemporaries as dangerous and possibly mad. That he should refuse to accept what everyone believed is what causes modern critics to praise his 'eminently sane and courageous mind', but at the time, his nonconformism was deeply suspect. The existence of demons and witches was not just approved by the church but also by royalty. Louis XIII's devoutly religious wife, Queen Anne, took a keen interest in witchcraft and possession, and in England James I was a fervent believer in sorcery. He even penned a learned treatise on demonology which was published in 1597. Shakespeare's shrewd decision to present three 'secret, black and midnight hags', on stage in *Macbeth*, was a direct appeal to the king's well-known fascination with witches. Cyrano's lifetime saw the beginning of a widespread popular debate on the subject of witchcraft, comparable to the modern fascination with aliens and alien abduction. Carl Sagan has produced some fascinating research detailing the extraordinary similarities between the two phenomena. Just as those on trial for witchcraft faithfully reproduced the details recorded in popular demonology texts, so alien abductees unfailingly claim to have encountered aliens whose spaceships and personal appearance correspond very closely to whatever representation has most recently appeared on film. Not only that, but striking similarities emerge between the actual accounts of victims of 'possession' and of 'abduction', for which Sagan gives eminently rational physiological and psychological explanations, with no need for the intervention of creatures from hell or the heavens. Cyrano would be delighted.

Throughout the 1630s and 1640s, intermittent poor harvests and recurring outbreaks of the plague had led to terrible hardship for rural communities across France. From time to time a natural occurrence, such as a devastating hailstorm, would unleash a paroxysm of terror in the beleaguered communities of the rural poor. This climate of fear and uncertainty triggered off widespread popular witch-hunts. In Burgundy, Champagne and Gascony travelling witchfinders were active and hundreds of suspects were sent for trial. Others were almost certainly dealt with in a more direct and deadly manner. Retributive killings were not uncommon in rural communities when a flashpoint was reached as the result of the loss of vital crops or livestock. The local people would take it upon themselves to bring the suspected 'evildoers' to justice.

In the village of Rouze in 1643 a witchfinder assembled all the inhabitants of the area in order to identify those responsible for the poor harvests, hardship and general misery which blighted the region. He picked out thirty-five women, charging 100 écus for the privilege of his services. The women were saved from the flames thanks to the timely arrival of the local bishop who interrogated the 'witchfinder' and forced him to admit that he was a charlatan. The thirty-five pseudo-witches were released and the pseudo-witchfinder was fined and imprisoned. In the mountains of the Languedoc region in September a court order had to be issued to force the lord of the manor of Rombret and Rouergue to release six prisoners (five women and one man) from the dungeons of his castle. The order came too late to save two of the six who had not survived the horrifying torture inflicted on them in order to extract their confessions. The *parlements* of Dijon and Toulouse reacted to the 'witch-craze' by ordering the arrest of all witchfinders, some of whom were summarily executed and hundreds of accused were set free. It was almost equally common, however, for murderers who claimed their crimes were committed against witches to be pardoned. In December 1630 in a village in the Franche Comté region, a woman suspected of witchcraft was beaten by a group of villagers and left to die in the snow.

Such horrors help to explain why Cyrano felt the need to engage in this particular debate and why he was convinced that witchcraft was an illusion. The letter 'Against Witches' gives a still clearer explanation of why Cyrano was so keen to expose popular superstitions about witches and demons as unfounded nonsense. He cites the examples of three famously scandalous witchcraft cases: the sorcery of Louis Gaufridy, the demons of Loudun and the bewitching of Madeleine Bavent.

These three cases in particular took the public imagination by storm, because in each instance there was something more to the story than the all-too-common scapegoating of a harmless, marginal individual by a troubled, rural community. The scandals which exploded in Aix, Loudun and Louviers became national sensations, partly because they concerned the apparent insurgence of Satan and his minions into the very heart of the religious mainstream, igniting as they all did within the confines of a nunnery. But they also generated such intense interest because key members of the church chose to disseminate the shocking details as widely as possible. Priests, who were supposed to be responsible for calming these explosive situations determined instead to add fuel to the fire, staging showy public exorcisms and allowing the publication of the salacious 'confessions' of the victims. The theory was that, the greater publicity given to the mysteries of demonic possession and witchcraft, the greater the public's consequent fear of the devil. The reality was not so simple.

In Aix in the summer of 1609, a young girl named Madeleine Demandolx de la Palud complained to the mother superior at the Ursuline convent, in which she was staying, that she had been suffering from night terrors and hallucinations. A series of exorcisms was set under way. In the spring of 1610, the 'devil' in Madeleine denounced a curé from Marseille as the source of her suffering. The priest whose name was Louis Gaufridy had been her family's confessor and a close friend of her mother's. The exorcisms continued attracting large crowds and two more girls also fell victim to 'possession'. One of them, Louise Capeau, accused Madeleine of having bewitched her.

By early 1611, Gaufridy had been incarcerated and subjected to torture sessions designed to elicit a full confession. After a couple of months Gaufridy broke down and admitted to having signed a pact with the Devil in order to be able to seduce any woman he wanted. He claimed to have chosen to sell his soul in order to satisfy his overwhelming lust for certain young girls, including Madeleine. The Devil had then apparently granted Gaufridy the power to seduce any woman he desired just by blowing into her nostrils. The priests in charge of the case stage managed the exorcisms to the terror and fascination of large crowds, with the intention of 'converting' as many unbelievers as possible and instilling a healthy fear of the Devil into the masses. In a spectacular *coup de théâtre* which would later be repeated in Loudun, Gaufridy was brought out to stand before his accuser. On seeing him again Madeleine lost the power of speech. Stripping away the 'supernatural' elements of Gaufridy's crime a skeleton of sexual obsession and abuse is revealed, an all too common element in witchcraft confessions. Gaufridy describes how he won the trust of Madeleine's family in order to get close to her, seducing her mother in order to have free access to the young girl. On 30 April 1611, Gaufridy was burned at the stake. His confession was printed and sold like hot cakes.

Although the Gaufridy case took place before Cyrano was born its notoriety was such that it was far from forgotten in his lifetime; an account of his trial, condemnation and execution had been published in 1611 and a salacious 'biography' entitled *The horrible and appalling witchcraft of Louis Goffredy* appeared later in the century. In Cyrano's teens another possession scandal erupted in the town of Loudun and it is hard to believe that he would not have followed the progression of the affair as breathlessly as anyone else. This time, the accused was another priest and the 'victim' was Jeanne des Anges, the prioress of the Ursuline convent in Loudun. The town had been struck by the plague in 1632, and later the same year, perhaps influenced by the resulting climate of fear and horror, Jeanne des Anges had declared herself possessed by the Devil and subject to disturbing erotic hallucinations.

When the exorcisms began, she eventually pointed the finger at the handsome young priest named Urbain Grandier, whom she had previously attempted to engage as the convent's confessor and spiritual director. Jeanne seems to have fixed on Grandier as the focus of an erotic obsession fuelled by the town gossip about his many sexual conquests among female parishioners that she had eagerly garnered at the gates of the convent. At the time of her accusation Jeanne des Anges had never even met Grandier. She had been keen to meet him and had gone as far as to write to him, offering him the position of confessor to the convent. Grandier's high-handed refusal probably sealed his fate. Urbain Grandier's crimes were rather more mundane than demonic. He was an intelligent, handsome and successful individual, essentially guilty of nothing worse than arrogance and womanizing. His quarrelsome nature and his unshakeable conviction of his own superiority had made him various important enemies in the town, enemies who were quick to seize on the excuse offered by the accusations made by the mentally unstable Jeanne des Anges. Urbain Grandier had been foolish enough to behave as if the rules didn't apply to him – even going so far as to pen a learned treatise against the celibacy of priests in order to reassure his pregnant lover. This weighed heavily against him at his trial. Just after his execution, one of his acquaintances summed him up in a letter to the great Pierre Gassendi as a man who 'had great virtues but who also had great vices'.[4]

The 'possession' did not abate after Grandier's execution and soon a large number of the nuns and a whole roster of the legions of hell were involved. Cracks appeared in the show exorcisms even at their height and dissenting voices were heard in the crowd casting doubt on the whole performance. One doubting nobleman, the Comte de Lude, even went so far as to trick the priest into letting him test whether some holy relics he possessed were really genuine by seeing how the Devil in Jeanne reacted to contact with them. The box containing the precious burden was duly pressed to Jeanne's head and she went into a more than usually dramatic round of howling and convulsing. When the priest handed back the box, he remarked how pleased the count must be with such a confirmation of the holy nature of his precious relics and asked to be permitted to see such a precious treasure. The count happily complied, opening the box to reveal that there were no relics within and that he had engineered the occasion to expose the 'possession' as a fraud. The exorcisms were popular theatrical events which attracted large crowds, most of whom were much more easily convinced than the count. The celebrity of the prioress reached such a pitch that Queen Anne summoned her to a royal audience in Paris.

Some years earlier, while awaiting the execution of his sentence Grandier had penned an urgent appeal to the king himself. The eloquent desperation with which he pointed out the numerous flaws in the accusations against him and the impossible catch-22 in which the priests had caught him, was sadly not enough to save him. It is doubtful that the king ever even read the letter. As Grandier pointed out in his plea, his trial was a farce and the accusations made against him by Jeanne and her fellow nuns were inconsistent and contradictory. The women had withdrawn their identification of him as their tormentor on more than one occasion but this was discounted on the grounds that Satan was the prince of deceit. When the 'demons' named Grandier they told the truth but when they pronounced him innocent they were lying. A similar paradox was used to deal with the results of interrogation under torture, confession was proof of guilt but refusal to confess under torture was also proof of guilt since only the devil could be responsible for such inhuman resistance.

The great philosopher Montaigne, an important influence on Cyrano's own thinking about the subject, had pointed out the terrible flaw in the use of judicial torture: 'What would one not say, what would one not do to flee such terrible pains? [. . .] Suffering forces even innocents to lie.'[5] Montaigne had even undertaken to research the whole issue of witchcraft and possession personally. He went to see some prisoners accused of witchcraft to examine them for himself. He was unconvinced by what he saw and argued strongly in favour of scepticism and tolerance, suggesting that it is putting too great a faith in conjecture and hearsay to see a man burned alive on the strength of them. It was the terrible arrogance of the priests standing in judgement over their fellow man that Cyrano objected to so virulently and in the letter 'Against Witchcraft', he states categorically that he does not believe that any of the three famous possession cases were genuine.

The third outbreak of satanic interference in a nunnery took place in Louviers, a small town with a previous history of demonic possession. In 1591 a young serving girl named Françoise Fontaine, who was being wooed by a rich merchant of the town, convinced herself that she was possessed by a demon and the ecclesiastical authorities arranged an exorcism. Her story was well known in the town and had even been published in the local chronicle in the early 1600s. A local priest had attended some of the earliest exorcism attempts at Loudun in 1633–4 and brought back with him terrifying tales that ran like wildfire through the town. Whispered accounts even filtered into the confines of the Convent des Hospitalières de Saint Louis et Sainte Elisabeth where Madeleine Bavent was a nun. It was at this point that the first problems began in the convent with isolated incidents of a similar nature to the events at Loudun. At first the spiritual director of the convent, Mathurin Picard, a calm and moderate man succeeded in controlling the situation. Recognizing the link between the manifestation of 'satanic' attacks on the nuns in his care and the news from Loudun, he suppressed the affair and refused to hold exorcisms or to inform the religious authorities. In this way peace reigned in the nunnery until Picard's death at the close of the year 1642.

With the calming presence of Picard removed Madeleine's 'possession' broke out once more and six other nuns were also afflicted. Exorcisms were arranged and after ten days of investigation Madeleine was condemned for witchcraft and locked up in the town dungeons. The affair dragged on for three more years as Madeleine's various accusations were investigated. This led to the distressing battle over the disinterment of Picard's body; his family had to fight through the courts to prevent him from being burned posthumously on a pyre in the town square. Eventually the convent was disbanded and the building sold.

In Cyrano's lifetime the burning of witches was generally regarded as a just punishment, in keeping with biblical commandment and with God's will. As Henri Boguet put it in response for calls for moderation,

> No, no, witches are walking abroad in their thousands, multiplying on the earth like the caterpillars in our gardens, it is a disgrace to the Magistrates to whom the punishment of crimes and misdemeanours belongs; because when we have no less than the express commandment from God to put them to death as his greatest enemies why do we continue to endure them any longer, rendering ourselves disobedient to his most high Majesty?[6]

Boguet was a witchfinder reputedly responsible for as many as 600 deaths. Although documentary evidence of only twenty-eight of his cases has survived, these include the harrowing account of the 'witches' who committed suicide rather than face Boguet and the trial process.

Cyrano's stance against the ignorant superstition and hideous violence of the witch-hunts stems from his awareness of human fallibility. In the letter 'Against Witchcraft' he writes, 'our fathers were wrong in times past, their descendants are wrong now; ours will be wrong one day.'[7] Given Cyrano's family background, his decision to highlight the three highly controversial possession cases can be seen as doubly provocative, and his comment about the errors of fathers and their offspring seems to take on a particularly personal significance. Thanks to the intervention of humane individuals like Cyrano the tide of opinion would eventually turn against witchcraft, although the last case in rural France occurred as recently as the 1950s. Looking back over the events of the century, Voltaire remarked that philosophy had ultimately prevailed and cured the judges of 'this abominable illusion', teaching them that 'one should not burn imbeciles'.[8]

10

A madman named Cyrano

In 1647, nine-year-old King Louis XIII was gravely ill with smallpox, his younger brother Philippe was also very sick, and, as a result, the throne looked to be in serious danger. Around this time, Cyrano had begun work on a blood-soaked classical tragedy in five acts. He entitled the play *La Mort d'Agrippine* (*The Death of Agrippina*) and in it he explored ideas about power and corruption and expressed ideas that were a direct challenge to the Catholic hegemony. The work is very dark and extremely violent, but critics have commended its 'strange and savage beauty'.[1] The plot revolves around the devices and desires of Agrippina, widow of the Germanicus Caesar and mother of the depraved future Emperor Caligula. Agrippina is at the heart of a failed revolt against the tyrant Tiberius, along with the tyrant's traitorous favourite, Sejanus, and Sejanus's murderously bitter former mistress Livilla. Sejanus is an unrepentant atheist anti-hero, who declares that man created the gods, and not the other way around. He argues, as did other creations of Cyrano's, that life after death is a figment of the imagination – that what awaits us after death is just the same as what we experienced before birth: nothingness. Cyrano put a typically double-edged bit of provocation into the mouth of his hero:

These lovely nothings that we worship without knowing why,
These creatures athirst for the blood of our slaughtered beasts,
These gods that man created, who did not create man,
Even the most solid State rests upon this absurd fantasy,
Fie, fie, Térentius, who fears them, fears nothing.

The final line is deliberately ambiguous and, in isolation, could be read as a harmless homily; that the godfearing man need fear nothing. The context of the speech reveals a far more radical argument: that he who fears the gods is afraid of a figment of his own imagination. There are no definite records of the play in performance so we have no indication when it might have been staged or where. It seems likely that it was withdrawn early in its first run and it has been largely neglected ever since.

According to an anecdote, which may be apocryphal since it is first recorded as late as 1715, the play attracted large audiences at first, due to its controversial theme. The writer La Monnoye describes large numbers of uncultured playgoers enthusiastically determined to attend and be scandalized, knowing that there were 'dangerous' passages in the *The Death of Agrippina* but failing, in their simplicity, to notice the real blasphemy and instead finally seizing on a perfectly innocent use of the word 'hostie' (a poetic synonym for 'victim' but also coincidentally the word for the sacramental host). Thus when Sejanus declared his intention to strike his victim, he was apparently greeted with cries from the audience of 'Oh! The wicked fellow! Oh! The atheist! Listen to how he speaks of the holy sacrament.' Another anecdote, told by Tallemant des Reaux, relates that, once the play was printed, it sold out almost immediately precisely because of its scandalous notoriety.

> A madman named Cyrano wrote a play entitled *The Death of Agrippina*, in which Sejanus said terrible things against the gods. The play was a bit nonsensical. Sercy who printed it said to Boisrobert that he had sold out the impression in no time at all: 'I am astonished to hear it,' said Boisrobert; 'Ah! Sir,' replied the bookseller, 'there are some lovely impieties in it.'[2]

Cyrano's fierce poetic tragedy, like his writings about witchcraft, contributed to the contemporary debate about faith versus freethinking. Having left the army and begun to study and eventually to write himself, Cyrano was rapidly caught up in the excitement of discovery and questioning. As a result he was to find himself at odds with the age in which he lived. Cyrano fought the orthodox mainstream not just as a rebellion against paternal authority, nor purely from a desire to stand out from the crowd, even if both of those things were part of his nature. In taking a stand against the Catholic Church, Cyrano was acting on humanitarian principles and it was idealism, rather than the cynicism for which the libertines were so often reproached, that led him to criticize a corrupt and bloodthirsty institution. In his attack on the freethinkers, the Jesuit priest Father Garasse decried the 'outrageous' ideas which formed 'the ordinary talk of the libertine', among them 'that heretics should be treated with leniency, that it is barbarous to persecute the Huguenots, that the Inquisition is a barbarously cruel thing'.[3] This puts the 'degeneracy' of the libertines into a whole new light.

In 1625, Louis XIII's physician, the scholar Gabriel Naudé had published a book in which he identified the accusation of witchcraft as a convenient label with which to dismiss the achievements of minds that were ahead of their time. In his *Apology for the great men who have been falsely suspected of Magic* he commented on the political suppression of free thought, noting that it particularly applied to those attempting to expand the horizons of knowledge.

> All these great minds aim at such a high degree of perfection that the ignorance of their century becomes angry that they have emancipated themselves so much further than others and will always suspect them of impiety in their speculations and their theory, and magic in their actions [. . .] It is hardly astonishing – since all the propositions of these great minds have always been rejected, despite being very solid and true . . . just for being met with in this century when all witticisms and exceptional knowledge are held as suspect and dubious – if most philosophers, mathematicians and naturalists have been falsely suspected of magic [. . .] this calumny is so particular to those who make these disciplines their profession, that it seems almost an essential attribute for them to be reputed magicians.[4]

The freethinkers were a beleaguered and mistrusted minority, exposed, as Naudé puts it, to calumny and suspicion. Regardless of the danger, Cyrano remained tremendously forward-thinking and determined to see new ideas accepted. His thirst for novelty, and for scientific progress in particular, led him to play a part in the invention of a whole new literary genre. As the author of one of the first ever works of science fiction, at a time before the word science even came into general use (science was known as 'natural philosophy' in Cyrano's time), Cyrano was a radical innovator and, as such, bound to come into conflict with the authorities. The heretical ideas of the new science were viewed with deep suspicion. Cyrano's science-fiction novel appeared in two volumes: *The Voyage to the Moon* in the late 1640s, later followed by *The Voyage to the Sun*. During Cyrano's lifetime they were initially circulated in manuscript form, and only published after his death in a heavily censored version.

As a mature writer, Cyrano expressed the conviction that blasphemy was the best way to take advantage of the dubious system of papal indulgences. Since the Pope was prepared to sell divine forgiveness to the highest bidder, Cyrano reasoned that it must be worth getting your money's worth first. 'It is good to offend the Pope since he has so much indulgence.'[5] In making this sarcastic reference to the corrupt system of indulgences Cyrano also highlighted the fact that indulgence in the sense of Christian forgiveness was not always forthcoming from the papacy. The torture chambers of the Holy Inquisition were notorious and France, as a Catholic nation under the spiritual guidance of the Pope, also enthusiastically pursued the policy of torturing and executing dissenters. The fact that Cyrano could make jokes about offending the Pope with apparent impunity is thoroughly deceptive. It appears that ultimately his fondness for provocative statements of this nature may well have cost him his life. Cyrano's was a character marked by rebellion and difference; from his earliest years, he had constantly set himself apart from his peers. Even in death Cyrano de Bergerac was not to follow the expected route. Given the provocative anti-religious content of his work, Cyrano could easily have ended his days at the stake. He seems almost to have expected it and he made frequent references to such a death in the course of his fiction. As, for example, in Dyrcona's flippant comment on the possibility of being burned as a sorcerer: 'it would be doubly annoying to die for something that I absolutely don't believe in', and the extended meditation on the subject in *The Voyages to the Moon and Sun*, where the hero is imprisoned and put on trial for his life on three separate occasions.[6] Instead, Cyrano's independence of mind would indeed have fatal consequences, but the final blow would not come from the expected direction. Cyrano was never prosecuted for blasphemy and he never faced the Holy Inquisitors. The question is – how on earth did such a controversial figure manage to escape the flames?

In 1598 the Edict of Nantes had brought the French wars of religion to a close. The conflict had been devastatingly bloodthirsty and bitter. Paradoxically, with the return of peace came a fresh wave of religious controversy. As well as unleashing the carnage of civil war on the nation, the Protestant Reformation had also served to highlight the corruption endemic in the Catholic Church. Consequently, a series of reforming measures were undertaken, designed to correct centuries of damage caused by the fact that all too often in the past, senior Catholic clergy had been elected through intrigue and nepotism. As a result of this reformation within the French Catholic Church the new century became known as 'the century of saints'. In seventeenth-century Europe the mounting death toll, as countries were riven by religious dissension, prompted even the most devout to reflect on the perversity of religious extremism. In 1620, Sir Thomas Browne, a moderate Anglican and a devout believer declared: 'Men have lost their reason in nothing so much as in their religion.'[7]

Cyrano, who combined a distinct lack of religious feeling with the powerful antipathy for violence of an ex-soldier who has seen bloody combat, became convinced that religion was all too often the root cause of man's inhumanity to man. In the atheistic speech made by an enlightened extraterrestrial, who serves as Dyrcona's mentor and guide on the moon, the central problem of the uncertainty of divine revelation is remorselessly followed through to its logical conclusion. 'But, according to your faith my little animal, if belief in God were so essential to us, in short if it meant eternity, wouldn't God himself have infused everyone with a light as clear as that of the sun which does not hide from anyone? Because if not then you are imagining for yourself a god who is either stupid or malicious.'[8] This expression of disillusionment must also be set in the context of an age in which religious strife was the main source of violent civil and international unrest.

In France in 1572, the wedding of Charles IX's sister Margaret of Valois to the Protestant Prince Henri (the future King Henri IV) had been intended as a symbol of a new harmony between the opposing faiths; instead it became the flashpoint for a series of horrifying events. Six days after the ceremony, on the eve of the feast of St Bartholomew, Admiral de Coligny, the leader of the French Protestant faction, and a number of other leading Huguenot nobles were murdered outside Coligny's Parisian home by royal troops. The violence spread throughout the city, whole families were slaughtered and, when the news reached the provincial towns of Lyons, Rouen, Toulouse and Bordeaux, they followed suit with massacres of their own. It is undeniable, and perhaps unsurprising that, with the end of overt religious conflict, when the converted Protestant King Henri IV began to impose a series of measures promoting religious tolerance, came a noticeable rise in blasphemy and irreligion. Prosecutions for the crime of heresy rose steadily from 1599 onwards.

A verdict of 'lèse-majesté divine' – that is atheism or heresy – was not always indicative of the repression of religious dissension. In a number of cases, an allegation of blasphemy was added to the charges against a criminal, as a means of highlighting the gravity of their offence. Of the sixty-three convictions in the first half of the century, at least sixteen fall into this category, where atheism was a secondary charge. Specifically, seven were found guilty of false testimony, three were accused of being sorcerers, one was an assassin, another had been caught stealing church silver, one was a woman found guilty of infanticide, two were robbers who had made the mistake of choosing Christmas Eve for their heist, and finally two were men who had been convicted of kidnapping and assault in a monastery. Although this catalogue of misdeeds reveals no common link and no direct evidence of religious dissension, damnable conduct was seen as the natural corollary of suspect ideology. In Cyrano's time the punishment of blasphemy followed a set series of stages with the penalties escalating according to the persistence of the offender. A rigorous system had been worked out over the years to establish the gravity of an offence of blasphemy and the nature of the punishment merited.

The French anti-blasphemy laws have their origins in a ruling pronounced by King Philippe VI on 22 February 1347, which established punishments for heresy ranging from public humiliation in shackles or the pillory, to incision of the lips and removal of the tongue. On 6 April 1594, Henri IV had issued a declaration establishing a system whereby the first two offences of blasphemy were punishable by a fine and the third by an unspecified corporal punishment. On 10 November 1617, the blasphemy laws were further refined by the sixteen-year-old King Louis XIII. The fines were increased and were to be reinforced by imprisonment, however recourse to corporal punishment was put back from the third to the fourth offence and the nature of the physical chastisements remained unspecified, allowing judges the freedom to maintain a degree of clemency. However, in 1636 when Cyrano was seventeen years of age and on the brink of his military career the laws were considerably altered in response to pressure from senior Catholic clergy to protect the sanctity of 'the century of saints' from the rising tide of impiety and irreligion.

On 19 May 1636 a new proclamation brought a new degree of order and rigidity to the punishment of heretics. The first four offences were punishable by fines which were doubled, then tripled and then quadrupled; on the fifth offence the fine not only rose to five times the original sum but was accompanied by an unspecified period of confinement in shackles. This would involve the victim being imprisoned in a sort of wooden neck brace linked by chains to the hands and feet and then secured in a public place. The assembled masses would then have the opportunity to pelt the criminal with rotten fruit or vegetables or even with stones. The rigour of this public retribution would depend on the notoriety of the offender and the description of their crime, hung on a placard around their neck. By the sixth offence the prescribed punishment had escalated to a deliberate and permanent disfigurement. The upper lip would be seared with a branding iron and the unfortunate victim would then be confined in the pillory (or stocks) to display their ignominious brand to the world. The pillory offered a still more painful confinement than the shackles and the same possibility of public retribution. On the seventh offence the lower lip was to be slit and on the eighth the tongue was to be torn out. Given this escalating scale of dire reprisals, one might imagine that incidences of persistent irreligious behaviour would simply not occur. The extraordinary career of the Chevalier de Roquelaure provides flamboyant proof to the contrary.

Roquelaure's numerous outrages against the holy church ran to a long and colourful list. He sang obscene rhymes in church, he was frequently heard to utter blasphemous oaths and phrases, he arranged mock baptisms and weddings for his dogs, he attempted to bribe a mendicant priest into denying God by a lavish donation of alms and he even conducted a parody of communion as the finale of his frequent orgies. The chevalier was arrested in Toulouse but within four days of his arrest he had escaped from prison and fled. The chevalier's father was a marshal of France and this may help to explain the fact that Roquelaure's flight was apparently aided by eight officials who included lawyers, members of the council and even prosecutors from the *Parlement* itself. The chevalier was consequently tried *in absentia*. He was convicted by default and condemned to be beheaded. Roquelaure was recaptured in Paris and imprisoned for a further twenty months, during which time the Parlement of Paris failed to reach a decision on whether to confirm the original sentence pronounced in Toulouse. Before they could decide, Roquelaure escaped again and this time he made sure not to reappear.

Roquelaure's egregious escapades took place in the mid-1640s just at the time when Cyrano was composing his own heretical masterpiece and the laughing atheist may have served as some degree of inspiration for Dyrcona, the hero of Cyrano's *Voyages to the Moon and Sun*, who is also condemned by the Parlement of

Toulouse and who also escapes from prison on more than one occasion. Not all those found guilty of blasphemy were lucky enough to have influential friends strategically placed to aid a daring prison breakout. The case of the Chevalier de Roquelaure was exceptional but it serves to highlight a commonly acknowledged fact of the times. 'Libertine behaviour was a luxury for gentlemen . . . before attacking God it was prudent to assure that one had protectors among men.'[9] Cyrano as a lowly writer was far from enjoying the extraordinary freedoms that Roquelaure had so abused. As a result Cyrano's rebellion was considerably more cerebral and initially more private; this may give some clue as to why, unlike Roquelaure, he was not to receive an official death sentence.

When Cyrano was still a child two very significant heresy trials took place, both of which resulted in the deaths of the accused. The two very different condemned men were both to provide models for Cyrano's own subsequent career of free thought and irreligion. The first was Giulio Vanini who died at the stake in 1619, the year of Cyrano's birth. While Cyrano was a newborn baby mewling out his first faint cries in Paris Vanini's howls were dying away in distant Toulouse. Vanini, a disgraced Carmelite monk was burned at the stake in the town square. In a letter written to a friend at the time of the trial the chief prosecutor who had been responsible for conducting extensive interviews with the condemned man described him as 'the finest and the wickedest mind I have ever known'.[10] As well as this ambivalent accolade, numerous other manuscript accounts of Vanini's notorious fate have survived, among them the following graphic description of the condemned man's final agonies:

> At the last moment his face was wild and horrible, his soul tormented, his speech confused and, though he frequently proclaimed that he would die like a philosopher, he died like a beast. Before the fire was lit, being ordered to submit his tongue

> to the knife, he refused and pincers were used to drag it out; having seized it the executioner sliced it off. Never was heard a more horrible cry; one would have said the bellow of a stricken ox. The fire consuming the remains; the ashes were scattered to the winds.[11]

The motivation for recording these hideous details can be deduced from the description itself. There is no shred of pity for the victim's horrible fate expressed by the writer, just a grim satisfaction that the dangerous radical got what he deserved. This harrowing description is, in fact, an early example of gutter-press journalism. It was written to flog to a bloodthirsty population keen to devour the latest gory details of someone else's private tragedy. This lucrative business ultimately served the same purpose as the public spectacle of execution itself. Firstly, it offered a horrible warning to other nonconformists and secondly it served as propaganda, confirming the justice of the sentence. In spite of the obvious bias in the telling of the story it is nonetheless very revealing.

We learn, for example, that Vanini's tongue was cut out before he was put to death. The surgical removal of the tongue and the burning or slitting of the lips was seen as a symbolic and fitting reward for blasphemy, hence its permanent enshrinement in the stricter blasphemy laws of 1636. The operation also conveniently prevented the victims from addressing any dangerously inspired or eloquent last words to the crowd. In an age before mass communication had become an everyday reality the opportunity to address the assembled hordes at an execution was one of the few instances in which a wide and varied audience could be reached directly. Our eyewitness account also reveals that Vanini saw himself as a 'philosopher' but that his torturers deliberately relegated him to the level of a 'beast' by denying him mankind's defining characteristic: speech. The decision to execute such determined sinners by immolation was also deeply significant since it brought vividly to life the imagined future of the damned, burning in a lake of hell-fire. In this way the authorities stage-managed a live-action, tangible vision of hell for the masses. Why leave the horrors of damnation to the imagination when you can bring the real thing to the town square of your choice? This also explains why the eye-witness account speaks of Vanini's horrifying pain in metaphysical terms, insisting that not just his flesh but 'his soul was tormented'.

A second outrageous dissident was famously condemned for blasphemy in Cyrano's childhood. Théophile de Viau perished in exile in 1625 when Cyrano was six years old, his health having been fatally undermined by a long period of imprisonment. Cyrano certainly read Viau's works and would have been vividly aware of the fate of his predecessor. It was the shocking content of the provocative verses collected in the *Parnasse des Poètes Satyriques* that had brought Théophile and his fellow authors to the attention of the authorities. The four main writers behind the collection were lucky enough to benefit from the patronage and protection of the powerful Duc de Montmorency and as such all of them succeeded in escaping Paris when the inevitable storm broke. They were tried *in absentia*, Théophile was identified as the ringleader and was the only one of the four to be condemned to be burned at the stake. In the absence of the man himself an effigy was hanged and then burned.

In September 1623 Théophile was arrested in Saint Quentin and brought back to Paris. In March 1624 the Parisian Parlement began the lengthy process of interrogation, in the course of which the chief prosecutor Mathieu Molé recorded his conviction of a strong connection between Théophile and Vanini. Among the allegations against the poet was that of considering nature as 'the sovereign power over men and all that is mortal, just as much as over animals, in accordance with the doctrine of his master Vanini'.[12] For over a year and a half Théophile was held in a dungeon and periodically interrogated. He held out against this ordeal and made no damning admissions, nor could anyone be found to testify against him; as a result his sentence was reduced to perpetual banishment and he was eventually released in September 1625. However, the horrific conditions in which he had been held had totally destroyed Théophile's health and he died shortly after his release.

In 1736 Voltaire wrote to a friend asking him to send copies of Vanini's works expecting to find within them the outrageous blasphemies which had led to Vanini's considerable notoriety as 'such a depraved character'. On reading the works he was extremely disappointed. 'I am annoyed that they fried that poor Neapolitan but I would gladly burn his boring books.'[13] This reaction gives a clue as to a paradoxical divergence of fortune between Vanini and Cyrano. Vanini's works were heretical but Cyrano's were flamboyantly atheistic. Although Vanini's works were considerably less provocative, his life was one of precarious exile and his conduct was occasionally decidedly questionable, which left him vulnerable to official reprisals. Cyrano's outspoken condemnation of the practice of burning dissidents at the stake draws attention to the fact that in a case where the question of guilt or innocence is a subject of ideological debate the practice of setting the accused alight renders the debate null and void. 'Although their accusation is ridiculous, doubtless the result of their stupidity, I shall be none the less dead when a dozen men of wit who have seen me grilled observe that my judges are fools. All their arguments proving my innocence will not resuscitate me.'[14]

In *The Voyage to the Sun* Cyrano dramatized the enthusiastic reception of *The Voyage to the Moon* and the public hunger for the challenging ideas it contained. His hero/alter-ego Dyrcona is accused of sorcery, and although this is a fictional work it is not too far-fetched to assume that there were important autobiographical elements in the account. It was long supposed that the imprisonment for the crime of sorcery which Cyrano describes in such graphic detail was a pure invention, but new evidence has recently come to light which suggests that Cyrano probably was incarcerated at a late stage in his career. Cyrano wrote his novel in the first person and christened his intrepid space traveller *Dyrcona*, an anagram of D. Cyrano. In choosing a thinly veiled version of his own name for his space-travelling hero he identified his protagonist's riotous interplanetary progress with his own terrestrial explorations and adventures.

Cyrano was always acutely aware of the image-making process. From an early age he showed a fascination with the possibilities for self-publicity that the right name could offer. Throughout his duelling career and his later incarnation as a mordant satirist, he retained a sense of theatre that contributed to the creation of a legend that would outgrow him and take on a life of its own after his death. At different times in his lifetime he signed himself in each of the following ways: Alexandre de Cyrano Bergerac, Hercule de Bergerac, de Bergerac, de Bergerac Cyrano, De Cyrano de Bergerac, Savinien de Cyrano, the last being the only name that was officially his by right. Cyrano was no respecter of officialdom and he refused to give up the name de Bergerac just because he no longer had a legal claim to it. He also decided to appropriate more dashing forenames: Alexandre (as in Alexander the Great) and Hercules both having obvious connotations of power and military might that Savinien did not. Savinien was a popular Christian name in the small provincial town of Sens where the Cyrano family had first established itself on arrival from Sardinia. Cyrano may have shrugged off the name as a way to prevent anyone from making the connection.

In the manner of modern-day spin doctors and publicists Cyrano recognized the importance of presentation. As such he was happy for his readers to identify Dyrcona, the inventor and philosopher whose travels explore some of the most controversial ideas of his time with himself. In keeping with Naudé's analysis, Cyrano realized that an accusation of witchcraft was the sign of a great mind and was therefore something to be flaunted and celebrated. In typical, iconoclastic fashion he also found in the subject an inexhaustible source of comedy. He gleefully mocks the ignorance and superstition of the unenlightened. The fearful suspense and tension created by the arrival of town officials to hunt down Dyrcona and lead him off to the stake are swiftly undercut by hilarity. Colignac, the hero's noble friend and host is unable to control his amusement when one of the officials, failing to understand Colignac's reluctance to denounce his friend, offers the following friendly consolation as an incentive for him to reveal the sorcerer's whereabouts: 'The magician is a person you love; but you have nothing to fear; things will go easily with respect to you: you just need to deliver him into our hands and for love of you we will engage upon our honour to get him burnt without a scandal.'[15] The rest of the officials' arguments are drowned out by Colignac's peals of laughter. Dyrcona's friend does not betray him but the hero is separated from his friends when they decide to leave the area, and finds himself cornered by a fanatical priest and some angry peasants. A superbly knockabout chase sequence ensues in which he is captured, escapes, is captured again, escapes a second time and then is finally recaptured. His influential friends succeed in getting him moved out of his slimy dungeon into a comfortable cell in a high tower and they insist on him being allowed all the books and materials he requires. As a result the adventurer succeeds in constructing a flying machine which, rather than simply aiding his escape as he had intended, carries him off into the skies and all the way to the sun. In this way a second adventure in outer space unfolds.

In reality of course a visit from the ecclesiastical authorities was no laughing matter. In Italy the career of the great Galileo Galilei, one of Cyrano's heroes, was famously dogged by many such unwelcome visits and in 1633 after having published his *Dialogue concerning the two chief World Systems* (1632) he ended up on trial and facing a death sentence. Galileo had presented his controversial scientific findings in the form of a fictional debate between invented characters. In spite of these precautions he still fell foul of the Catholic authorities and ended up seeing his works banned and living out his days under house arrest. Galileo was an extraordinarily talented, visionary man of science who risked his life to publish his astronomical findings for the benefit of the growing community of natural philosophers. Cyrano de Bergerac was a science popularizer, a writer who used his abundant imagination to try to communicate the excitement of the scientific revolution. While Galileo worked on analysing the raw data of his astronomical observations and drawing fascinating and startling conclusions therefrom, Cyrano and others like him enthusiastically attempted to assimilate some of the implications of the new science and to analyse the imaginative possibilities of this extraordinary broadening of mankind's perspective on the universe. Unlike Dyrcona, who had powerful friends and a spaceship to aid his escape, the real Cyrano was to find himself abruptly abandoned by those who might have been able to shield him when the storm clouds of sectarian disapproval started to gather threateningly above.

Even today the act of publishing a book, albeit a work of purest fiction can potentially be fraught with danger, as the novelist Salman Rushdie can attest. Books are powerful. Books are dangerous. Books can get a person into a lot of trouble. Small wonder that Cyrano, a lifelong devotee of rebellion and troublemaking, would grow to love them so dearly. Dyrcona is nearly torn to pieces by a group of yokels for possessing a book. It is a copy of Descartes' *Physics* but the peasants, who can't read and, lacking the ability to recognize the work for what it really is, assume that the diagrams it contains must have occult significance and the owner of the book is therefore condemned as a witch. They are preparing to execute him when he makes his escape. The incident is deliberately farcical, but this does not undermine the satirical intent with which it was conceived.

Even in our own increasingly secular age, examples abound which teach us that the absolute certainty of the zealot can unleash unspeakable evil. Cyrano was born into a society in which religious extremism occupied a position not at the marginalized terrorist fringes but at the very heart of the ruling classes. As such, his free-thinking stance was all the more heroic and inspirational. Religious conviction can strike like lightning; one moment the sky is lit with divine brilliance, the next a smoking corpse lies cooling on the ground. Throughout history belief has been a dangerous business with a determined few prepared to die for their faith and an even larger number happy to kill for it. As Cyrano points out in *The Voyage to the Moon*, it is a little too late to argue the rights and wrongs of ideological execution once the accused has been set alight.

11

I fell from the moon

On 20 July 1969 Neil Armstrong and his fellow astronaut Buzz Aldrin revealed to a fascinated public their first-hand observations of the surface of the moon. Television screens across the globe relayed images of a barren, rocky landscape marked by gigantic craters, the vivid scars of ancient asteroid strikes. Over three centuries earlier Cyrano de Bergerac had revealed to an equally fascinated public that the lunar landscape was lush and verdant and extraordinarily similar to that of the earth. He entranced readers with the revelation that the moon was inhabited by intelligent extraterrestrials, who were superbly scornful of humanity. Although Cyrano's imaginative exploration of the moon may have been a long way from scientifically accurate there was one common element between Cyrano's journey to the moon and that of *Apollo* 11. Both Cyrano and the American astronauts had taken the opportunity to look back at the earth from above and to reflect on the insights to be gained from this extraordinary new perspective.

As the great seventeenth-century astronomer Johannes Kepler realized, there has never been any shortage of people whose reaction to the spectacular panorama of the night sky is to look up at the stars and imagine heading off out into the vast interstellar emptiness to explore, leaving the earth spinning below. As early as 1610 Kepler wrote: 'Let us create vessels and sails adjusted to the heavenly ether and there will be plenty of people unafraid of the empty wastes.'[1] Astronomers like Kepler and Galileo Galilei had given the world more detail than ever before to enhance such imaginings. Today the thirst to get out there among the 'empty wastes' is so great that a certain privileged few are prepared to pay enormous sums of money to the chronically underfunded Russian space programme and in doing so secure themselves a seat on a vessel which can take them out of this world. Space tourism has recently become a reality. In 2004, Richard Branson announced his intention to launch the first purely commercial space flights. Over 350 years earlier several men possessed only of the vast wealth of their imaginations set off on space tourism's earliest missions. It is fair to ask the question why. Exactly what was it that inspired Cyrano de Bergerac to write about a trip through the 'heavenly ether', so many years before the possibility of such a trip could be realized?

Despite writing a fantastical description of rocket propulsion three centuries ahead of its time, Cyrano was no rocket scientist. The best efforts of the talented philosopher-mathematician Pierre Gassendi infused Cyrano with a passionate enthusiasm for the ideas of the new science, but failed to introduce any kind of scientific rigour into Cyrano's 'turbulent mind'. He may not have had any great technical or mathematical abilities but Cyrano had a riotous imagination and so it was that his work saw the first description of a hot air balloon, over 130 years before the Montgolfier brothers would develop the first workable prototype. He dreamt up the concept of the mobile home, pleased with the idea of whole cities being transported under their own power, with each house on wheels travelling great distances, allowing the inhabitants an enjoyable sense of freedom. He also described the peculiar sensation of weightlessness in zero gravity in terms that were echoed by the first astronauts some 300 years later. He even imagined personal stereos, although his vision of the device that lunarians carried about with them might not be immediately recognizable to the MP3 generation. Its primary purpose was not to play music but rather talking books; it was the fantasy of a voracious reader. Cyrano came up with the idea as a way for the super-intelligent people of the moon to read and do other things at the same time, thus considerably expanding the amount of time in the day that could be devoted to this uniquely enriching activity.

Cyrano amused himself dreaming up elaborate ways to escape the confines of the earth, which range from the sublime (a solar-powered spaceship complete with a small sail for steering, whose rectangular box-like form echoes that of Doctor Who's *Tardis*) to the ridiculous (smearing his naked body with marrowbone jelly, as a remedy for the bruises sustained in a previous unsuccessful lift-off and then, having escaped the earth's atmosphere by rocket power, discovering that the moon's influence operating on the marrowbone draws him into a lunar landing softened by a fall through the branches of a tree). Given the endearingly high level of confusion and misapprehension in Cyrano's 'scientific' writings, one might wonder why it was that he chose subjects for which he was so manifestly ill-qualified. He was attracted to such subjects because he sensed both their phenomenal potential and their tremendous scope for provocation. Cyrano recognized that the vehemence of popular hostility to the controversial themes of natural philosophy was a good indicator of its seminal importance. There is no doubt that the scientific discoveries of the era precipitated one of the most dramatic paradigm shifts in the history of human understanding.

The late sixteenth and early seventeenth centuries witnessed a flowering of new ideas about the world. Ancient methods of enquiry inherited from diverse disciplines from philosophy to natural magic and alchemy began to coalesce and transform into a rational system. This system was known as natural philosophy and is recognizable as the root of all modern science, from astrophysics to zoology. Natural philosophy represented an entirely new way of looking at the world; the most important characteristic of a natural philosopher was a tendency to ask questions, lots of questions. Previously, European conceptions of knowledge had largely been defined by biblical insistence on the authority of 'the Word'. Essentially, all knowledge had to derive in some way from an existing written source, preferably the Holy Scriptures or failing that the works of Aristotle. The great minds of the Renaissance had started to challenge this extremely limiting notion. Various flamboyant characters had embraced natural philosophy: they were beginning to recognize the value of poking things with sticks, setting things on fire, and generally having more fun than was to be had in merely accepting whatever conclusions were reached in ancient texts, solely on the basis that 'it is written'.

In the early sixteenth century Leonardo da Vinci had been one of the first thinkers to advocate this essential shift in scientific methodology. Leonardo writes scathingly in his notebooks about the misguided masses who fail to ask searching questions, who look to books instead of to the real world for knowledge and understanding. Perhaps the greatest of all Leonardo's inventions was his invention of the scientific experiment. He recognized that the true scientist must seek knowledge through direct investigation of the natural world. This innovation was to become increasingly popular over the following decades. In Cyrano's fantastic voyages, the hero Dyrcona succeeds in inventing a spaceship through a lengthy process of trial and error. Such investigations were not without risk however; natural philosophers who turned away from written authority and chose instead to look to the real world and the deductions of human reasoning in their search for truth all too often came into violent conflict with the religious authorities. Galileo's clashes with the Holy Inquisition are well known. Less familiar is the fate of Giordano Bruno, one of Galileo's most important influences. Cyrano was probably first introduced to Bruno's works by Gassendi and he seems to have studied them thoroughly. Bruno's thinking runs through Cyrano's science fiction like an underground stream, providing a wellspring of inspiration.

Giordano Bruno was a disgraced ex-monk and a talented scientist. As a young man, his insatiable fascination for natural philosophy led to his expulsion from a Dominican monastery in Naples. Having fallen foul of the religious authorities, Bruno was a wanted man. Rather than face the potentially fatal consequences of a heresy trial, he fled the country. In the course of a life spent on the run, Bruno's extravagant intelligence secured him access to the royal courts of Henri IV in France and Elizabeth I in England, where he showed off the power of his phenomenal memory and fascinated and aggravated courtiers and royalty alike. Bruno eventually returned to his native Italy where the Inquisition finally caught up with him. His published works reveal that he was unequivocal in embracing the new methodology: 'Arguments are presented in the name of tradition; but the truth is far more often to be found in the present and the future than in the past.'[2]

This rebellious rejection of the authority of the ancients appealed enormously to Cyrano. Early in his career Bruno had published a satirical comedy for the stage, entitled *Il Candelaio*. The play enjoyed considerable popular success, largely thanks to the fact that it was a lively knockabout farce with an incredible number of absolutely filthy jokes, penned by an ex-monk. *Il Candelaio* was an important influence on Cyrano. The French translation had appeared in 1633 under the title *Le Pédant Joué* – it was no coincidence that Cyrano chose to give his own first satirical comedy the exact same title. The two plays share a common theme – in which an unappealing central character is mercilessly tricked and outwitted by his social inferiors. Cyrano did not plagiarize *Il Candelaio*, but in using the same title he scrupulously acknowledged Bruno's influence.

Bruno's works on natural philosophy reveal his overpowering confidence in his conclusions. Throughout his lifetime, in addition to performing stunts to show off his prodigious memory to courtly audiences and working as a freelance tutor for aristocratic pupils, Bruno devoted himself to a rigorous programme of study and calculation. His enthusiasm for natural philosophical investigation had led him to place an innovative focus on 'evidence' and 'reason' in his quest for knowledge and understanding. A key statement in which he explains this focus also holds the key to his ultimate decision to face death rather than renounce his convictions: 'If the evidence is missing, if reason and the senses are mute, we should know to doubt and wait. Authority is not outside of ourselves, but within us. A divine light shines in the depths of the soul to inspire us and guide our thoughts. That is the true authority.'[3]

Bruno's faith in the illumination of this 'divine light' was total. Ultimately, he was condemned for his adherence to a new scientific theory which the Inquisition considered atheistic and dangerous, a theory which emerged as a direct result of the new form of scientific investigation, with earth-shattering consequences.

The ancient Ptolemaic model of the universe described the earth as the still point around which the entire universe rotated. This was in strict accordance with the Holy Scripture, and, having been outlined by Ptolemy in AD150 in an impenetrably complicated work entitled *Almagest*, it was also acceptably ancient. The essence of Bruno's heresy was his rejection of Ptolemy. Bruno's earliest conflicts with his religious superiors had sprung, not from a lack of faith, but rather from an excess of faith. Specifically, Bruno was convinced that since God's power was infinite he had naturally created an infinite universe, within which there would naturally be an infinite number of habited worlds. His studies led him to the conviction that Ptolemy's closed system with its seven spheres and rigid boundaries was unworkable and inaccurate. Bruno rejected outright Ptolemy's convoluted system of epicycles and, in doing so, found himself overwhelmed by the awe-inspiring possibilities of an infinitely expanded horizon.

A radical alternative to the geocentric system had been suggested by a mathematician named Nicolaus Copernicus in 1543. Copernicus taught that the sun was the centre of the solar system and that the earth was just one of several astronomical objects rotating on its own axis and proceeding in an orbit around the sun. Copernicus had published his new heliocentric system in a work entitled *De revolutionibus orbum coelestium*. This was a ferociously technical work, which came stamped with the discouraging warning 'For Mathematicians Only' on the title page. Hardly surprisingly therefore that the Copernican system had been largely ignored until the explosive events of the early seventeenth century brought this astronomical controversy vividly to life. Bruno's vociferous support for the Copernican system had awakened the attention of the European intelligentsia to the debate.

In 1592, at the age of forty-eight, Bruno had begun to tire of his nomadic existence and he gave in to the repeated requests for a private tutor made to him by the nobleman Giovanni Mocenigo. Sadly the job offer turned out to be a trap designed to lure Bruno back to Italy where he could stand trial for crimes against the faith. Mocenigo was almost certainly in the pay of the Inquisition and he spent months convincing Bruno to take up his offer of a well-paid post, only then to testify against Bruno to the Venetian Inquisition. Once Bruno was back on Italian soil and Mocenigo had had some time to gather as much incriminating evidence as possible, the reaction was swift and decisive. Bruno was arrested and imprisoned. Had he stood trial in the comparatively liberal state of Venice, he might have been spared but Bruno had been a wanted man ever since his initial flight years before and in 1593 he was transferred to Rome and imprisoned at the headquarters of the Holy Inquisition. His trial dragged on for a further seven years; the methods of the Inquisition are well known and Bruno was certainly tortured during his incarceration. Nevertheless, he refused to capitulate. Instead on the 21 December 1599, just two months before his execution, Bruno's tormentors noted the following statement which reveals his overwhelming obstinacy in the face of years of violence and oppression; the prisoner declares that 'he does not wish to repent and that it is not for him to repent, that he has nothing to repent, and that he is unaware what he is supposed to repent of.'[4] On 17 February 1600, Giordano Bruno was burned at the stake.

Cyrano's work reveals a keen engagement with Bruno's ideas about the universe, and he would certainly have admired Bruno's extraordinary courage and extravagant style. The cruel irony of Bruno's fate was that it was his absolute devotion to his faith which killed him. He was by no means an atheist or an enemy of the faith. He had been so inspired by the revelations of the new cosmology that he formed the conviction that it was to the greater glory of God to have created a universe which far exceeded the scope of mankind's previous petty imaginings. Bruno was an enthusiast and a profoundly religious man. If he had cared less about the glory of God, he would have been able to recant his statement and save his life. It was just eleven years after Bruno's murder that Galileo published a book detailing findings which seemed to support the controversial Copernican system. Naturally, the example of Bruno's hideous fiery death loomed large in the minds of those engaged in astronomical studies. Hardly surprising then that Galileo chose to make no mention of Bruno in his work.

At the beginning of the seventeenth century, the moon had become the focus of an impassioned debate. Galileo's telescope had revealed mountains and lakes and other geographical features on the lunar landscape, which seemed to suggest that the moon was a planet like the earth. In fact, these mountains and lakes were actually impact craters and the moon is a satellite rather than a planet. The importance of Galileo's work was that, in accordance with the new methodology, he had used applied mathematics and observational proofs to support and underpin his scientific reasoning. All of Galileo's discoveries, from the mountains on the moon, to Jupiter's satellites, to the phases of Saturn were crucial bits of evidence in a much bigger argument. Galileo was looking at the concrete mathematical proofs that had been previously been lacking to confirm that the earth was in motion and not the centre of the universe. Essentially the question of whether the moon was a world like the earth was of vital significance because it seemed to hold the key to the triumph of the Copernican world-view.

Cyrano was not the first author to dream of travelling into space to resolve the argument first-hand. An English author, Bishop Francis Godwin, had written a book entitled *The Man in the Moon*, describing the adventures of a cocky Spaniard, Domingo Gonsales, who hitches a lift to the moon by ensnaring a flock of geese. Godwin had been a student at the University of Oxford during the period when Giordano Bruno tried with customary bravado, but without success, to convert the professors of that institution to Copernicanism. Although Bruno failed to win over the professors, it seems he found some sympathy among the students. Francis Godwin's work had appeared a good decade before Cyrano's and was an important source of inspiration to the Frenchman, a fact which Cyrano acknowledged with characteristic flair.* In the course of Cyrano's *Voyage to the Moon*, his hero encounters the hero of Godwin's work and the two are imprisoned together by the lunar inhabitants who have mistaken them for monkeys. Cyrano gives the following revealing explanation for the Spaniard's presence on the moon: 'In reality what had forced him to flee across the whole Earth, and eventually to abandon it for the Moon, was the

* *The Man in the Moon* was first published in 1638 and a French translation was published in Paris in 1648. We do not know for certain if Cyrano understood English; if he did not, then he had perhaps already begun his own moon voyage story before he read Godwin's work. Either way, he made no secret of his admiration for Godwin's work.

fact that he had been unable to find a single country where the imagination itself was free.'[5] Rather than try to hide the debt he owed to Godwin, Cyrano used it as a source of comedy. Cyrano's hero jokingly reproaches Gonsales for having preceded him, complaining that in looking for a way to reach the moon he had been forced to take the trouble of building a flying machine because Gonsales had already taken the easy option of flying there by harnessing migrating geese.

These poetic exiles had fled to the moon to discuss radical natural philosophy ideas with freedom. Unfortunately, for them lunar society turns out to have restrictions of its own and Dyrcona is eventually put on trial for insisting that he comes from earth. In a neat reversal of the terrestrial controversy, Dyrcona insists that their moon (the earth) is a world to his people and vice versa; this throws the religious authorities of the moon into confusion. Dyrcona is forced to recant, but the form of the address which Cyrano's man in the moon makes to his assembled public is steeped in irony and underlines the futility of a forced capitulation of this kind. 'People, I declare to you that this moon here is not a moon, but a world; and that that world down there is not a world but a moon. That is what the priests think it good you should believe.'[6]

These lines and the situation of Dyrcona's trial on the moon not only present an eloquent argument in favour of freedom of the imagination, they also have a very specific contemporary significance. Cyrano's readership would instantly have recognized the reference to a dramatic event in which one of the most renowned and respected thinkers of the age had been compelled, on pain of death, to pronounce a disavowal of his most firmly held convictions. In 1633, when Cyrano was a rebellious student at the Collège de Beauvais, Galileo Galilei had been put on trial by the Papal Inquisition. It was the second time that the great scientist had faced the wrath of the Holy Office and this time he would not escape unscathed. One of the key elements of Galileo's work to which the inquisitors objected was his contention that the geography of the moon, observable through his famous telescope revealed striking similarities to the geography of the earth.

Not only does Cyrano's account echo the fact of Galileo's forced renunciation, it also recalls the popular belief that, after pronouncing his formal statement that the earth was the unmoving centre of the universe, in strict accordance with biblical tradition, the great scientist muttered, '*Eppur si muove*!'* As Cyrano wisely pointed out, however repressive the regime, however dire the threatened punishments, the state could still only control the ideas that its people expressed, it could never control their private beliefs. In the course of Dyrcona's trial on the moon, his defence is led by an erudite extraterrestrial who has taken pity on the hopelessness of the poor human and who does his best to convince the lunar authorities of the unreasonableness of attempting to control the private convictions of its people: 'Since every man is free, is he not also free to imagine whatever he wishes? What? Can you compel him to have no visions but your own? You can certainly force him to say that the moon is not a world, however he won't believe it for all that.'[7]

To a modern readership this defence of free thought seems rational and just, and consequently unremarkable. However, in the contemporary context this emphasis on the freedom of the individual imagination was dynamite. The Jesuit priest Father Garasse, who wrote numerous attacks on the freethinkers, highlights this very idea as 'the quintessence of atheism': 'The first moronic doctrine of these supposed wits: that there is nothing more free than belief and that no one should be forced or compelled to believe this or that.'[8] Although Cyrano had put his argument into the mouth of an extraterrestrial his polemical intention is clear.

Cyrano repeatedly emphasized the overwhelming and entirely unjustified arrogance of humanity. The aliens, encountered by his

* 'But it does move.'

hero, serve to highlight the numerous failings of the human race. Cyrano shows humanity to be unbearably self-satisfied, he constantly decries 'the insufferable pride of human beings'.[9] This appeal for humility springs from the teaching of the new science. Just as Bruno tried to argue that sometimes it can be better to doubt and wait, than to leap precipitately to a wrong conclusion, Cyrano tries again and again to suggest that human understanding is all too often flawed and unreliable. These reflections form the most heretical aspect of the new cosmology. The papacy was not against the act of modelling a saner solar system mathematically. In fact, the notion of a heliocentric universe predated Christianity. The real controversy lay in the perceived implications of the heliocentric model. The public imagination was not likely to be gripped by Copernicus's complex series of mathematical workings, but as more accessible texts began to appear, exploring the implications of the new cosmology, the church had to fight a rising tide of speculation about mankind's place in the universe, not to mention the shock of a direct contradiction of biblical authority.

The scientific revolution that so enthralled Cyrano was not solely the result of a new conception of methodology. A series of factors combined to produce a tremendously fertile climate for scientific discovery. For example, optical instrumentation had become increasingly sophisticated and this enabled early modern astronomers to work with more detailed mathematical information than ever before in making their calculations. One technological advance in particular was crucial: the 'perspective glass' (or telescope as it came to be called) was invented by a Dutchman in the late sixteenth century. When Galileo trained his telescope on the stars and realized that the Copernican model of the universe came much closer to offering an explanation of the observations he made, that revelation produced a profoundly important epistemological shift towards a new humility and awareness that mankind's perception was actually extremely limited and his role as lord of creation perhaps not so assured. For rebellious radicals like Cyrano the sun-centred universe was an electrifying place of possibility and wonder.

Johannes Kepler, a younger man than Galileo and a citizen of Protestant Germany was inspired by his greater distance from the horrors of the Papal Inquisition to take the new cosmology a stage further than Galileo could have risked doing. In his letter written in reply to Galileo's work and published as *Conversations With Galileo's Sidereal Messenger*, he admits the possibility of a plurality of inhabited worlds, but is careful to maintain the earth's privileged position as the home of mankind, deducing 'that this world of ours is the most excellent of them all if there should happen to be plurality of worlds'. In the same letter he also refers directly to the fate of the devout monk Giordano Bruno. He does so in order to underline the extent of his commitment to the truth of Galileo's observations. He implies that he would die to defend Galileo's results. 'If you had discovered any planets revolving around one of the fixed stars there would now be waiting for me chains and a prison amid Bruno's innumerabilities, I should rather say exile to his infinite space.'[10]

Privately, Kepler was less circumspect, becoming one of the earliest of many authors to succumb to the allure of an imaginative exploration of the moon. His *Somnium* (*The Dream*) is another of Cyrano's important influences; it was one of the earliest texts to combine serious scientific thought with vivid speculation about the possibility of life on the moon. Unlike Cyrano, Kepler scrupulously avoids any challenge to mankind's position as 'lord of creation' from the lunar inhabitants. They are depicted as an unprepossessing bunch of giant, slimy monsters. Kepler did not publish this work in his lifetime but it did circulate fairly widely in manuscript and despite his precautions it almost certainly contributed to his mother being put on trial for witchcraft. She narrowly escaped being condemned to death. It took all of Kepler's ingenuity and influence to save the eccentric but harmless old lady.

In its early years scientific enquiry was fraught with very real danger. Those who became involved with the new cosmology were men whose impressive intellect was equalled by their great courage. Small wonder then that the new cosmological ideas were so appealing to Cyrano. One of the most inflammatory aspects of Galileo's work was his observation of distinct similarities between the observed surface of the moon and the familiar geography of the earth, because this gave rise to speculation that the moon might very well prove to be an inhabited planet like our own. This idea, which directly contradicted biblical authority, was to prove enormously seductive, but it was left to the next generation, and radical authors such as Cyrano, to question the received wisdom that revelations about the moon could not challenge mankind's position as the 'primary rational creature' and dead centre of the turning universe.[11]

12
The secret illness

Aside from the works themselves, for which we have no definite composition dates, there is a lone surviving shred of concrete evidence relating to the period 1641 to 1648. The document, an IOU dated 1 April 1645, has been particularly inflammatory despite its relative brevity. The paper is an acknowledgement of a debt owed to the barber surgeon Elie Pigou by a patient, who signs himself Alexandre de Cyrano Bergerac. According to the document, Cyrano was lodged, fed and treated by Pigou for a period of four months and the resulting debt amounted to 400 livres. According to the terms of the contract, Pigou had 'treated, dressed, medicated and cured him of the secret illness with which he was afflicted'.[1]

The phrase 'secret illness' has naturally attracted a great deal of speculation as to what exactly may have been wrong with Cyrano. The nineteenth-century scholar Frédéric Lachèvre who first published this document assumed that a secret illness must imply venereal disease. He extrapolated out from this clue and described Cyrano as a rake: a lecherous womanizer, who drank, gambled and whored away his inheritance and ended up catching the pox. For

Lachèvre the 'secret illness' had to be a sexually transmitted disease and the sexually transmitted disease had to be syphilis. Lachèvre shores up this chain of reasoning with a further 'proof': the existence of a poem entitled 'Le Pauvre Malade' signed with an initial C. This poem was initially attributed to Cyrano by another academic, Lacroix, who had seen in it the description of Cyrano's fatal wounding of 1654 and dated it accordingly. Lachèvre decided that the poem was about the pox and dated it to 1645. The opening line of 'Le Pauvre Malade': 'Magdelon, I am very ill' does offer a vague echo of the first line of Théophile de Viau's poem about the pox, albeit in a far less aggressive register. Théophile's poem begins with the unambiguous statement: 'Phylis, It's all fucked, I am dying of the pox', and ends with a deliberately inverted and obscene parody of a repentant prayer for forgiveness. Lachèvre's interpretation of 'Le Pauvre Malade' is seriously undermined by the lines

People who see me in the street . . .
. . . Imagine that it must be the pox

This phrase clearly implies that an added humiliation and increase of the poet's sufferings is that his weakness and fever cause him to be mistaken for a syphilitic. The signature C. does not appear in all volumes in which the poem appears and in 1901 the poem was attributed to the Abbot Testu who was suffering not from the pox but from diseased lungs.[2]

The contract with Pigou is not proof that Cyrano was suffering from syphilis and 'Le Pauvre Malade' even less so.

There are two other possible explanations of the contract: Cyrano may have been receiving treatment for a disease other than syphilis or his illness may have been linked to lingering health problems caused by the severe injuries he had sustained in the army, as suggested by Le Bret in his biography. Certain critics have read the document as a proof that Cyrano's 'secret parts' had been damaged by the musket shot he received in the war; they trace themes of castration through the work and speculate that he may have been rendered impotent by the injury. Ultimately, the contract with Pigou does not contain sufficient information to resolve the question but the 'secrecy' of the illness may well imply that it was of a sexual nature.

A key link in the chain of inference that eventually saw Cyrano labelled a syphilitic is the fact that a common and devastating symptom of tertiary syphilis is insanity. In the late stages of the disease, once neurosyphilis sets in, the patient experiences bewildering mood swings, delusions of grandeur, paranoia and eventually dementia. There were no references to Cyrano's madness during his lifetime, perhaps because no one wanted to risk reprisals from the great swordsman, and the first reference to Cyrano as a syphilitic was not to appear until over two centuries after his death. The first accusation of insanity dates from sometime between 1657 and 1659. In his *Historiettes*, composed between these dates, but not published until the early eighteenth century, Tallemant des Reaux referred to the scandal caused by *The Death of Agrippina* and described the author as 'a madman named Cyrano'. Given the context it is clear that Tallemant's remark was chiefly intended as a comment on the outrageousness of Cyrano's work and the provocation it contained. In his attempt to get himself released from the clutches of the Inquisition, Charles Dassoucy had written an attack on the atheists of his time in which he described Cyrano as having 'died insane'.[3] However, Dassoucy's evidence was obtained by the Inquisition whose techniques are well known, and in any case the man is the very definition of an unreliable witness. There is no shred of evidence to suggest that Cyrano was either syphilitic or suffering from any kind of mental illness, if anything he was only too lucid.

While certain minds recoiled in horror from the new science and its devastation of the old certainties, Cyrano was one of the few truly adventurous thinkers who considered the idea of mankind cast adrift in an infinite void as an extraordinary liberation. As the fictional lunar explorer Domingo Gonsales tells Cyrano's hero – outer space was the only remaining refuge for the freethinker. Cyrano has the Spaniard lament the impossibility of finding a country on earth where the imagination is truly free. Gonsales explains that his scientific interests had nearly landed him in the clutches of the Spanish Inquisition. He remarks that if an outsider (i.e. not a member of church or university) expresses any interesting ideas he will instantly be dismissed as 'an idiot, a madman or an atheist'.[4] Cyrano was accused at various times of being all three and yet he found a way to use such accusations to his advantage. If only a madman, a fool or an atheist would uphold and explore the possibilities of the new science then the solution was to try to make the repressive censorship of the time work in the author's favour – by penning a text so foolish, crazy and atheistical that the very excesses of his provocation would serve to protect him. It is not for nothing that the first edition of *The Voyage to the Moon* published by Le Bret was retitled *A Comical History* – it was essential to underline the humorous nature of the text in order that the authorities might be tricked into dismissing Cyrano's imaginings as too outrageous to be taken seriously.

Le Bret includes a detailed list of all the authors from Lucian to Gassendi who have supported the idea of a world in the moon in order to legitimize his friend's work and even goes so far as to insist that out of all the illustrious company to have considered the idea he is 'all the more to be praised because he treated in an amusing way a chimaera which they handled all too seriously'.[5] This is disingenuous in the extreme – for, although the overall tone of Cyrano's madcap adventures in outer space is playful, the burlesque buffoonery of the voyages conceals a serious purpose: a determined and provocative iconoclasm. His imaginary exploration of the newly expanded universe afforded Cyrano not only an opportunity to contribute to the ongoing debate about Copernicanism, but also a vehicle for some biting satirical comment on a society with which he found himself increasingly at odds.

If further testimony, aside from the passionate hilarity of Cyrano's science-fiction masterpiece, is needed, we may turn to a text written by Charles Dassoucy. Dassoucy had been a vivid presence in Cyrano's youth but a bitter quarrel divided them. After Cyrano's death Dassoucy penned a number of mocking attacks on his erstwhile friend and in particular, whilst languishing in the dungeons of the Holy Inquisition in Rome, he wrote an address to the Pope entitled *The Thoughts of Monsieur Dassoucy in the Holy Office in Rome* in which he admitted to having been connected to some notorious free thinkers but detailed at length the sharp contrast between their dubious ideas and his own strict adherence to the principles of the true faith. Allowances must be made for the desperation of a man on death row. Dassoucy's betrayal of Cyrano (who was already dead in any case) and others was of little consequence since he was careful not to name names. His description of Cyrano is interesting because he dismisses him as a madman, and in order to prove this insanity he details the extent of Cyrano's Copernican convictions:

> He had such a powerful imagination that there was nothing neither so ridiculous nor so extravagant that he would not consider as an unassailable truth; and he was not content with being entirely convinced if others were not also as convinced as him. He wanted everyone to believe that each star is a world and that on top of that there were an infinity of others, and that there were numerous suns and no matter what I fed him he would quarrel with me and would not have thought twice about breaking off with me if I did not agree to allow that there was a world in the moon.[6]

This vision of Cyrano's aggressive commitment to the new science contrasts sharply with Le Bret's deliberate attempt to tone down the controversial nature of his friend's work by describing it as having been written without serious intent, purely in order to 'amuse'. Religious opposition to the new cosmology was only part of the battle; ancient convictions about the nature of knowledge itself also needed to be overturned before the new science could begin to grow into a truly creative enterprise. Writers like Cyrano and Francis Godwin (the original creator of Domingo Gonsales) deliberately blurred the boundaries between truth and fiction in order to open up a space within which the essential new scientific concept of 'probability' could be explored.

In his *Novum Organum*, published in 1620 when Cyrano was only a year old, Francis Bacon had reflected on the inadequacies of the old optical technology and of the old conceptions of knowledge, 'the human understanding is like a false mirror, which, receiving rays irregularly distorts and discolours the nature of things by mingling its own nature with it'.[7] Bacon's acute perception of the limitations of the human perspective led to his dream of a coordinated programme of utilitarian cooperation and discovery. In *The Voyage to the Moon* Cyrano's befuddled space traveller is told that his attempts to comprehend the mysteries of the universe using his woefully limited sense perception are like a blind man's attempts to describe colour or the beauty of a landscape. Despite his identification of 'vain imaginations' as one of the 'distempers of learning' Francis Bacon was unable to resist the temptation to pen his own 'science fiction' fantasy. In the *New Atlantis*, published posthumously in 1627, Bacon outlined his utopian vision of a devout Christian society dedicated to progress through scientific research and experimentation. The story describes the wonders achieved by the men of 'Bensalem', a remote island community in the South Pacific, thanks to their adherence to Bacon's own scientific ideas. Ironically, despite his extraordinarily perceptive theories on scientific development, Bacon, like Cyrano, was far from possessing a truly scientific mind and the 'false mirror' of his own perceptions led him into a misguided dismissal of the central importance of mathematics. Bacon was profoundly hostile to the work of mathematicians, regarding it as divorced from the reality of natural philosophical investigation. Furthermore, Bacon considered the attainment of certain absolute principles as the true aim of such investigations. In contrast with practitioners, such as Robert Hooke, who had begun to recognize that approximation and probabilistic ideas were the key to scientific development, Bacon refused to accept that absolute certainty was a concept of little or no value to the natural philosopher. The authors of fictional accounts of the world in the moon were engaged in the development of a conception of knowledge reliant on intelligent, imaginative speculation.

Johannes Kepler acknowledged the comical works of the classical author Lucian as the literary source which first inspired the composition of his own account of exile to the freedom of the world in the moon, *The Dream*. 'Later I came across the two books of Lucian's *True Hisory* written in Greek, which I chose as my means of mastering the language . . . These were my first traces of a trip to the moon, which was my aspiration in later times.'[8] The application of satirical techniques to the new science was a radical achievement of early modern authors and formed the earliest roots of the 'thought experiment', an essential tool of modern-day astrophysics. Lucian's *True History* plays with notions of truth and lies, and many of the readers of early science fiction must have anticipated precisely the same pleasure which Lucian promises his readers: 'to heare so many notorious lies perswasively set down'.[9]

The decision to treat urgent scientific inquiry in a lighthearted manner sprang not just from the necessity imposed by censorship but seems also to be the result of a determination to disseminate the radical ideas of the new science as widely as possible. The work of Bernard le Bovier de Fontenelle was perhaps the first text to openly declare its intention to popularize scientific ideas. By choosing to address a specifically female audience in the person of the Noble Lady with whom the discussions take place, Fontenelle aimed to demonstrate that a specialized education (of the sort unavailable to women) was not essential to an understanding of the new ideas about the universe. Furthermore, Fontenelle recognized the value of a blending of fictional and factual elements in the explication of scientific theory. He acknowledged that such a method was central to his endeavour without being able to explain adequately why this should be the case. 'The visions themselves that I have added, have something of a real Foundation in them; the True and the False are here mixed . . . I do not undertake to justifie a Composure so fantastical: This is the most important Point of this Work, and 'tis only this that I cannot give a Reason for.'[10]

His description of his method recalls that of Kepler, who was called to account for allowing his imagination too free a rein in his writing. He acknowledges this fact at the start of a letter written in response to Galileo's *Sidereus Nuncius*, 'my friends cautioned me that it seemed a little too unconventional in conception'.[11] The astronomer was unapologetic about his extravagant, irreverent style and defended the importance of humour to the discussion of serious scientific subjects: 'Whereas most debaters get all heated up, I regard humour as a more pleasant tone in discussions. Other authors strive for impressiveness in the exposition of philosophy by the weightiness of their assertions; yet they often prove amusing, unintentionally. I seem by nature cut out to lighten the hard work and difficulty of a subject by mental relaxation, conveyed by the style.'[12]

Cyrano's work was nothing if not 'unconventional in conception' and he recognized that humour could prove a powerful means of persuasion. Just as Cyrano's hero frequently reveals his own limited 'earthbound' perspective in his inappropriate mocking laughter, so he is in turn the butt of the joke to the superior beings he encounters. Cyrano dared to imagine that seen from space, mankind was not much more than a cosmic joke. In the world of *The Voyages to the Moon and Sun* (just as in Douglas Adams's *A Hitchhiker's Guide to the Galaxy* in our own time) the rest of the universe is shown to be laughing at the puny race of upstarts who have the colossal ignorance and arrogance to imagine that they are the centre of the universe. While conversing with the lunar courtiers about the physics of the universe, Dyrcona disingenuously admits that, were it not for the fact that their ideas are contrary to the teachings of the Catholic faith, he would consider their explanations 'far more reasonable than our own'. He then gamely tries to use a biblical reference to contradict their rationalistic account of the origins of the universe to little effect: 'I asked him what he could reply to the authority of Moses and that this great patriarch expressly declares that God created the world in six days. Instead of answering me the ignorant fellow only laughed.'[13] Laughter in this instance is used to signal the flimsiness of the church's arguments against the new science. Paradoxically the intent is at once polemical and self-mocking.

The one subject that Cyrano consistently refused to take seriously was that of the terrible risk involved in contradicting the teachings of the church. Cyrano clearly took great pleasure in using the freedom of fiction to laugh in the face of his opposition. As for example, when Dyrcona finds himself surrounded by threatening hordes who look set to tear him limb from limb, or at the very least deliver him into the hands of the religious authorities who have vowed to burn him at the stake. The peasants' suspicion and fear of the cornered 'magician' and his demonic black horse mount to fever pitch, the priest leading them screams a garbled exorcism that ends in a threat to eviscerate Dyrcona if he moves a muscle. The hero cannot flee for his life, not because he is intimidated by the priest's vehemence, but because he is laughing too hard. Weak with hilarity at the ignorance and superstition of his enemies, he is easy prey and is quickly caught and bound hand and foot. Meanwhile, in a revealing little background vignette the priest's servant secures Dyrcona's black horse for the vicarage stable, the peasants being too frightened to stake their own claim on the valuable animal that the priest has convinced them is satanic. It was not only Cyrano's fictional hero who would set laughter above his own safety. The serious comedian himself would eventually pay the ultimate price in the real world as a result of his comical irreverence.

Cyrano's frequent laughter is occasionally edged with bitterness and like many a modern stand-up comedian he is often at his funniest when he is at his angriest or most exasperated. In particular, one episode which occurs during *The Voyage to the Sun* allows Cyrano to elaborate his most comprehensive attack on the 'presumptuous stupidity' of mankind. In a comic reversal of fortune man is for once in the power of the beasts. In a direct contradiction of the Old Testament the 'fowl of the air' rule over mankind, whose God-given dominion over the natural world suddenly starts to look rather shaky. The birds who capture Dyrcona have a democratically elected leader, a sophisticated judiciary and an unrelenting contempt for mankind. He is put on trial for the crime of 'being human' and his only hope of reprieve is to convince them that he is in fact a monkey. Throughout *Voyage to the Sun* references to the Old Testament account of creation abound only to be swiftly subverted and turned to ridicule.

Dyrcona's confrontation with the republic of the birds serves partly as a satirical comment on the human tendency to dismiss difference as a sure sign of inferiority. The less enlightened birds condemn the captive purely on the basis that he doesn't look like them declaring: 'That it was horrible to believe that a beast who did not have a face made like their own could be in possession of reason. "Ha! What," they murmured to one another, "he has no beak, no feathers, no claws and yet his soul should be spriritual? O gods! What impertinence!'"[14] But there is another deeper purpose to the encounter. Here is yet another example of Cyrano using comedy in order to address issues of contemporary philosophical debate. In the late sixteenth century Montaigne had made the controversial assertion that animals were not only rational and moral beings but that their morality and reason were superior to that of humans. In Cyrano's lifetime this idea became the focus of a vivid controversy sparked by the great philosopher René Descartes. Descartes dismissed Montaigne's ideas and asserted that not only were animals neither rational nor moral but that they were not even conscious. Cyrano was an admirer of Descartes and mentions him in *The Voyage to the Sun* as 'this famous philosopher of our time'.[15] But when the hotly contested dispute about animal consciousness and the nature of the soul arose, setting Descartes at odds with his old mentor Pierre Gassendi, Cyrano naturally sided firmly with Gassendi and the animals.

In 1641 Descartes had published a book entitled *Méditations métaphysiques* in which he argued that the soul and the body were entirely separate and that only mankind was possessed of an immortal soul while animals were no more than automata or machines. Gassendi wrote a detailed response in his *Disquisitio metaphysica* in 1644. Among other objections he offers up the charming example (that he had personally witnessed) of a dog that had learnt to bark along in imitation of a trumpet. He points out that just because animals do not possess human reasoning it does not follow that they possess no form of reasoning at all – just as the fact that they are unable to speak human languages (despite occasional feats of imitation like that of the musical dog) does not preclude their communicating in languages of their own, which we in turn cannot speak nor understand. Cyrano takes this process of argument a stage further. He highlights the absurdity of some of Descartes's propositions by putting them into the mouths of the birds who condemn his hero Dyrcona to death for the crime of being human. They reverse Descartes's own argument, insisting that although a man may imitate birdsong he doesn't understand it and is therefore not a rational creature and certainly not possessed of an immortal soul. Dassoucy also mentions this debate in his document written to get him out of the claws of the Inquisition. With his characteristic humour he pokes fun at the libertines for their affection for the natural world: 'As they do not believe in God or the Devil. They do not believe in the the immortality of the soul either; and what is amusing about them is that there is no man so vile or stupid but he believes himself above all the animals, but these men, with all their haughtiness and their wit do not draw any distinction between their own souls and those of their horses.'[16]

Dassoucy was certainly not a partisan of the animal faction at any time and his choice of a horse as an example is not without significance. In his semi-autobiographical novel he laughs at himself for the 'cowardice' which meant that he never rode if he could possibly avoid it. In one instance he congratulates himself on wisely refusing to take to the saddle after having spotted the nasty look on the horse's face. In contrast Cyrano's overwhelming affection for the natural world is a strong theme throughout his work and one is left in no doubt as to his allegiance in the debate. When the birds encountered in *The Voyage to the Sun* sit in judgement on the 'monster' that is man, some focus on Dyrcona's unfortunate lack of a beak and feathers and this serves as a satirical comment on humanity's tendency to react badly to physical difference. However, the more intelligent members of this avian community despise his self-appointed (biblical) role as lord of creation and this gives rise to a sophisticated critique of mankind's engagement with the natural world:

> Man . . . so stupid and so vain, that he convinces himself that we were all created for him; man, so clear-sighted that he can not even distinguish between sugar and arsenic, and who would swallow

> hemlock that his fine judgement would have him take for parsley; man who insists that we reason only through the senses and yet who has the weakest, the slowest and the falsest senses of all creatures; man in short, whom nature created for the sake of variety like other freaks, but in whom she nevertheless instilled an ambition to rule over all other animals and to destroy them all.[17]

This is a determinedly non-Christian viewpoint, attributing the creation of humanity to 'nature' not to God and thereby directly contradicting more than one biblical teaching. According to the Bible man was made in God's image, here he is seen as an aberration of nature, a monstrous freak. The Bible teaches that man is given dominion over the animals by divine right, the birds, however, see mankind as abusing his natural (not divine) strength and intelligence, striving to dominate and destroy the rest of the natural world. The passage also highlights man's flawed sense perception, a central preoccupation of the new science.

The environmentalist focus of this passage seems extraordinarily modern even if Cyrano could never have anticipated the extent to which his criticisms of mankind's ignorant destruction of the natural world would become relevant on a global scale. His denunciation of 'the insufferable pride of human beings which persuades them that nature was created only for them' is all the more starkly relevant in our own time when technological advances have only increased mankind's devastating power to ravage and destroy the environment.[18] Cyrano could never have predicted the horrors we have inflicted on the planet and yet he was not only ahead of his own time in his criticisms but ahead of ours too.

Cyrano's search for a naturalistic, irreligious explanation to replace the biblical account of creation leads him elsewhere in *The Voyage to the Sun* to an imaginative vision of the creative power of 'chance', which could almost have been written by Darwin himself:

> But, you will say, how could chance have assembled in one place all the things that were necessary to produce this oak tree? I reply that it is no marvel that the material should be assembled in such a way as to form an oak, but rather that the material being so assembled the marvel would have been great indeed if the oak had not been formed. A little less of certain forms and it could have been an elm, a poplar, a willow, an elder, some heather or some moss; a few more of certain other forms and it had been a sensitive plant, an oyster, a worm, a fly, a frog, a sparrow, a monkey, a man.[19]

Cyrano may not have been a talented physicist, but his profound love of nature and his careful observation of the natural world and the intricate connections between all forms of life made him a truly excellent naturalist. He may not have anticipated Darwin but it cannot be denied that this is an eerie precursor of the theory of natural selection. He contrasts the infinite variety of possible forms with the relatively small number of actual forms seen in nature, one of the favoured arguments of the renowned evolutionary theorist Richard Dawkins:

> You are surprised that this matter, mixed up pell-mell by chance, should have built up a man, since so many things are necessary to the construction of his being. But you do not know that this matter moving towards the design of a man has stopped a hundred million times on the way to form, sometimes a stone, sometimes lead, sometimes coral, sometimes a flower, sometimes a comet, for the excess or the lack of certain forms which were necessary or superfluous to the design of a man. It is not marvellous that an infinite quantity of matter changing and moving continually should have met together to form the few animals, vegetables and minerals that we see.[20]

Dyrcona's trial is delayed at first because according to the rules of the avian court he cannot be judged in case the miserable weather influences the jury to be harsher than they might be otherwise. This impressive ideal of impartiality is ever so slightly undermined though by the choice of advocates in his case. The prosecution is led by a partridge who has recently escaped from earth where an encounter with a hunter has left him with a vicious throat wound. It is interesting that Cyrano chose to gift the prosecutor with the exact same injury that he himself had suffered. Meanwhile the defence is undertaken by a starling, an apparently anodyne choice except that 'starling' was a synonym for chatterbox or 'bird brain'. Despite the pronouncement of a death sentence Dyrcona is ultimately reprieved by the last-minute intervention of a parakeet whom he had previously released from captivity on earth. Here again Cyrano reveres 'freedom' as the highest moral ideal and also shows the birds to be more 'humane' than humans – no last-minute reprieve had been forthcoming for Vanini or for Giordano Bruno.

It is Cyrano's endless inventiveness and wit that save his satire from becoming morose. His dark vision of mankind may occasionally recall that of the pitiful figure of the card sharp who appears in Dassoucy's 'adventures'. Having been found cheating and badly beaten, the card sharp defends the dishonesty of his profession on the basis that 'The world is nothing but a great forest where men, a hundred times more dangerous than wild beasts, devour each other like wolves.'[21] The negative view taken by the lowly criminal reflects that of one of the greatest philosophers of the time. In *Leviathan* (1651), Thomas Hobbes had argued that 'without government, human life is solitary, poor, mean, nasty, brutish, and short'.[22]

Of the three imprisonments to which Cyrano's hero is subjected, it is at the hands of men that he suffers the most injustice and it is only the parliament of birds who show mercy, tolerance and understanding. Although Cyrano constantly compares humanity to a variety of beasts and although his hero is mistaken at various times for a monkey, an ostrich and even a monster, he retains a faith in nature which seems to provide him with the same inspiration and reassurance as other men found in religion. Cyrano's letter, 'On the reflections of the trees in the water' is a delirious prose poem, a hymn to an upside-down world, where 'the fishes stroll through the woods'.[23] In the letter 'On a house in the country' he not only laughingly refers to the rejuvenating power of the countryside (a theme he returned to in *The Voyage to the Moon*) but also to its ennobling effect, such that 'a rural gentleman is an unknown prince'.[24] In order to underline the superiority of lunar society Cyrano chose to describe the delicious luxury of a bedchamber, not draped with the silk and velvet that might have been expected, but where the beds are made from deep piles of jasmine and orange blossom and the room is lit by glow-worm-filled lanterns. This preference of the 'natural' to the artificial was a characteristic feature of the freethinkers whose extensive classical reading caused them to dream of a golden age of Arcadian simplicity before the corruption of court and city could pervert the 'natural' virtue of mankind. In Théophile de Viau's 'Elegy to a Lady' he paints a vivid portrait of this naturalistic libertine ideal,

I wish to write verses that are not forced,
Let my mind wander through little pathways,
To seek out secret spots where nothing bothers me,
To spend an hour staring at my reflection in the water,
Listen in a dream to the course of a stream,
Write in the woods, break off, be silent,
Compose a quatrain without thinking about it.[25]

The solitude and isolation essential to the libertine ideal of creation and virtue seem to have been the rule by which Cyrano chose to guide his own writing life. Just as Le Bret had described him in the guardhouse voluntarily isolating himself from his companions to work on a sonnet, so Cyrano's own letter 'On a house in the country' asks the absent lord of the manor: 'O Gods! Is it possible that a philosopher like you should prefer the vanity, sorrows and trouble of the court to the peace and quiet of such an agreeable retreat?'[26] Despite having initially tried hard to live up to the standards of courtly life, following the traditional 'gentlemanly' path of a career in the armed forces and disguising his humble origins under a self-created myth of noble Gascon lineage, Cyrano ultimately turned his back on 'worldly' success and chose to revel in the independence and freedom the decision offered him. No surprise then that in his fantasy world dressing luxuriously in the latest fashions was a mark of ignominy nor that in his ideal society no poet ever starves as long as his inspiration lasts because original thought is a currency worth more than gold. Nor that he should dream of a superior alien society in outer space where, rather than recommending each other to the care of God (*Adieu*), Lunarians bid one another farewell using the phrase 'Remember to live free.'[27]

13

A profane brotherhood

To a certain extent Cyrano's status as a marginal member of society was fixed even before his birth. His grandfather's Protestantism had cast the family into the heart of a repressed and hated minority. Certain members of the younger generation (notably Cyrano's father and siblings) seem to have rejected this alienation and striven to eradicate the stain of difference by an intense devotion to the Catholic norm, but Cyrano displayed a 'dangerous tendency' to isolate and differentiate himself still further. Refusing to define his beliefs, his sexuality or even his biography, he embraced and exaggerated the role of outsider. As Le Bret would put it, 'as he had nought but exceptional sentiments, so none of his works were ever commonplace'.[1]

On occasion, Cyrano seems to have gone out of his way to be as outrageous and offensive as possible, almost as if he were determined to test the limits of his audience. He repeatedly made jokes which defied even the most sacred teachings of the church. In their condemnation of Dyrcona the parliament of birds reveal their conviction that the human belief in life after death springs from the fundamentally servile nature of mankind. The birds suggest that humanity's 'false hopes of immortality' spring less from the 'horror which un-being inspires in them than from the fear of having no one to order them around after death'.[2] The birds of paradise sent to console Dyrcona on his deathbed express the same atheistic notion as the character Sejanus in Cyrano's tragedy *The Death of Agrippina*. They whisper that Dyrcona should liberate himself from his fear of death by accepting that: 'in the blink of an eye after your life ends you will become that which you were a blink of an eye before it began'.[3] This is an idea that in our own time many might find disquieting, but that in Cyrano's lifetime could have led to its author being tortured, having his tongue cut out or being burned at the stake.

Cyrano's desire to think the unthinkable sometimes led him into very dark imaginings indeed. His account of the funeral rites on the world of the moon is a perfect example. At first his introduction of the pagan idea that cremation is a pure and noble end and that only criminals should be buried in the earth seems to be a simple reversal of expectations, intended to vindicate the heretics whose death by fire was supposed to be the proof of their damnation. This alternative viewpoint also neatly undermines the triumph of the religious authorities. Cyrano even includes a nightmarish vision of Christian burial designed to call the notion of 'resting in peace' sharply into question: 'Can you imagine anything more hideous than a corpse crawling with swarms of worms, at the mercy of toads that gnaw at its cheeks; in short, the plague dressed in a man's body?'[4] As a battle-hardened soldier Cyrano would have been all too familiar with the horrific reality of a putrefying corpse.

And yet this is not the last of the provocation; not only does Cyrano deliberately dwell on the physicality of death but he even dreams up a vision of vampirism to rival Bram Stoker's wildest imaginings. He explains that while cremation was the usual funeral rite on the moon another fate awaited the mortal remains of the most noble. The friends of a moribund philosopher would gather round his deathbed and his closest friend would watch for the moment when the dying man was on the brink of death in order to plunge a dagger into the failing heart and drink his friend's life blood. A ritual would then take place during which all the dearest friends of the departed would partake in an orgy of lovemaking and cannibalistic feasting in an attempt to see the dead reborn in the form of a child conceived during one of the ritual couplings. This is a grim, literal rereading of the Catholic doctrine of the holy sacrament of communion – with the friends of the dead man consuming his body and his blood in order to guarantee a 'resurrection'. Perhaps the choice of an attack on the doctrine of transubstantiation also reveals the traces of Cyrano's Protestant roots.

It is possible that this morbid focus on the rituals of death and decay may have been inspired by the death of Cyrano's father on 18 January 1648. Although the exact composition dates of *The Voyages to the Moon and Sun* are unknown, the most likely periods are 1642–3 and 1648–9 for the *Moon* and 1648–54 for the *Sun*; no doubt the loss of a father with whom he had never enjoyed an easy relationship must have been a spur to Cyrano's creativity. Grief is all the more devastating when mixed with anger and self-reproach. It is impossible to reconstruct the complex nature of Cyrano's feelings for his father but the hints in his work seem to imply a strong element of conflict. A codicil in Abel senior's will mentions a theft from his house that took place during his final illness and states that the victim wished to conceal the identities of the two culprits. The discovery of this document has led to accusations that Cyrano and his brother Abel II were guilty of taking advantage of their father's weakened state. No concrete evidence can be found to support this interpretation of the mysterious document but its existence casts a dark shadow over the family. Cyrano's mother had died at an earlier unknown date and he and his brother Abel were the sole beneficiaries of their father's will. Their two other siblings, Denis and Catherine, were both members of religious orders and therefore ineligible to inherit any part of the estate.

Cyrano chose to sign his first published work, a short introductory piece for his friend Dassoucy's poetic work *The Judgment of Paris*, not with his family name but with a pen name that he had chosen for himself for its combination of a Gascon surname and a truly heroic forename. He set down in black and white his rejection of the homely Savinien de Cyrano in favour of a name to conjure with – *Hercule de Bergerac.* The letter is addressed 'To the stupid reader and not to the wise' and in it Cyrano explains that only idiots will not appreciate Dassoucy's work and recommends therefore that they leave it well alone, rather than risk revealing their ignorance in misguided criticism of his friend's talents. Cyrano jokingly concludes with a wish that all idiots could be lumped together to form a single monster that he might slay in true Herculean fashion.

Although this was Cyrano's first printed work it is extremely unlikely that it was his first composition. By 1648 he had already begun to establish a reputation for himself due to the circulation of his works in manuscript form. The preface was also the first concrete link tying him to Charles Dassoucy. His close association with Dassoucy is one of the keystones of the argument for his homosexuality. Certain references and jokes within Cyrano's works, as well as the comments of some of his contemporaries, do seem to point to his having been involved in one or more passionate same-sex relationships. The anecdote most often cited to support the idea of Cyrano's involvement in a gay love triangle with Dassoucy and Chapelle is the 'Chapon' incident, as related by Dassoucy himself in his semi-autobiographical novel *The Adventures*. To explain the bitter enmity between himself and Cyrano and the duellist's frequent threats to kill him (which he admits to taking seriously enough to flee the country) Dassoucy describes an obscure practical joke:

> The late B[ergerac] had good reason to wish to kill me, since in his worst fit of famine I was inhuman enough to hide away from his need a de Mans capon straight from the spit, that I hid under my bed in vain since the steam that roused his appetite and at the same time hardened his heart made him well enough aware that he had in me nothing more than a cruel and barbarous friend.[5]

The fact that the word *chapon* meaning capon could also be used to signify a young man combined with the alliterative link Chapelle/chapon has led to this anecdote being read, not just as a fling at Cyrano's poverty and near starvation – humiliating accusations in themselves which would be taken up by other enemies of Cyrano after his death – but as the key to the relationship linking the three men. According to this interpretation the clash between Cyrano and Dassoucy would have as its origin their rivalry for Chapelle's favours.

As further corroboration of Cyrano's disappointed love for Chapelle a literary portrait of the young man has been identified in the character known only as the 'son of the host' who appears towards the end of *The Voyage to the Moon*. There does seem to be a parallel between the situation of the fictional young man who entertains Dyrcona at a dinner with an elderly sage and that of Chapelle, the son of François Lhuillier who played host to the philosopher Gassendi and his circle. The glamorous and intelligent youth described in Cyrano's prose rules his household with a rod of iron, he takes precedence over his ageing father and the elderly philosophers who discourse wisely with the space traveller. The author's admiration for his good looks, vitality and outstanding promise is clear. He is also by far the most irreverent and provocative character encountered by the hero, and it is the 'son of the host' who offers the most daring challenges to religious orthodoxy. In the uncensored original ending of *The Voyage to the Moon* a particularly blasphemous exchange between Dyrcona and the young man is brought to a sudden and dramatic end. In response to Dyrcona's half-hearted evocation of the word of God the young man retorts, 'Not so fast . . . you are still at "God has said"; you must first prove there is a God, which for my part I wholly deny.'[6] This prompts the hero to consider his interlocutor more closely and to reflect that he is not so attractive as he had seemed at first, and the dramatic tension is built up as Dyrcona starts to become thoroughly alarmed by the young man's 'devilish opinions'. He is torn between fear and admiration and threatens the young man with 'a bad end' only to be interrupted by the arrival of the Devil himself who seizes the atheistic young man in his claws and flies off with him to hell. Dyrcona can't bear to let his friend be carried away and so seizes him by the waist in an attempt to save him from the Devil's clutches but only succeeds in being carried off along with him. In reality, the monster that was to seize Chapelle in an unbreakable hold was that of alcoholism.

The real Chapelle was certainly an attractive and witty young man who inspired profound attachments. Dassoucy wrote of their relationship 'I could not live without him and he had trouble living without me' and this passionate phrase echoes that used by Bernier in his description of Chapelle's friendship with Molière: 'the illustrious Molière could not live without Chapelle'.[7] In later life Chapelle became an embittered alcoholic whose notorious excesses were to spoil his early promise. There is a story that while attending a banquet at Molière's house in the country Chapelle had stayed up drinking into the early hours with a group of friends. When Molière was woken at four in the morning and went down to check on them, Chapelle informed him that since the world was such a terrible place and life such a burden the group were all determined to drown themselves in the river. He begged Molière to join them in their noble plan. Molière diplomatically agreed that it was an excellent idea but managed to persuade them that it would be as well to retire for the night and put off the group suicide until the next day, since it would be easier to get to the river in the light. When the revellers eventually resurfaced the trip to the river was mercifully forgotten.

Cyrano's intimacy with Chapelle and Dassoucy dates from the early 1640s to 1651. The end of their friendship is fairly clearly defined. Early in 1650 Cyrano penned another contribution to support one of Dassoucy's publications. This time an eight-line poem signed simply *de Bergerac*, but in 1651 manuscript versions of Cyrano's letters appeared, including bitter attacks on both Dassoucy and Chapelle. We will return to the nature of their falling out, for now it will suffice to note that in 1653 Chapelle wrote a poem for another of Dassoucy's publications, and so the initial rupture clearly involved Cyrano alone. A few years later Chapelle also fell out with Dassoucy and wrote a travelogue with his friend Beaumont in which he ridiculed Dassoucy for his misadventures in Montpellier. Dassoucy had been forced to leave Paris and tour the provinces having fallen out of favour at court and having been imprisoned for sodomy on more than one occasion. In Montpellier his notoriety had reached fever pitch and the townspeople were baying for his blood. He was saved from death at the stake at the last minute by the intervention of his noble patron. In *The Adventures*, Dassoucy refers to this incident, as well as to Chapelle's betrayal, in terms which do nothing to dispel the rumours of his forbidden sexuality, but rather serve to draw his two friends into the controversy with him:

> Friend C[hapelle] was not yet seventeen when the late B[ergerac] who was already eating his bread and using his sheets gave me the honour of an introduction. That is why no one should be astonished if I made the most of the situation. Since at that time he was very generous, when he had kept me late supping at his house and the hour being unsuitable for me to return home he gave up very liberally half of his bed to me. This is why after

> having long had proofs of the nature of my desires and having several times deigned to honour me with his bed, it seems to me that it's rather for him to justify me than for the magistrates of Montpellier with whom I have never slept. But what! One must pardon something to one's friends; we are not always in our right minds, the brain does not always enjoy an even temperature; my friend C. has like others, good and bad moments.[8]

It should be noted that Dassoucy is anything but a reliable witness and the 'capon' anecdote was written at a time when he was at odds with Chapell and Cyrano; Chapelle he dismissed as a 'spoilt child', mocking his cowardice and his 'inextinguishable thirst'.[9] The attacks were all written after Cyrano had died and he could therefore make no objections or corrections to the story. The style is typically flippant and forms part of a fictional work. It cannot be considered much more than circumstantial evidence of a personal element to the dispute. Cyrano's own works offer another possible explanation in the form of a bitter professional rivalry.

Cyrano's determined refusal to conform and his passionate longing for freedom possibly lend weight to the theory that he was homosexual. If he were gay or bisexual this additional element of difference would in some degree help to account for his lifelong isolation and rebellion. In seventeenth-century France 'sodomy' was a capital offence, although power and influence could buy a level of immunity as Dassoucy's repeated escapes from death row demonstrate. That anyone should dream of a legitimate alternative to heterosexual relationships was heretical in the extreme. In outer space of course anything was possible and at one point in the world on the moon Cyrano's hero finds himself ordered by royal command to enter into a gay relationship. Having been mistaken for monkeys, both he and the Spaniard Gonsales are being kept as pets by the royal court. Dyrcona is taken for the female and the Spaniard for the male and the king orders that they should they share a cage in the hope that they will breed:

> . . . the King commanded his monkey-keeper to take us away, with strict orders to make the Spaniard and me lie together to multiply our species in his kingdom. The Prince's command was carried out in every point and I was very glad of it for the pleasure I took in having someone with whom to converse during the solitude of my brutification.[10]

Love cannot be legislated against and, despite the official repression of homosexuality, the Collège de Lisieux, which Cyrano attended in his early twenties, was notorious for the numerous affairs which flourished among its all-male population.

Another element in identifying Cyrano as a member of a group of homosexual friends and lovers was a letter written by Montigny in 1656 which was aimed at disgracing the notorious womanizer Lignières by identifying him as an acolyte of the dangerous pervert Cyrano. 'It is an irregular way of life unknown to our fathers [. . .] and a sort of profane brotherhood, of which Cyrano had been the founder.'[11] The reference to a monk-like brotherhood (*moinerie*) conjures up ideas of celibacy and poverty both of which Le Bret refers to in his preface. Montigny's attack is clearly not intended to suggest self-denial however, rather it is the rejection of worldly success coupled to the frank enjoyment of male friendship and probably love that cast Cyrano beyond the pale. Cyrano's decision to turn his back on courtly success and to refuse early offers of patronage had laid him open to allegations of failure and penury and even paradoxically of parasitism. In *Menagiana*, Gilles Ménage stated that Cyrano was penniless and mad at his death and there was even an allegation that he ended his days in the poor house. Much has been written about Cyrano's poverty and his dilapidation of his inheritance but there is in fact little evidence to support these allegations.

That Cyrano quickly frittered away his share of his inheritance leaving his brother Abel saddled with extensive debts has been a persistent element of his legend but this is easily refuted. A legal document in which Abel gifts two of his children with money from the family inheritance shows that the rents were undiminished in 1680. This means that on Cyrano's death his share of their inheritance must have been returned to his brother (sole beneficiary of Cyrano's will) largely untouched. To some extent evidence of payments made by Cyrano towards large debts seems to have clouded the issue. In fact, the irregularity of the payment of rents from the family estate would mean that on occasion debts would build up. Therefore it would sometimes be necessary for Cyrano to deal with other agents. This was commonplace in an era when much banking and many financial transactions were the province of individuals acting as moneylenders rather than a modern banking system as we would understand it. Professor Madeleine Alcover has examined in detail the various surviving shreds of Cyrano's accounts, including bills for lodging and food, and she concludes that the evidence proves that Le Bret's following remarks about Cyrano's frugal habits were entirely accurate:

> He was always considered a man with a rare mind: nature had also gifted him with a happy control over his senses such that he was always able to submit his appetites as much as he wanted to his will, with the result that he drank wine but rarely, because as he said, in excess it stupefies the mind, and one needs to take the same precautions as one would with arsenic (that was what he compared it to) since one should fear poison in whatever form it might appear.[12]

Le Bret also noted that Cyrano was 'no less moderate in his eating habits' and in particular remarks on his avoidance of 'stews' and preference for simpler dishes, a sensible move in an era when heavily spiced or strongly flavoured dishes were often the means of concealing food which had gone bad. These ascetic habits do not sit easily with the caricatured image of the hedonistic libertine. That Cyrano should have been rather serious and self-denying is a contradiction of the various accusations that have been thrown at him.

The forms of greeting used by the inhabitants of the moon offer an insight into the two guiding principles of Cyrano's existence. To say 'Hello' the lunarians say 'Love me sage as I love you' and to say 'Goodbye' they say 'Remember to live free'.[13] Neither affection nor freedom were ever simple and in Cyrano's case devotion to freedom cost him firstly his liberty and ultimately his life, while devotion to friendship (as he himself boasted) was to gain him bitter enemies. Cyrano's friendships were, according to Le Bret's account of him, the most important thing in his life and a close reading of his works entirely supports this idea. Whereas references to romantic love of the sort celebrated by Rostand's play are rare, references to friendship are both frequent and insistent. In the enlightened republic of birds one of their number is condemned for a crime described as 'the most serious that can blacken any bird. He is accused . . . but good gods! Even to think of it makes my head-feathers stand on end . . . he is accused of having not deserved to have a friend for the last six years.'[14] In Cyrano's ideal society such a heinous crime would carry a suitably harsh penalty. In his prologue Le Bret names twenty-five different people whose friendship and support of Cyrano he wishes to acknowledge publicly. Among these names some are familiar – the poet Lignières, Cyrano's patron the Duc d'Arpajon, his cousin Madeleine de Neuvillette, the war hero Maréchal de Gassion, and Monsieur de Bourgogne the eye-witness of Cyrano's famous duel with one hundred men. Certain other names are notable by their absence, in particular those of Chapelle and Dassoucy.

It is possible and even probable that some of Cyrano's celebrations of masculine friendship are the outpourings of his repressed homosexual romanticism. If he could not write openly in support of gay relationships at a time when to do so would cost him his life, he still included enough elements in his fictional works to reveal a profound conviction that whether gay, straight or bisexual what matters most in the relationships we form is honesty, courage and selflessness. Le Bret describes Cyrano's selflessness as being carried to such a pitch that he cared nothing for personal possessions and considered that whatever belonged to him was less his than it was the property of whichever of his friends (or lovers) might happen to have need of it. His generosity was, according to the testimony of his oldest friend, his most noteworthy characteristic. Le Bret paints a picture of a warm-hearted, intrepid and thoroughly noble individual, respected, admired and held in great affection by all who knew him. There is no reason to disbelieve any of Le Bret's complimentary references to his friend's kindness and wit but naturally the elegy composed by Cyrano's grieving friend is only half the story.

Cyrano certainly seems to have been a loyal and much cherished friend to many people but he could also be an extremely venomous enemy when he chose, a fact which Le Bret naturally leaves out of his eulogy. Cyrano's works include a certain number of virulent attacks on those he considered beneath contempt: among them the coward, the plagiarist, the ingrate and the pedant. Like the love letters these were compositions written for public consumption and do not represent an individual correspondence, but rather the carefully crafted expression of Cyrano's values, or at least those values by which he wished to be known. On the whole the letters are the expression of a general idea and no specific target can be identified for their towering wrath but there are notable exceptions to this rule.

The letter 'Against a fat man' is generally considered to be aimed at the famously corpulent actor Zacharie Jacob de Montfleury. In 1694, Gilles Ménage had alleged that Cyrano had taken a dislike to the actor Montfleury and forbidden him to appear on stage for a month. When the ban was disregarded two days later, he apparently interrupted a performance to threaten Montfleury with violence if he didn't leave the stage. Rostand dramatizes the confrontation between Cyrano and the fat actor in the opening scene of his play and identifies the source of their enmity as partly due to Cyrano's indignation at Montfleury's spectacular lack of talent and partly due to a jealous reaction to Montfleury having dared to rest his lascivious gaze on Roxane.

In reality Montfleury was a very successful and talented actor who was praised by contemporaries for having the rare ability to shine in both tragic and comic roles. Born in Anjou in 1600 he had joined the theatre of the Hôtel de Bourgogne in Paris around 1638. This would put him in the right place at the right time for a clash with Cyrano that is likely to have been professional rather than personal. Cyrano had composed two plays, a comedy and a tragedy, and it seems probable that he may have attempted to interest the illustrious players of the Hôtel de Bourgogne in staging one or both of them. If Montfleury were instrumental in rejecting Cyrano's work and if in doing so the celebrated actor treated the unknown fiery young playwright with disdain then the sublimely comical letter 'Against a fat man' with its inventive insults and its dire threats of a bastonnade or worse, may well have been the natural result. In the course of the letter Cyrano also reproaches Montfleury with having written a play which is nothing but an anthology of ideas and incidents stolen from other authors. That the fat actor should have succeeded with a second-rate, unoriginal work while his own compositions languished unperformed would have been a bitter pill indeed for Cyrano.

Cyrano's epistolary rants also include examples where the targets are identified still more directly. His quarrel with fellow burlesque author Paul Scarron remains obscure. There is no reference to Cyrano anywhere in Scarron's works but in the manuscript version of the letter 'Against Scarron' Cyrano states that Scarron had accused him of writing works which 'stank of the moneybag'.[15] Scarron was a lifelong invalid whose infirmity was believed to have originated with an ill-advised midnight swim. The story is excellent and it is characteristic of Scarron's self-deprecating humour; he describes how he had decided to disguise himself as a bird for the carnival of Le Mans in 1638 and so had smeared himself in honey and then rolled in some feathers. Later in the evening the worse for drink he was set upon by thieves and in order to escape and to remove his embarrassing costume he plunged into the River Huisne. He blamed the chill that he caught for his debilitating condition. In reality his disability was far more likely to have been the result of a genetic disorder. Cyrano's vicious mockery of Scarron's physical disability does not reflect at all well on the author and reveals that his much-vaunted generosity did not extend to his enemies. He was not one to forgive and forget. Scarron remains the only subject where the published version of Cyrano's satirical letter against him proves harsher than the manuscript original. The legendary hero was only human after all, and although he was capable of greatness he was equally capable of petty meanness.

Cyrano reserved the lion's share of his spite for his former friend Dassoucy. They had begun on excellent terms and Cyrano had written congratulatory verse for him. Yet Cyrano chose to attack Dassoucy again and again. The key to his hatred of Dassoucy seems to lie in the phrase with which he opens the letter 'Against an ungrateful person': 'By the affection in which I held you of which you are unworthy, I have made you deserve to be my enemy.'[16] The bitterness of Cyrano's hatred was, as he states it here, the curdled remains of love and respect. Dassoucy was an accomplished seducer. He had a gift for self-deprecation and wit that causes the reader of his works to laugh and pity the hapless protagonist even at the same time as an element of disquiet is sounded by the presence of Dassoucy's 'evil spirit' Pierrotin. The boy was the star of Dassoucy's retinue of choirboys, young men and boys who worked for him performing the music he composed and whom he 'adopted'. Thankfully Pierrotin was able to exact a degree of revenge on the man in whose power he found himself – he was personally responsible for seeing Dassoucy jailed on numerous occasions and were it not for the intervention of noble patrons might even have seen him condemned to death. Both Pierrotin and Cyrano seem to have experienced the sickening disillusionment that follows the initial seduction in an abusive relationship. There is certainly an element of terrible indignation, anger and an overwhelming sense of betrayal in the climax of the letter in which Cyrano promises to see Dassoucy punished even if it means being judge, jury and executioner himself:

> And yet you boast of my friendship. O heavens! Punisher of heresies, punish this one with thunder! I loved you then? I brought you my heart as an offering? [. . .] you will have in me alone,
>
> Your prosecutor, Your judge
> And your executioner[17]

Having seen the capacity for human beings to do each other terrible harm it is perhaps not surprising that Cyrano felt greater companionship with animals. The birds on the sun dismiss humans as 'those vile beasts' and the most touching love story Cyrano ever created featured a bird and an alien prince rather than human lovers.[18] It is the tale of a nightingale who defies death to follow his beloved. However, the nightingale he has fallen so hopelessly in love with turns out to be a shape-changing alien prince who tries to explain that their love is impossible. The nightingale simply refuses to accept this rejection and ultimately his stubborn devotion wins through. It seems certain that whatever the emotional connection between

Cyrano, Dassoucy and Chapelle, the letters against plagiarism reveal an important intellectual rivalry that exploded into accusations and fury. Given the real Cyrano's incandescent reaction to the idea or the fact of plagiarism it is all the more ironic that his legend was to become so hopelessly entangled with recurring literary thefts.

14

'What the devil was he doing in that galley?'

In 2002, when Evan Mark Katz decided to leave his job in the customer service department of an Internet dating site and set up on his own, he chose to name his new company e-Cyrano.com. Katz had spotted a gap in the Internet dating market. His daily conversations with dissatisfied customers had made him realize that although there were many sites offering hopeful singles the chance to find true love online, none of them gave advice on how best to present oneself and one's expectations in the process. The idea of e-Cyrano was not to write fake descriptions of clients enabling them to hoodwink unwitting strangers into going on doomed dates, but rather to provide them with an honest but infinitely more eloquent account of themselves to send out into the ether: 'Making personal ads more personal' as their strapline puts it. The prevalence of e-mail and the extraordinary growth of online communication has seen something of a renaissance in the lost art of the love letter and Katz sees his role as that of a latter-day Cyrano de Bergerac.

In Rostand's play Cyrano offers to help Christian express his true feelings for Roxane – the complication is that his own emotion colours his intermediary role and he strays from helping Christian to open his heart into the more dangerous territory of revealing his own deepest feelings. The plot of Rostand's play revolves around an unwitting act of plagiarism as Christian passes off Cyrano's passionately sincere declarations of love as his own, with the result that Roxane falls deeply in love. Rostand had chosen to present his fictional version of Cyrano as a man prepared to connive in plagiarism and deception. Audiences are easily reconciled to this fact since the act of deception is motivated by a poetic ideal of self-sacrificing greatness. Cyrano's deceit is paradoxically honourable and generous as well as beautifully unrealistic.

There is a further paradox in the fact that the real Cyrano abhorred plagiarism above all things. In a satirical letter 'Against a plagiarist of thoughts' he once wrote that plagiarism should be considered a mark of esteem since the thief wouldn't make off with stolen ideas unless he saw value in them but he then went on to develop a virulently scathing attack. There was no legal notion of copyright in Cyrano's time and consequently plagiarism was commonplace. As an author who always placed the highest value on originality Cyrano considered the plagiarist as the lowest of the low. Le Bret's biography echoes the famous line from *Othello* 'who steals my purse steals trash', in order to explain that Cyrano felt strongly that there are worse crimes than the tangible, concluding that 'since glory is a more precious possession than a cloak, a horse or even than gold',[1] then plagiarists who attempt to steal that glory should be punished with harsher penalties than highway robbers.*

In contrast, at the end of Rostand's play the fictional Cyrano is informed of Molière's theft of an entire scene from his comedy *The Pedant Tricked* and responds that he approves of the plagiarism, asking only if the scene went down well and humbly acknowledging Molière's superior talent as a playwright. At the play's tragic

*The punishment for highway robbery was hanging. Apparently Cyrano envisaged a fate worse than death for the 'thief of thoughts'.

climax the fictional Cyrano sums up his entire lifetime as having been spent patiently waiting in the shadows while others thrust themselves into the sunlight realms of love and recognition.

> Cyrano: *My life – all of a piece – a shaft*
> *Of sun, a puff of air, and then not even*
> *A memory. Roxane – do you recall*
> *That night – the balcony, the ivied wall,*
> *Christian? I stood in the shadows, underneath,*
> *And left it to another to climb and claim*
> *The kiss of glory. It happened again and again –*
> *The shadow for me, for others the applause, the fame.*
> *There's a kind of justice somewhere. Even in the teeth*
> *Of what's to come I can say: Gentlemen,*
> *Take down this truism in your commonplace books:*
> *Molière had genius; Christian had good looks.*[2]

The regrets expressed by the real Cyrano on his deathbed were of an entirely different nature. In retelling Cyrano's story Rostand was engaged in rescuing a neglected author from literary oblivion. As the above lines from Cyrano's death scene are spoken the audience inwardly protest against the hero's gloomy vision of himself. Rostand skilfully manipulates his audience into recognition of his hero's greatness precisely by having him deny and reject that greatness. Moments later, as death finally overpowers Cyrano he rebels one last time and, refusing to go quietly, he launches into one last poetic tirade, raging against the dying of the light. He is established as an unforgettable hero even as he anticipates his own oblivion. Rostand's ending is sublime but profoundly anachronistic. Molière's act of plagiarism really did take place, but not until sixteen years after Cyrano's death. Rostand's deliberate decision to ignore this historical detail was the result of his determination to throw the contrast between the two writers into sharp relief. It was natural that Rostand should focus on the contrast between Molière the 'genius' and popular favourite and Cyrano the neglected, heroic failure. In the nineteenth century at the time of writing, Cyrano was an obscure author, a quirky footnote in literary history, whereas Molière was a mainstream popular success.

Today this balance is being slowly redressed, Cyrano's genius is now more generally recognized and his innovative and provocative writing is more and more widely read. The difference between his and Molière's positions in the literary canon are no longer considered to be a simple question of superior and inferior talent. Molière was a comic genius and his brilliantly observed characters remain as popular and as funny on the modern stage as when he wrote them. This extraordinary achievement is in no way diminished by the revelation that he was a frequent plagiarist and a court toady. The two men may well have been friends, they certainly frequented the same circles and had friends in common, but they had very different literary careers. Molière started out as an actor and he learned his art through a long apprenticeship touring the provinces. He was a determined and ambitious individual who rose to lead his own theatre troupe. He became a wealthy celebrity, a favourite with royalty and the populace alike. The king commissioned Molière to write for court entertainments and the royal family subsidized his Parisian theatre. Molière always wrote with the reaction of his audience very clearly in mind. As a leading actor in his own plays he was able to judge and refine the nuances of dialogue, and his version of the stolen scene is consequently the superior in polish. Cyrano worked in isolation and rebellion; hardly surprising then that his provocative and uncompromising works should slide slowly into near-oblivion while Molière's crowd-pleasing witticisms would go on delighting audiences for centuries to come.

Even today, despite the revival of interest in Cyrano's writing, his artistic reputation is utterly eclipsed by that of Molière. The latter's works are a standard at both school and university and very few people are aware of the various clever thefts dotted throughout Molière's *oeuvre*, still less that a frequently quoted line from one of his plays was actually originally written by Cyrano de Bergerac. The scene stolen from Cyrano appears in *The Schemings of Scapin*, which was written and performed in 1671. Sixteen years had elapsed since Cyrano's death, not only allowing audiences sufficient time to have forgotten the original – *The Pedant Tricked* premiered some twenty-six years earlier – but also showing that Molière had the sense to realize that if you are going to steal from the greatest swordsman of the day, you wait until he is safely dead and buried first. Molière's biographers have attempted to save the great playwright's reputation by inventing the unconvincing theory of a collaboration with Cyrano, which they date to the time when the young men were studying with Gassendi in the early 1640s. According to this theory, first suggested in the early eighteenth century by Grimarest, Cyrano used the scene first but it was written by Molière and thus he did no more than reclaim it for his own later play.[3] That Molière should have 'esteemed' Cyrano's works highly enough to steal from him was a difficult pill to swallow for those who chose to see in Molière the flourishing genius and in Cyrano the dangerous outsider, penniless and probably insane. Nowadays critics are prepared to acknowledge Molière's numerous thefts and to recognize that like Shakespeare, who also relied heavily on earlier works for his inspiration, his luminous talent remains undimmed by such revelations.

The central character of Cyrano's play and the hero of the stolen scene is the cantankerous, selfish and miserly college professor Granger. In the scene that caught Molière's fancy, Granger junior has staged an elaborate hoax in order to trick his tight-fisted father into handing over some money. He achieves this by sending his crafty servant Corbinelli to his father to recount the story of his terrible abduction by bloodthirsty Turks and to demand a ransom to free him from their clutches. The colourful story that the two conspirators concoct hinges on the fact that galleys or slave ships were a common phenomenon at the time. Corbinelli tells Granger senior that he and his master had both been captured and taken prisoner, condemned to serve out the rest of their lives as galley slaves. Corbinelli explains that he owes his own escape to his suggestion that he should be set free in order to go to Granger to obtain an impressive ransom.

In spite of the fact that his son's life apparently hangs in the balance, Granger senior displays great reluctance to part with any cash, as well as comic incredulity at finding *himself* in such a terrible position, repeatedly asking how his son could have let such a thing happen: '*Que Diable, aller faire en cette galère*?'* This phrase as reformulated by Molière '*Que Diable allait-il faire en cette galere*?' has become proverbial and is still in current usage in France to express incredulity at someone who allows themselves to get caught up in any particularly disastrous situation. The word '*galère*' on its own has become convenient shorthand for misfortune and difficulty.

And so a joke written by a supposedly 'forgotten' author survives and flourishes over three and a half centuries later. Molière also plagiarized a comic type that Cyrano had invented for the play, a wily old peasant called Mathieu Gareau who speaks in a tortuously thick accent and creates much hilarity with his combination of idiocy and impenetrable self-confidence. Cyrano's name for this character also came to be proverbial in his lifetime, denoting a sly or cunning peasant.

Just like Molière, Cyrano read widely and was not above taking his inspiration from his reading. The difference was that Cyrano was always scrupulous in acknowledging his debts. Determined never to commit the crime that he considered worse than highway robbery, Cyrano came up with a range of inventive solutions to the problem of citing his influences and most often he chose to do so

* 'What the devil was he doing in that galley?'

through a comic device. Where he did repeat an idea, he was also ready to joke about it. In the *Comical History of Francion* by Charles Sorel the idea of using poetry as an alternative form of currency appears as one of the many crack-brained notions of the character Hortensius. Cyrano liked the idea so much he included it as one of the idiosyncrasies of the civilization on the moon. Somewhat cheekily, he refers to his original source by having Dyrcona speculate that Sorel must have got the idea from the lunarians – 'O really!' I said to myself, 'that's just the money that Sorel makes Hortensius use in *Francion*, as I recall. This must be where he stole the idea from; but who the devil could he have learnt it from? It must have been from his mother, because I have heard it said that she was something of a lunatic.'[4]

Le Bret informs us that although Cyrano abhorred all instances of intellectual theft he never blamed a work too much if he found one original thing in it. Cyrano also seems to have understood that following in the path of a literary predecessor could sometimes be a spur to creativity, forcing an author to be more inventive in order not simply to repeat what has gone before. In spite of Cyrano's own feelings about the subject, his legend remains hopelessly entangled with instances of plagiarism both real and imagined. The central conceit of Rostand's play, Christian passing off Cyrano's words as his own, is one of the most familiar aspects of the Cyrano legend and yet it is also one of the most striking divergences between the real and the fictional Cyrano.

At one time, critics could have pointed to the existence of the *Mazarinades* poems and letters as proof that the real Cyrano was prepared to lend his voice to another, in this instance to the political interests hoping to dislodge the all-powerful Cardinal Mazarin, chief advisor to the regent Anne of Austria. These works have always been somewhat controversial since they directly contradict another letter that Cyrano wrote in defence of the cardinal. As a result, Cyrano has been accused of opportunism and being a political turncoat. No definitively convincing case has ever been made to support their inclusion in the canon of Cyrano's work (beyond the flimsy coincidence of their being signed with the initials B.D. and D.B.). The attribution of these works to Cyrano (always dubious), may now be dismissed out of hand.[5]

The real Cyrano reacted with characteristic wit to the real or imagined thefts from his work made by Beaulieu and Chapelle (the two men named as the targets of his two letters 'Against a thief of thoughts'). The highlight of the letter against Chapelle is a spectacular tirade in which Cyrano declares that Chapelle is compelled to plagiarize because he lacks the intelligence, the inspiration or the wit to do otherwise. 'He never opens his mouth but you'll find a theft, and he has become so accustomed to this pillage that, even when he doesn't speak, it is in order to steal the silence from some poor mute.'[6]

Cyrano's former friends Beaulieu and Chapelle were not the only ones who had good reason to be grateful that France never did take up Cyrano's suggestion that plagiarists should be subject to a punishment worse than hanging. In 1902, an international scandal erupted as the hugely successful play *Cyrano de Bergerac* became the focus of a plagiarism trial. Edmond Rostand stood accused of having stolen the essentials of his hit play from an American work entitled *The Merchant Prince of Cornville*. The trial took place in Chicago and under advice from his lawyers the complainant had finally decided not to bring his action against Rostand himself but against the American actor Richard Mansfield, who had bought the rights to stage a production of the play in New York, in which he played the starring role. Mansfield's moment of glory was short-lived, as he found himself threatened with a huge damages claim by the author of *The Merchant Prince*, a successful Chicago businessman named Samuel Eberly Gross. Gross, as rich men will, employed some clever and unscrupulous lawyers who duly pointed out to Mansfield that if he agreed to put forward no defence to the charges they would drop the original astronomical damages claim down to a single cent. Mansfield, as an impecunious actor, had no choice but to agree and the case was therefore decided in Gross's favour and Rostand's play was consequently banned from the American stage for twenty years.

Unlike *Cyrano de Bergerac*, *The Merchant Prince of Cornville* is a terrible play and had quite naturally been rejected by all the theatre producers who ever had the misfortune to have it thrust under their noses by the irrepressible Samuel Gross. And yet the plagiarism accusation has a grain of truth in it. A close analysis of the two texts reveals that Rostand almost certainly did take a few scraps of straw from *The Merchant Prince of Cornville* and spin them into the box-office gold of *Cyrano de Bergerac*. Possibly the similarities between the two plays are nothing more than coincidence, and Rosemunde Rostand's charming tale of her husband's intervention in the floundering love-life of a tongue-tied young friend may be the true origins of his play, but the evidence against Rostand is compelling.

Having failed to interest theatre producers in Chicago and New York of the merits of his play, Samuel Gross had decided that his work was simply too subtle for his fellow Americans and that it would certainly have a better reception from the more sophisticated Europeans. In 1889 he took the opportunity of a business trip to Paris to leave a manuscript copy of *The Merchant Prince* at the very playhouse which would later see the spectacular success of *Cyrano de Bergerac*, the Théâtre de la Porte St Martin, whose director Coquelin would create the role of Cyrano. Gross never heard back from Coquelin and a few years later he took matters into his own hands. In 1896 Gross travelled to London, rented a theatre, hired some actors and produced his play himself. The reception it received was sufficiently dire to convince Gross to close after one night. He paid for the play to be printed and distributed copies to various friends and acquaintances. There the matter might have rested but for the fact that when *Cyrano de Bergerac* hit the New York stage, two of Gross's friends who had read his play wrote independently to draw his attention to the similarity between the hit French play and his own work.

When the scandal first erupted, Rostand went to some lengths to disprove Gross's claims. He argued that he didn't speak a word of English. This seems distinctly implausible given that he had attended an English kindergarten for three years as a child and employed an English au pair in his own family to ensure that his children would be fluent in the language. He also misquoted the date that Gross had left the manuscript at the theatre, and asked for a copy in translation to be provided offering to recommend it to his own publisher. The facts remains that the play had been waiting at the theatre for a translation and there is no great leap of faith required to imagine that Rostand may have picked it up and flicked through it. He would then no doubt have cast it aside as worthless but he may also have retained the odd good idea that he could improve upon and use in the context of his own work. At worst Rostand took a few ideas and the odd phrase from Gross's work and these he transformed so utterly that Gross's lawsuit should by rights have been thrown out immediately as laughable and pointless.

When the twenty-year ban was nearly up the case was retried in New York and on a closer examination of the evidence the judgement in favour of Gross was reversed. After the initial flurry of excitement caused by the scandal the press were unanimous in deciding in favour of Rostand. One London journalist even remarked 'It wants a bit of believing, Eh? Presently we may hear that Cyrano himself has arisen to ask for an injunction against Rostand.'[7] Once the initial anxiety had died down Rostand gained the necessary confidence to dismiss the case as laughable and prepare a light-hearted and witty response to the controversy. In a letter published in *Le Temps* he wrote:

In the four years which this affair has lasted, I have always refused and I still refuse to take it seriously . . . In the meantime I am ready to admit that I have taken Cyrano de Bergerac, his name, the panache, the Hôtel de Bourgogne, Montfleury, the Rôtisserie de Ragueneau, the soul of *préciosité*, Roxane kissing Cyrano's words on Christian's lips, the trip to the moon, the siege of Arras, the Gascon cadets, in fact our whole seventeenth century from Mr Eberly Gross of Chicago.[8]

If nothing else the controversy certainly puts a new spin on Rostand's decision to have the dying Cyrano accept Molière's plagiarism with such angelic grace. He was to learn from his own experience with Gross just how unlikely a scenario this was.

In the memoirs that Rosemunde Rostand wrote about her husband, she included her own artful defence against the accusations of plagiarism. She gives her own version of the play's genesis, insisting that the painful love triangle at its heart was actually inspired by a far from tragic incident in Rostand's own life. A young friend named Amédée had apparently confided in the great poet his despair over a hopeless love affair. He explained that he was madly in love with an intelligent and spirited young woman, but that he was failing miserably in his attempts to win her heart. Rostand taking pity on the young man asked him for more detail.

'Alas!' cried the young man, 'I talk, I plead all in vain, she doesn't even listen to me.' What do you say to her? asked Rostand who found himself acknowledging the young girl's cruelty.

'I tell her that I love her.'

'Then what?

'I repeat the same thing!'

'And then what?'

'That's it.'

> 'When she loves you that will be enough,' concluded the poet. 'But for now she needs something else. I know her; she is pedantic, affected, she is even snobbish. She requires flowery language, paradoxes. When she is simplified by her love for you she will only require a single word but for now she needs lots of them.'[9]

And so began a collaboration in which Amédée returned every day to consult the poet for his lesson in the art of wooing, leaving with his head stuffed full of witty remarks and poetic speculations. A little while later, the poet encountered the young woman and overheard her confiding to a friend that the admirer whom she had originally considered so dull and uninteresting had turned out to have wonderful hidden depths – Amédée was a poet, a thinker and a prodigious talent. Rosemunde does not describe what happened next to the young lovers. We are left to wonder whether they lived happily ever after, or whether, once the lessons were over, Amédée reverted to type and his sweetheart got bored and ran off with a cavalry officer. Instead, Rosemunde concludes her story with the triumphant, but probably disingenuous declaration: 'The first idea for "Cyrano" had been found!!'

Whatever the truth of the play's origins and, aside from his own feelings about the ethics of the situation, there was another more compelling reason for Rostand to include the story of Molière's plagiarism in his play. As his biographer Sue Lloyd reveals in her book *The Man Who Was Cyrano*, Rostand was obsessed with what he termed '*les ratés*' – life's failures. For Rostand, Cyrano was an excellent example of such a failure and the comparison with Molière served as additional confirmation of this 'fact'. Throughout his life Edmond Rostand was haunted by bouts of depression and a crippling fear of failure. The poet fêted by an entire nation and beloved of high society and ordinary folk alike, always aspired to be the champion of the underdog, the lost cause, the failure. For this reason Rostand's works were to provide comfort and inspiration to many a doomed soldier amidst the horrors of the First World War. Rostand was not eligible for military service because of his poor health, but he wrote hundreds of letters of support and encouragement to the men in the trenches. Lloyd recounts how Cyrano was to become an important symbol of French heroism and courage during the war. Rostand received letters from men at the front describing how they carried his works in their backpacks and drew strength from the example of the legendary hero.

Two infantrymen composed a parody entitled *Cyronac de Bergerot* to entertain the troops and in 1918 Joseph Suberville published a one-act drama entitled *Cyrano de Bergerac in the Trenches*. The play was performed at the front and published in the review *The Ideal* in March 1918. The action dramatizes a conversation between Cyrano (freshly arrived from the moon) and a French infantryman. There is a terrible poignancy to Cyrano's initial bewilderment at the scene of devastation he sees around him as he wonders aloud, 'perhaps I have landed on the wrong planet . . .' The two military men discuss heroism and warfare and conclude that although battles in the modern age may have become a bloodier and still more horrifying business than in the age of the musketeers the innate heroism of the soldiers fighting for freedom remains the same. There is no room in such a context for the real Cyrano's complex feelings about the life of a soldier and his ultimate rejection of codes of chivalry and honour as a fraud designed to send men willingly to the slaughter for the sake of a political futility. In such a historical moment it is the hero of Rostand's play who must step forward to represent the self-sacrifice and the courage of those lost young men dying in their millions for the sake of freedom. In a time of universal tragedy the power of such an emblem is significant but it should not be forgotten that Rostand's noble hero has his origins in the life of a real man. While the fictional hero of *Cyrano de Bergerac in the Trenches* is confounded by the cynical battlefield humour of the infantryman the real Cyrano would have understood only too well, the real Cyrano would have had no difficulty in relating to exactly what those young men were going through.

In the play, when asked the cause of the war the infantryman replies by evoking a patriotic vision of the pastoral beauty of his beloved homeland.

> *. . . Because*
> *Our fields were too green and our sky too blue,*
> *Because too intoxicating blood flowed from our vines*
> *And because for the French the earth was benign*
> *While she sulked on the other side of the Rhine!*

This recalls the speech made by Rostand's Cyrano when he needs to calm and encourage the troops on the eve of their last desperate assault at Arras. The words of the fictional infantryman chime with those of the fictional Cyrano but if we turn to the words of a real First World War soldier we find a more accurate echo of the real Cyrano. An English journalist named A. M. Burrage wrote a memoir of his time fighting in the trenches in France entitled *War is War*. At one point he asks,

> Who will ever forget Arras who saw her then in the middle days of the war? The whole rows of houses with their façades torn off so that one could see into every room, as in an architect's sectional drawing; pictures hanging askew, beds with the clothes dragged aside and left just as when their occupants leaped up and ran for safety, perhaps more than a year since; open wardrobes and garments still hanging on the pegs; intimate medical appliances left ruthlessly exposed [. . .] Arras was a more poignant sight than Ypres. Ypres was a bleeding corpse and Arras was still writhing in her death agony.[10]

Cyrano's own experiences in the same place underline the tragic fact that three centuries on nothing has changed. Cyrano's reflections on the futility of war, his plea for the recognition of this fact, his insistence that true nobility in mankind would be for us to understand that we are all citizens of the world rather than citizens of one nation or another, remain sadly as urgent and as little heeded as ever. Time moves on and the technology of war advances horribly but the individuals caught up in the fighting can no more hope to understand or accept their situation now than they could in Cyrano's day.

Burrage's experience of war forced him to take refuge in cynicism and black humour notably similar to Cyrano's own. Burrage explains how essential it was to maintain this protective barrier of mockery and wit in order not to break one's heart with anguish. Both men also join in denying that courage exists in warfare, stating that abject terror is more natural and more current on the battlefield. Burrage published his account anonymously under the pseudonym 'Ex-Private X' and explained that he did so in order to be free to tell the truth about his experiences. 'If any young man should ask an old soldier, "Was it really like this?" and the old soldier answers, "Yes, it's all true," this book will have served its purpose. And I shall not mind if the young man exclaims, "What a very unpleasant fellow the author must be!" Perhaps I am.'[11] Just like Cyrano, Burrage was a man who put his duty to tell the hard, painful truths that society might not want to hear above the fear that he might be considered an 'unpleasant fellow'.

15
An ambush vile

It was in the period leading up to his untimely death that Cyrano's literary career began to take off. In 1653, he had finally accepted the assistance of a noble patron, the Duc d'Arpajon, and was preparing his work for print publication. Two volumes duly went before the censor for official approval in late 1653, and in early 1654 Cyrano's *Diverse Works* and *The Death of Agrippina* were published by the bookseller Charles de Sercy. The finished products were elegant quarto editions featuring the duke's coat of arms and, in the case of the *Works*, a specially commissioned portrait engraving of the author by his friend Zachary Heince. *The Death of Agrippina* was a great success thanks to rumours about its scandalous atheistic content lending it sinful notoriety. The volume of letters, accompanied by *The Pedant Tricked*, also found favour.

An English edition was published in 1658 by the bookseller Henry Herringman under the title *Satyrical Characters, and Handsome Descriptions in letters, written to severall persons of quality . . . Translated by a person of honour.* The accompanying translator's note 'To the Reader' promises plentiful wit 'in these essayes, cloathed by the Author, in smooth and significant expressions, and such high and unthought-of raptures you'll meet with . . . for like Pliny's fish he carries teeth in his tongue', as well as concluding on the plaintive note that 'Those that can judge of the Originall will I believe grant, that 'tis almost as hard a Book to translate well, as any in prose that is extant in that Language.'[1] This is not just a final self-congratulatory flourish but also an important acknowledgement of the complexity and intricacy of Cyrano's writing.

Cyrano's new patron, the Duc d'Arpajon, was an ex-soldier who had fought valiantly in Turkey and earned himself the dignities of Knight of the Grand Cross and Knight of the Order of Malta. One of his contemporaries described d'Arpajon as the slow but steady type: 'of easy relations with his superiors, never compromising them, more tenacious than enterprising, prudent, cunning even, self-centred, painstaking; he was one of those men who barely shine, and yet who, marching with a firm tread from degree to degree, without great leaps but without pause, finish by accumulating favours, rank and dignities'.[2] In short, he was the exact temperamental opposite of Cyrano.

Tallemant des Réaux also recorded a less than flattering story about the duke in his *Historiettes*. One evening d'Arpajon invited Sarasin and Pellisson, two well-known authors to dinner. The duke complimented Sarasin on a recent work entitled *Springtime*, only to be told indignantly that it was the work of a different author, the poet Montplaisir. He tried again, praising *The Temple of Death* (by Habert) with the same result, and it was only with a whispered hint from Pellisson that he was able finally to come up with praise for the *Sonnet for Eve*, a piece that Sarasin had actually written. It was a common enough phenomenon for great men to frequent authors, since it was considered gentlemanly to take a certain interest in literary matters. John Evelyn's *Diary* contains a sarcastic passage in which he bemoans the fact that all too often the great noblemen were content to construct libraries purely for show, paying no attention at all to the content of the books as long as their bindings were acceptable and they filled up the space becomingly: 'He doth not much amuse himself in the particular elections of either Authors or Impressions; but having erected his cases & measured them, accords with a Stationer to furnish him with so many gilded Folioes, so many yard of quarto's and octavo's by the great, till his Bibliotheke be full of Volumes.'[3] It seems fair to suspect that d'Arpajon might have been one of those who bought his books by the yard. He clearly wished to appear cultured, but he seems to have contented himself with patronizing impecunious writers without necessarily taking the trouble of actually reading their work. Such a man was ideal for Cyrano's purposes; what could be more apposite for the provocateur than a patron who would not read his works too closely (if at all) and would therefore be unlikely to raise any objections, or worse, suggest any modifications. Also, Cyrano's friend, the poet Tristan L'Hermite whom he greatly admired, had previously accepted d'Arpajon's patronage; Tristan dedicated *Heroic Verses* to d'Arpajon in 1648. This precedent must have been important to Cyrano and significantly he once described Tristan as 'the only free man' in France.[4]

For Cyrano a patron was a necessary evil; d'Arpajon took him on as a part of his household. As a '*domestique*' Cyrano lived in d'Arpajon's home but was neither servant nor honoured guest – his was an intermediary and subordinate position. In such circumstances an author was expected to earn the generosity of his noble sponsor. One way in which to do so was by writing a suitably fawning letter to the patron to be printed at the start of the works. In return for these dedications, nobles would then show their gratitude in the form of a 'gift' of hard cash. Cyrano had been living with d'Arpajon and his family for nearly a year at the point when he composed his *Dedicatory Epistle* to the duke. In his dedication, Cyrano dismissed his own works as a haphazard collection of 'caprices', the product of his youthful folly. This was a fairly standard stance for the author to take in a dedication. The necessary combination of grovelling and false modesty led to the very common ploy of dismissing the work, as nowhere near good enough to recompense the extraordinary honour paid by the distinguished patron in accepting the dedication. In Cyrano's case, there is a ring of truth to his rejection of the letters and plays.

By the time he came to publish them, he had progressed enormously in his art and was working on a far more original and daring project – his science fiction novels. In the second volume of these novels, Cyrano writes about the experience of being a well-known author, whose portrait has been circulated and whose works have caused a controversy that has overtaken the whole town. He is rather scathing about his readership, complaining that certain ignorant souls initially praised the work to the skies without understanding a word of it, purely in order to seem intelligent and cultivated. He describes how these 'idiots' then grew to resent the author's success and their own ignorance and consequently performed a spectacular U-turn dismissing the work as ridiculous and the author as a madman. It is tempting to read an indirect reference to d'Arpajon in this little vignette because, from having been Cyrano's champion, albeit one who undoubtedly had little affinity with his protégé's work, d'Arpajon had eventually reversed his allegiance and thrown a gravely injured Cyrano out of his house.

Cyrano's disgrace and expulsion from the house of d'Arpajon seems to have been the direct result of a dramatic incident that took place in early 1654, right at the point when his works had finally made it into print. Until the discovery of the uncensored version of Le Bret's biography, d'Arpajon's decision to kick the dying Cyrano out of his house was extremely difficult to account for. According to the facts as related in outline, Cyrano had suffered a blow to the head that had left him seriously ill, and it was in this condition that he was suddenly sent away from the duke's household in disgrace. How a terrible accident could prejudice Cyrano's patron against him was a vexed question and one to which no satisfactory answer had been found. The syphilis theory was one way of explaining the facts away differently but this directly contradicted Le Bret's assertion that the cause of *both* Cyrano's illness and his disgrace was a serious head injury. Those who chose to accept the slightly confusing version of events offered by Le Bret's censored account duly dreamt up the theory of the falling beam or roof tile. According to that theory, a beam was dislodged in the course of either renovations or a fire (depending on whose account one favours) and Cyrano had the misfortune to walk underneath at just the wrong moment. It is thoroughly appropriate that in Rostand's play this fictional falling beam also fells the fictional Cyrano, but Rostand also understood enough about the real Cyrano to guess at the real cause of his death, and in the play the beam did not fall but was pushed. Cyrano's death is the result of an ambush, as the hero himself declares:

> *Monsieur de Bergerac*
> *Was foully, ignobly*
> *Murdered.*[5]

The uncensored version of Le Bret's biography cast a stronger doubt than ever before on the theories of Cyrano's death by disease or accident. Further documents, recently come to light, add convincing detail to corroborate the theory of a botched assassination attempt. It had always seemed significant that after the 'accident' which destroyed Cyrano's health he was no longer welcome in d'Arpajon's home. Le Bret states quite explicitly that the incident 'caused his disgrace'. The timing alone of Cyrano's injury and subsequent ejection from the d'Arpajon household seemed to imply that the source of his serious injuries was known and feared – since a genuine accident would surely have inspired sympathy and a greater degree of support rather than this summary dismissal. A shred of rhymed gossip recorded by the poet Loret in his *Gazette* paints a picture of a late-night attack on the duke's carriage that ended in death and disarray.

> *Sir d'Arpajou* [sic.] *by simple chance*
> *Heading rather late to his residence,*
> *Encountered some armed men*
> *Who caused him pandemonium*
> *As they dared his coach to attack.*
> *But on a sudden he forced them back.*
> *Four horsemen of his retinue*
> *Made the ten men flee without ado,*
> *Excepting, of their number, two;*
> *One of whom, a reckless fool,*
> *Was overthrown, left dead in the mud*
> *Wearing a most miserable expression;*
> *The Other, like a night prowler,*
> *Straight to Prison was led further.*
> *But in this same war as well,*
> *One of his own men also fell,*
> *Mortally wounded, they said,*
> *By a bloody blow, a musket shot.*
> *And even, a valuable horse*
> *Shared in the misfortune of their sort*
> *It was the one (so I heard)*
> *On which the duke's equerry rode.*
> *Whether such an unfortunate fight,*
> *Taking place under bright moonlight,*
> *Was madness or an ambush vile,*
> *The suspense continues yet awhile.*[6]

The horse-drawn vehicles of the aristocracy were cumbersome and not easily manoeuvrable in the narrow streets of Paris; carriages were therefore vulnerable to attack. The lack of street lighting and the myriad, interconnecting crossroads and alleyways formed the perfect setting for a clandestine attack. As the poem reveals, the underhand plot involved the waylaying of the duke's carriage in the dark streets and the result was not a robbery, as might have been anticipated in such circumstances, but a single member of the duke's retinue shot at close range. That wounded man was almost certainly Cyrano. There was a well-known royal precedent for a murderous ambush of this kind in the streets of Paris. On 14 May 1610, King Henri IV's carriage had been held up in a narrow lane and the fanatical monk Ravaillac leapt into the carriage and repeatedly stabbed the king and then gave himself up to the guards. James Howell, writing in 1619, remarked on the frequency of traffic jams in Paris and the resulting potential for murderous ambush:

> A world of coaches, carts and Horses of all sorts that go to and fro perpetually, so that sometimes one shall meet with a stop half a mile long of those coaches, carts and Horses, that can move neither forward nor backward by reason of some sudden encounter of others coming a crosse-way; so that oftentimes it will be an hour or two before they can disintangle: In such a stop the great Henry was so fatally slain by Ravillac.

In Le Bret's biography, he describes Cyrano's injury as a gunshot wound, the timing and his description are in accordance with the account given by Loret: ten men sent to surround and stop the carriage and one of them to take the opportunity to fire the fatal bullet at close range – this is clearly testament to the great swordsman's fearsome reputation. After his extraordinary feat of bravery at the de Nesle gate, there could be no question of engaging him in swordplay; instead this dastardly method of eliminating him was chosen. The moment when the attack on the carriage happened, it must have become unpleasantly clear to d'Arpajon that supporting Cyrano was a risky undertaking with consequences far beyond those of literary scandal. Possibly the loss of his 'valuable horse' weighed more heavily with d'Arpajon than the loss of the troublesome poet. It is not clear from Loret's account whether the duke was in the carriage himself at the time of the attack, but if he was, then his precipitate haste in ridding himself of the seriously injured Cyrano is, perhaps, the more easily understood. Exactly who ordered the attack on Cyrano will probably never be known. When a criminal has escaped justice he is unlikely to be brought to book over 350 years later. But before the attack happened, Cyrano had already voiced his own suspicions that an attempt would be made on his life.

An extraordinary letter, that features in the manuscript collections but not in the printed editions of Cyrano's works, is entitled 'Against a murderous and slandering Jesuit'. This letter foreshadows the disaster to come in chillingly accurate detail – in the opening line Cyrano jokes that the murderous priest clearly takes him for a king since he is attempting to incite his acolytes to follow the example of Ravaillac. He goes on to suggest that one failed attempt has already been made on his life. He describes the priest having succeeded in convincing a 'savage', already guilty of one murder, that the key to his salvation was the assassination of Cyrano. The proposed 'ambush' apparently missed Cyrano as he provokingly reminds his enemy 'by one day' and so failed to 'redden the streets with my blood'.[7] He points out that if the Jesuit had been less tight-fisted and had seen fit to embolden his hired killer with ready money instead of with sermons, 'indulgences and medallions', then perhaps his chosen assassin would have been rather more dedicated to his task. Cyrano also points out the notable hypocrisy in the Jesuit's preaching this doctrine of justifiable homicide to his followers. If the priest really believed that Cyrano's death were for the greater good of Christianity, he should personally attempt to take Cyrano's life. If he dare not, for fear of eternal damnation, then he should not encourage others to run that risk on his behalf.

Another of Cyrano's accusations against the priest is that he is guilty of sexually abusing the pupils in his charge. Cyrano's vision of authority was that it was inseparable from abuse of power and he seems to have particularly distrusted the hypocrisy of those whose power was divinely sanctioned. In the 1640s in France, there were indeed Jesuit priests (such as Niccolo Baldelli, who may or may not be the same Nicholas B. to whom Cyrano's harangue is addressed) openly preaching the astonishing doctrine that murder was acceptable in certain circumstances to save one's honour.

The evidence is circumstantial, Cyrano's letter to the murderous priest is a damning indictment of the Jesuit brotherhood but it does not prove in itself that the Jesuits were responsible for Cyrano's death. It does prove that he felt that certain members of the brotherhood represented a very real threat and maybe even that he believed one attempt on his life had already been made, before the incident in which the duke's carriage was attacked.

One of the nineteenth-century editors of Cyrano's work, Paul Lacroix, investigated the bibliographical history of Cyrano's works. In particular, he was intrigued by the scarcity of surviving copies. Given Cyrano's popularity (there were at least twelve reprints of the complete works and numerous editions of individual works) Lacroix expected to find far more extant copies. His explanation for the disappearance of so many books was that it could not be an accident. He was convinced that editions of Cyrano's works had been 'systematically destroyed by the tireless efforts of the mysterious brotherhood of the Index'. If Lacroix is to be believed, the brotherhood pursued their vendetta against Cyrano beyond the grave. There is certainly compelling evidence that such campaigns against 'heretical' authors did take place. Even with a concerted campaign to consign Cyrano to oblivion in full force, his name at least lived on. But the impact on his readership was dramatic. In 1858, Lacroix wrote that: 'everyone knows the name Cyrano; but no one, or hardly anyone, reads his books'. After the explosion of

Rostand's Cyrano on to the stage nearly forty years later, this situation would only become the more acute. Despite the familiarity of Cyrano's name, his works were to languish under a cloud of oppression and censorship. It was not until 1977, when Jacques Prévot published an edition of the *Complete Works* based on precious manuscript sources, that Cyrano's fractured texts were finally fully reconstituted, uncensored and entire. Cyrano seems to have been the victim of a double assassination attempt, in which his enemies had chosen to act in the most cowardly and underhand manner imaginable, seeking to extinguish not just his life but also his literary legacy.

He was almost certainly the target of the d'Arpajon ambush, but in the darkness and confusion of the fray the ten men sent to destroy this rebellious spirit were not enough to totally silence him. Although his attackers left him drenched in his own blood and with a life-threatening head injury, he was still alive. Cyrano stubbornly fought for life for several crowded months more, during which a fresh catastrophe overtook him before he finally surrendered to the darkness. In his biography of Cyrano, Le Bret refers to the head injury his friend had sustained and a following period of serious illness caused by 'a long captivity', but the full account he made of these terrifying events was rapidly censored and lost to view for centuries to come. As a result, biographers chose to believe that Cyrano was either the victim of a tragic accident or of the deadly neurosyphilis. Perhaps madness is in the eye of beholder and Cyrano was labelled a lunatic because he consistently went out of his way to defy convention. Despite Cyrano's obvious allegiance to a notorious line of heretics who had died fiery deaths before him, he was never prosecuted for blasphemy. It is significant to note, though, that such prosecutions were in fact becoming increasingly rare from 1653 onwards, as a new, more insidious response to nonconformity had emerged. Blasphemy was beginning to be categorized as a mental disorder and therefore treated as illness more frequently than crime. Similarly, witchcraft was gradually becoming more the affair of the asylum than the stake. Cyrano's case may well have been on the cusp of this wave.

The experience of the author Bonaventure Forcroy, who wrote a *Life of Apollonius of Thyane*, offers a strong parallel with Cyrano. Forcroy's work was essentially a learned attack on the Christian idea of the miracle, an idea that Cyrano also disputed in his late works. Forcroy then wrote a thesis addressed to the doctors of the Sorbonne setting out seventeen 'doubts on religion' in which he asked the question whether natural law were not the 'sole veritable religion'.[8] In return for his provocative challenges to religious doctrine Forcroy was neither burnt at the stake nor thrown in prison. Nor was he left in peace to express his radical views. Instead, he was locked away in the lunatic asylum of St Lazare for six years until he showed himself docile and started taking the sacrament regularly. When he was eventually released he was banished from Paris back to his home town of Noyon.

Forcroy's case is relevant to Cyrano because it shows the authorities reacting to dissidence in a new way. Imprisonment and the label of insanity were as effective, if not more so, than the previous strategy – the criminalization of such individuals. Not least because the troublesome, rebellious elements of society were more effectively silenced shut away in a lunatic asylum, than when offered the oxygen of publicity. Criminal prosecution attracted the attention of the public, particularly when it ended in a big showy execution. Once the public's curiosity was aroused, a fascinated determination to read the scandalous works of the 'demonic' miscreants was all too often the result. Even years later, the lingering whiff of fire and damnation could lend a forbidden glamour to certain works. Voltaire acknowledged that his desire to read Vanini's writings sprang from his fascination with their author's notorious fate. Cyrano's own bookseller suggested that it was precisely the reputation of blasphemy and scandal attached to *The Death of Agrippina* that guaranteed its success. By the time Cyrano had published his own dissident writings, the authorities had perhaps begun to appreciate the fact that it was better to make such seditious subjects silently disappear, than to risk whipping up a frenzy of public interest in them – interest, which despite being nominally disapproving would only serve to draw attention to the criticisms and challenges to be found in the works of these passionate rebels.

Conditions inside the lunatic asylums of the seventeenth century were little different than those in the prisons. Dark, damp and disease-ridden, the cells in which the inmates were confined were occasionally little better than dungeons. In the opening of *The Voyage to the Sun* Cyrano recounts his hero's imprisonment in a 'black dungeon'; the experience has the vivid quality of a waking nightmare. The description of his imprisonment, as it emerges in Cyrano's fiction, is at once a wellspring of irrepressible black humour and a harrowing insight into the harsh reality of a society where freedom of expression did not exist; where corruption and oppression masqueraded as authority and justice. In the novel, the events that lead up to the imprisonment of Cyrano's protagonist Dyrcona are depicted with a combination of high drama and slapstick humour. A high-voltage chase sequence sees Dyrcona on the run from his jailers. He manages to trick his gullible guard into taking him to say a prayer in a local church with an elaborate story of angelic visitation (and the promise of a hefty bribe). Once outside the confines of the prison, he quickly gives his guard the slip and goes on the run through the streets of Toulouse. Although Cyrano had probably completed much of *Voyage to the Sun* before the date of his incarceration, it seems likely that he rewrote this opening section in order to include the new material inspired by his recent experiences. Dyrcona is not an autobiographical portrait of the author, yet comparisons between the two are unavoidable; both identify themselves as notorious due to their authorship of a text entitled *Voyage to the Moon*, whose accompanying portrait engraving has launched a degree of celebrity that is both uncomfortable and clearly a source of pride, and both were wrongly imprisoned. The first public portrait of the real Cyrano was that engraved by his friend Zachary Heince in 1653, to accompany the publication of the *Oeuvres Diverses*. In *The Voyage to the Sun*, Cyrano reflects that *The Voyage to the Moon* has sparked such controversy that the debate touches every household, dividing families and crossing social divides: 'From the gentleman to the monk . . . even women took their part'; all enthusiastically joining in the debate about the intriguing possibility of a world in the moon.[9]

Dyrcona discovers the downside to this sudden celebrity; he becomes aware that he is dangerously well known, thanks to the circulation of his portrait on the publication of his *Voyage to the Moon*. He is forced to disguise himself to escape detection: first of all as a peasant, then as a mute beggar and finally as a plague victim. His outlaw career is short-lived despite his quick thinking and terrified headlong flight. He has the ill luck to run straight into the head jailer but manages to escape once again, by tricking the crowd of onlookers into misinterpreting the jailer's initial consternation at the sight of his escaped prisoner and thereby neatly reversing their roles. He makes a quick-witted appeal to the crowd and various young hot-heads, eager for the reward that he tells them has been offered for the jailer's capture, seize on the unfortunate official and start beating him soundly. Meanwhile, Dyrcona sneaks away to seek refuge from the riot that he has set in motion. It is at this point that his good fortune utterly abandons him; he finds that in following a group of people, all trying to escape from the street fight into a nearby building, he has inadvertently returned himself to captivity. Dyrcona collapses, fainting with horror at this turn of misfortune. His fellow refugees from the brawl rush to his aid and the first to reach him is one of the town guards, who instantly recognizes him and arrests him on the spot. So ends his first prison break. The second, definitive escape takes place after his friends have discovered him in prison and paid for him to be transferred out of the dungeon and into a large well-appointed tower room, where he is allowed to have all his mathematical books and instruments with him. He orders materials delivered to his cell and manages to construct a spaceship (relying on a form of rudimentary rocket propulsion), which takes him on his second unintentional flight into outer space, this time on a voyage to the sun.

These elaborate escape fantasies probably reflect no more of the real Cyrano's actual experience of incarceration than the spur to his comical and fantastical imagination provided by isolation and deprivation. It is to be hoped that the description of his confinement in a rat-infested dungeon, where he is crawled over by lizards and snakes, where slugs and toads drip their slime in his hair and leeches suck his blood also owes more to imagination than reality. There is, perhaps, an element of wish-fulfilment in his portrait of an insouciant hero who reacts to the nightmarish horrors of this rancid prison with an unfailing stream of cheeky quips to his jailer and a witty refusal to be downcast. But there is one moment when it seems clear that the real Cyrano's experience of imprisonment intrudes on this fictionalizing process. He interrupts the description of Dyrcona's dungeon with the reflection that: 'to describe the rest is more than I can bear: it is beyond all belief; and I don't dare attempt to remember, I am too afraid that my conviction that I have escaped from my prison should prove to be no more than a dream from which I might be about to wake up'.[10]

Cyrano's description includes no elements of the trial that would naturally loom large in an instance of criminal imprisonment: this would not be part of the experience of incarceration in an asylum. The focus on visible punishment is the central difference between a blasphemy prosecution and imprisonment in an asylum. There was no programme of treatment for asylum inmates – beyond the regular ministrations of a priest – but at least there was, as Forcroy's case shows, the possibility of a 'cure' and consequent release. The living conditions may have been every bit as dirty, disease-ridden and dangerous as in the prisons, but the threat of torture or the stake was at least withheld. The inmates of asylums like St Lazare were an extremely varied population. Manuscript sources, detailing the proceedings that led to their incarceration, offer an interesting sample list of unfortunates: 'a persistent litigant', 'the most litigious man', 'a very wicked and argumentative man', 'a man who spends his days and nights deafening other people with his songs and uttering the most terrible blasphemies', 'a great liar', 'an anxious, melancholy and surly spirit', 'a billposter'.[11] With the possible exception of the troublesome singer or the melancholy soul, it is hard to see in these descriptions any elements recognizable to a modern conception of mental illness.

The asylums were perhaps becoming a convenient dumping ground for the disposal of those thorns in the side of the civil authorities whose conduct was not strictly illegal. As such, individuals who had the requisite money and influence could also use the asylums to settle private disputes. Such seems to have been Cyrano's case, although exactly who was responsible for arranging his incarceration remains a vexed question. The conditions in the asylums were undoubtedly unsanitary and appallingly grim. It must have been torture for the devotee of the woods and rivers of the beautiful valley of Chevreuse to be locked away from all light and hint of green, surrounded only by filth, decay and infestation.

16

Towards the sky

In order to retrace Cyrano's final months of life one can only rely on inference and the various hints strewn through the text of his final, posthumously published masterpiece *The Voyage to the Sun*. The shreds of documentary evidence that have survived are sadly few and far between. Censorship of Le Bret's biography has proved quite extraordinarily effective, shrouding Cyrano's death in a mystery that has endured to the present day. The rediscovery of the censored section of Le Bret's work reveals not only a clearer explanation of Cyrano's injury and illness, but also an accusation. Le Bret charges Abel II with having had Cyrano locked up in pretence that it was for his own good and as a result of his 'illness' but in reality as a low trick motivated by 'cowardly covetousness'.[1]

Essentially then, Cyrano seems to have gained his reputation as a madman, not because he was suffering from the dementia caused by neurosyphilis, but because his own brother apparently had him locked away in a lunatic asylum. The details were never entirely clear because of the rapid censorship of Le Bret's accusation, but now that the uncensored version has been recovered, it becomes possible to retrace the events with a little more clarity. In the

28. JAN 04.
10. JAN 06.
13. SEP 06.
13. SEP 06.
12. DEC 07.
04. MAR 08.
26. APR 08.

suppressed section of Le Bret's preface, he states that Cyrano's close friend Jacques Rouhault had been 'the first to discover the ill-treatment that his brother had subjected him to, and the one who, with all his friends, painstakingly sought the means to shield him from the cruelties of that barbarian'.[2] Le Bret also thanks Cyrano's benefactor Tanneguy Renault des Boisclairs, the man responsible for 'breaking the iron-fetters in which his barbarous brother was keeping him prisoner', and with whom Cyrano was then to lodge for the next fourteen months.[3] Tanneguy was distantly related to Cyrano through his uncle Samuel; he was also something of a philanthropist, and it is to be assumed that he broke those iron fetters with the help of a substantial sum of money, paid to free Cyrano from the asylum. Le Bret never specifies that Cyrano's 'captivity' was within the walls of an asylum, rather than a prison – hardly surprising that he would not wish to record such an ignominious fact. The balance of probability is nevertheless in favour of a mental institution, rather than a prison, as this would also fit with the later reputation of insanity that attached to Cyrano's legend, as well as with the apparent ease with which his friends succeeded in releasing him from his 'fetters'. If he had been facing criminal prosecution this would have been considerably more difficult.[4]

Le Bret's condemnation of Abel is extremely damning, but it is possible that he may have been mistaken. At first glance, Cyrano's case seems to fall into the fairly common category of families who despaired of a troublesome member, whose outrageous conduct was likely to bring disgrace and possibly prosecution upon them if not checked in time. In such circumstances, one solution was to turn to the asylums in the hope of a 'cure'. Chapelle's aunts apparently had him locked away in St Lazare for a time in an attempt to curb his worst excesses. Another family tried to arrange a transfer for their son when a dangerous prison fever swept the asylum of St Lazare because they didn't want to risk losing him. Contrary to what one might imagine, they genuinely believed they were acting for his good in having him locked away, as their plea for his transfer affirms: 'having no design to cause their son's death when they had solicited the order to have him imprisoned but only to correct and recover his wits that were almost completely lost'.[5]

Le Bret's accusation is that Abel acted maliciously and avariciously, under pretence of a similar concern for his brother's good. This feigned concern lends significant weight to the theory that Cyrano's nightmare in the 'black dungeon' took place within an asylum rather than a prison. In the censored section of his published letter to Tanneguy des Boisclairs, Le Bret draws a direct contrast between the selflessness of the philanthropist and the selfishness of Abel de Cyrano. He also suggests that Cyrano was devastated by his brother's betrayal and that this accelerated the course of his illness: 'Your generous care had stayed the swift course of his illness, that his vexation at the inhumanity of this wicked brother alone had rendered so violent, I consider you as a miracle of our time, and I console myself, amid the hard-heartedness of a century when men are generally so self-serving, when I see a friend so kind and so generous.'[6]

Le Bret's identification of Abel as the author of Cyrano's downfall was published in 1656, in his preface to the edited version of *The Voyage to the Moon* that he had seen through the press. Within a very short space of time, the offending sections of the preface had been cut out of copies of the work and replaced with a confusing shortened version, in which vague references to Cyrano's head injury and illness replaced the description of his captivity and Abel's barbarity. Only one surviving copy of the uncensored version has come to light since, and that only very recently. In 1662, Cyrano's bookseller (publisher) Charles de Sercy published a new edition of Cyrano's works, in which *The Voyage to the Sun* appeared for the first time. Sercy opened the volume with a letter addressed to Abel de Cyrano in which he speaks to him of his brother's numerous enemies, who cruelly persecuted him with their 'envy and malicious gossip'.[7] Sercy alludes to a plot against the two brothers, but he declares the failure of the 'deception' to harm a fraternal friendship that endures beyond death.

If the bookseller's comments are accurate, they suggest that the accusation against Abel was the result of a conspiracy against the family. It is perfectly possible that Le Bret's condemnation of Abel was unfounded, and that he had been presumed upon by enemies of the family, who had deliberately hidden their own involvement by casting the blame on Abel. If it wasn't Abel who was responsible for Cyrano's imprisonment, then these same shadowy enemies somehow managed to orchestrate Cyrano's commitment to an asylum under Abel's name, without Abel having genuinely given his consent. This would probably not have been a particularly difficult task and would only have required money and the knowledge of the right palms to grease. Cyrano's own suspects of choice, the Jesuit brotherhood, certainly had the funds and connections to pull off such a thing. Sercy argues that Cyrano's brother was no more than an unknowing scapegoat. Abel could have been complicit in the plot to silence his troublesome brother and rival for the family fortune. Sercy explicitly states that Abel was his brother's heir, inheriting not only Cyrano's half of the estate but all of his literary production too, and there is some indication that Sercy was unsure what Abel's reaction to the publication of the *New Works* would be.

In the course of his letter, Sercy makes his own contribution to the Cyrano legend. Following in the path laid down by Cyrano himself, he draws a comparison with Alexander the Great and points out the fact that, like his hero, Cyrano was not the sort to live to a quiet old age. In a sad presentiment of his own fate, Cyrano had written in celebration of legendary heroes such as Hercules, Achilles, Alexander and Caesar, who had lived fast and died young. All of them, he noted approvingly, died before the age of forty. Sercy conjures up a vision of Cyrano as an 'incomparable genius', who, having exhausted the limitations of the earth, the moon and the sun, was forced to flee to the 'palace of the gods' in order to escape from these worlds 'too narrow for his ambition'.[8]

Whether Abel was an ally or an enemy, his situation could not have been further removed from that of his brother. Cyrano may already have been on the run from the late 1640s onwards (the date of the initial manuscript circulation of *The Voyage to the Moon*). Records show that Abel married a certain Michelle de Marcy on 1 July 1649, and settled with her in his father's house, living the rest of his life in the same faubourg as his parents before him. The family home was in rue Saint-Jacques in the parish of Saint-Jacques du Haut-Pas. Abel fathered a son Abel-Pierre and a daughter Marie-Catherine, whose births Cyrano did not live long enough to see. Cyrano's life, unlike his brother's, was far from settled, and what few clues remain to his domestic situation in the last few years of his life speak of upheaval and instability. In August 1650, he was staying with Monsieur Barat in the main street of the Faubourg Saint-Jacques. During the winter of 1651, he was in a different parish, Saint-Nicolas-des-Champs, in the inauspiciously named Cemetery Street. The spring of 1653 found him still in the same parish, but in a different street, the rather more appealing sounding Fountain Street.

In Le Bret's preface, he goes to some lengths to establish the broad network of supporters and friends that Cyrano had succeeded in building up. He mentions some twenty-five of them by name. This is naturally, a testament to the great swordsman's dual nature; while he could be antagonistic, angry and difficult he could also be charming, funny and loyal. He had endeared himself to many of his contemporaries and the image of his friends' desperate search for him after his mysterious disappearance is a touching one, but not all of those who were involved in taking care of Cyrano in the final months of his life were motivated purely by affection.

Tanneguy des Boisclair's involvement with the dying rebel is at first glance somewhat difficult to explain. Temperamentally, the two men had little in common and, unlike Rouhault, Le Bret or Le Royer de Prade, Tanneguy did not have a long-standing close, personal relationship with the poet. Instead, Tanneguy was part of the circle of devout Catholics centred around the charismatic Mother Superior of the Convent of the Daughters of the Cross, in which Cyrano's sister and cousin were both nuns. La Mère Marguerite de Jésus was rumoured to be so persuasive and appealing that young women were afraid to pay a visit to her nunnery, for fear of being 'charmed' by her into giving up their chances of matrimony and a family by taking the veil. Le Bret refers to the Mother Superior as someone who took a particular interest in Cyrano, and mentions that she attempted to introduce him to various useful acquaintances. This determined and energetic old lady seems to have made full use of the privilege of her position to involve herself in the lives of those around her, in a fashion that verged on the managerial. She lends a crucial note of solid respectability to Le Bret's epitaph and the list of Cyrano's friends, but the devoted biographer has to tread a fine line between praising her involvement with his friend's destiny, and admitting that Cyrano resisted her interference and neglected to cultivate the improving acquaintances she had hoped to procure for him. Cyrano's patron the Duc d'Arpajon was a benefactor of the convent and, given that the works were still going through the press at the time of the attack on Cyrano and his subsequent imprisonment, it may be that Mère Marguerite had a hand in preventing him from cancelling publication altogether.

Le Bret also notes the presence of the real Roxane at Cyrano's side in the final months of his life and he eulogizes her as a supremely pious and charitable woman. He credits Mme de Neuvillette with effecting such a change in his friend that he began to see free thought as monstrous, and to be sufficiently disgusted with the world to be ready for the next. Le Bret's depiction of a penitent Cyrano, meekly responding to the insistent appeals for repentance made by this circle of devout Catholics, is not entirely convincing. He also seems to have engaged in a little censorship of his own, as the edition of Cyrano's works that he supervised through the presses has gaps left in the text where the most outrageous and blasphemous passages should be. Le Bret explains away these gaps with an implausible tale of a break in that had entailed the loss of some of Cyrano's papers. Le Bret was ordained in 1656, and it is hard not to see the timing as significant. Finally free of his friend's powerful anti-establishment influence, Le Bret returned to the Catholic fold. There is one simple fact that emerges in his account of Cyrano's supposed deathbed conversion that he cannot disguise, however hard he tries to lessen its significance. Just five days before he died, Cyrano had fled from Tanneguy's house and the ministrations of his cousin and her Mother Superior, in order to return to the peace and tranquillity of the countryside.

Cyrano breathed his last on 28 July 1655, at the age of thirty-six. The parish records show that he died at the house of his cousin Pierre, in Sannois, a small village just outside Paris, on the fringes of his beloved valley of Chevreuse. This last-minute flight from repentance and respectability speaks volumes, casting significant doubt on the accuracy of Le Bret's assurance that Cyrano died a truly Christian death, regretting his freethinking, rebellious past. Father Garasse once wrote that: 'True freedom of the spirit consists in simply and sensibly believing all that the Church proposes, indifferently and without distinction.'[9] It is difficult to imagine Cyrano renouncing everything he ever believed in and fought for to accept a position of such unthinking conformity. Le Bret attempts to shore up his vision of a repentant Cyrano by recounting an exchange that passed between them near the end. Cyrano apparently quoted the classical author Tibullus on wasted youth, adding: 'no one has ever regretted as deeply as I do, so many beautiful days squandered'. As evidence of Cyrano's supposed Christian resignation this is decidedly flimsy. Tibullus was a pagan philosopher-poet whose four books of Elegies deal with his turbulent love affairs and his profound attachment to the natural world. He longed for tranquility but lived a passionate and occasionally violent existence. Like Cyrano, Tibullus died in his mid-thirties and he wrote with anguished lyricism about the fleeting nature of human existance. Rather than repenting his sins and focusing on the afterlife Cyrano's thoughts seem to have been playing on the intellectual achivements he had left unfinished, as for example, his scientific treatise, 'the fragment of physics' that would never be completed, the third volume of his interstellar adventures, *The Voyage to the Stars*, that would never see the light of day, and the countless works of his overflowing imagination that he had not yet even begun to frame or capture.

Despite the terrible melancholy that seems to have gripped Cyrano as he felt his hold on life weakening, he continued to make jokes about death and Le Bret's preface opens with a comical vision of Cyrano's ghost, that he hints was directly inspired (possibly even dictated) by the man himself. Even in the afterlife, Cyrano is shown refusing to fall in with expectations. Rather than tormenting superstitious mortals with any of the classic ghostly activities like rattling his chains in an attic or knocking over furniture, his ghost is described as being 'in excellent humour as always'. Paradoxical to the last, the ghostly Cyrano attacks the sort of credulous fools who believe in ghosts.

Cyrano's attitude to death in his earlier works had always been deliberately prosaic and fearlessly flippant. In the letter 'On a Coward', his fictional coward makes a paradoxical boast: 'But does he think he will have beaten me when he has taken away my life? On the contrary, I will become all the more terrible and I am convinced that he will not be able to look upon me fifteen days later without being frightened by me.'[10] In the same letter, the coward contradicts the popular, gentlemanly notion that a glorious death is worth more than a long but insignificant life, remarking that, 'the least flea still living is worth more than Alexander the Great deceased'. This was written for comic effect but, by the time of his death, Cyrano was no longer the headstrong, reckless youth in pursuit of death or glory, who laughed at such cowardice. He had become a more mature and disillusioned man, who had seen the grim reality of such sacrifices and felt their tragic futility. Perhaps he also came to see the sense of lines that he had written originally in jest: that a man may risk his life before the age of thirty, because he does not know much of life, and so does not know what he stands to lose, but that to do so after that age, 'he would be crazy to risk it having known it'. Cyrano must surely have been aware that, if his life was ebbing away day by day, he had the freethinking rebellious stance that he had taken against the church to thank for it. Thus, it is hard to imagine that he would have found much comfort in the absolution promised by that same institution. It has been suggested that Molière modelled his atheistic anti-hero Dom Juan in part on Cyrano, and there is certainly an echo of Cyrano's provocative wit in the following exchange between Dom Juan and his manservant Sganarelle:

Sganarelle: People must believe in something in this world. What do you believe?
Dom Juan: What do I believe?
Sganarelle: Yes.
Dom Juan: I believe that two and two are four, Sganarelle, and that twice four are eight.[11]

In his short lifetime, Cyrano had succeeded in assuring that, for better or for worse, he would not soon be forgotten. He was a virtuoso of spin and the fact that he was known as a Gascon noble within his own lifetime is testament to the success of his image-making. Ultimately, that very success was to see him eclipsed by his own glory. Although he managed to project his flamboyant legend into the future, he could not control the direction it would take. But even in his lifetime, it already seemed clear that this was a man whose story would never die. Cyrano's good-humoured ghost has taken on many guises. His death was only the beginning of another story, a haunting that has so far lasted for three and a half centuries and counting.

In the immediate aftermath of his death more voices emerged praising his extraordinary, 'generous audacity', and admiring the brilliance of his 'uncommon mind', and the 'noble path to the heavens' that he had chosen to take. In the end, his independence and determined rejection of all authority and all conformity had led to his death. From Rostand's perspective, some two hundred years later, this made him the ideal symbol for every failure, every forgotten man who had ever struggled in vain against the vagaries of existence. But perhaps a more appropriate representation of Cyrano's 'failure' is that offered by the rebellious monk Giordano Bruno, who wrote, in anticipation of his own spectacular fall from grace: 'I am satisfied with my lofty enterprise; if the soul does not attain the desired target of its ardent zeal, what does that matter? It is enough to burn with such a noble fire; it is enough that I will have escaped towards the sky and delivered myself from the base multitude.'

Cyrano's own escape towards the sky did not prevent more earth-bound spirits from trying to drag his memory through the mud. A pamphlet circulated after his death, describing his apocryphal battle with a performing monkey. The first printed version of the pamphlet dates from 1704; it has been suggested that it may have circulated earlier in manuscript form and that the authorship may therefore be attributed to Dassoucy, who died in 1677. There is no proof to support this supposition. The pamphlet included a ridiculous description of Cyrano's appearance drawn for maximum comic effect: 'His head was almost entirely bereft of hair, one could count every strand from ten paces away. His eyes were lost under his eyebrows; his nose, wide at the stem and hooked, was rather like those of the green and yellow chatterboxes [parakeets] that they bring back from the Americas.'

According to the pamphlet, Cyrano found himself accosted by a crowd of lackeys gathered to watch the performing monkey on the Pont Neuf. One young man knocked off his hat while another flicked him on the nose and cried out: 'Is that really your everyday nose? What a devil of a nose! Back off a couple of steps won't you it's preventing me from seeing the show.' At which point, Cyrano prepared to fight single-handedly against his 'twenty or thirty aggressors' and found himself, in the confusion, stabbing to death the little monkey who was dressed as a cavalier. Sadly, such venomous attacks on Cyrano had as vigorous a life as the positive image-building he had achieved through his life and works. Théophile Gautier clearly used this parody as a source when writing his portrait of Cyrano in his *Grotesques*, and Rostand's Cyrano is a direct descendant from this distorted image. It is said that, in order to create just the right false nose for the actor Coquelin (the first ever incarnation of the stage Cyrano) the costume department tried and rejected over fifty different wax noses. In a letter published in *The Times* newspaper on 2 June 1931, a response is offered to a previously published letter that had posed the question 'Did Cyrano have a big nose?' The writer describes the 1654 portrait engraving of Cyrano, and reveals that he had personally demanded of Coquelin why he wore a big bulbous 'snout' rather than a high arched nose like that belonging to the real Cyrano – the answer given was that the arched version had made Coquelin squint.

The identification of Dassoucy as the author responsible for the tale of Cyrano's ignominious battle with the performing monkey is debatable, particularly since the pamphlet was first published some twenty-seven years after Dassoucy's death. There is no doubt, however, that Dassoucy was responsible for instigating the very first public criticisms of Cyrano after the great swordsman's death. In his memoirs, Dassoucy's references to Cyrano are designed to suggest that the great freethinker was little more than a dangerous madman. Dassoucy picks up on the idea of Cyrano's ghost continuing to haunt the land of the living and refers to 'the vengeful shade of that furious soldier'. The word 'furious' is weighted with significance since, at the time, it implied insanity as well as anger – it is the word that recurs most often in the descriptions of asylum inmates. In the context in which this reference appears, Dassoucy ridicules his own craven cowardice with his characteristic self-deprecating humour:

> But you also do not know how the late Mr D[e] B[ergerac], angry at having angered me, came to my abode to be reconciled with me. I was terribly afraid on seeing the pistol holster that he had brought with him because he was taking it to be repaired and this caused me to flee France for Italy; and even after his death, travelling from Paris to Turin by the light of the moon, my fear of my own shadow caused me to throw myself in a river, convinced that it was the vengeful shade of that furious soldier, terror of the living, and nightmare of the brave, who was at my heels in order to avenge himself for the capon affair.

Dassoucy's comical 'confession', that he fled the country out of fear of Cyrano, neatly conceals the fact that he was really forced to flee because of his conduct towards the retinue of small boys he kept as pages and trained as choirboys. Dassoucy's abuse of the young men he had in his power led to his imprisonment on more than one occasion and, if he left France, it was not to escape from Cyrano but from the scandal. He was pursued not by one vengeful shade but by many.

In the *Menagiana* of 1693, Dassoucy's suggestions were further embroidered upon in a fanciful account of Cyrano's death:

> I believe that when he wrote his *Voyage to the Moon*, he already had the first quarter in his head. He died mad. The first public sign he gave of his madness was to go to midday Mass at la Mercy in breeches and a nightcap without a doublet. He hadn't a penny when he fell into a severe illness from which he died; and without M. Sainthe-Marthe, who had the charity to provide for his necessity he would have been obliged to go to the poor house.[12]

A year later, on publishing a new edition of the *Menagiana*, the author had added a further inaccuracy: 'He died at the Hôtel d'Arpajon where the duke of that name had given him refuge.'[13] This is a neat illustration of the obfuscating powers of unbridled gossip in action. We have already seen that Cyrano was far from bankrupt when he died, the registers of the parish prove that he died at his cousin's house in Sannois, not at d'Arpajon's home in central Paris, and the picture of him attending mass in a nightcap is an amusing, but not particularly relevant or convincing detail. As for the statement that Cyrano was slowly falling under the influence of the moon in the course of his writing and died a full-blown lunatic, nothing could be further from the truth.

Thankfully, Dassoucy's merry spite was far from Cyrano's only epitaph. In 1703, an Englishman named David Russen published a book-length review of Cyrano's *Voyage to the Moon*, entitled *Iter Lunare*. Russen was an enthusiastic admirer of Cyrano, who declared it impossible to read *Voyage to the Moon*, 'without abundance of delight'. He also took issue with the work being labelled as 'a comical history', insisting that, since it contained 'many discourses worth the observation of the most learned', that 'though it be interlaced with much matter of mirth, wit and invention . . . yet it is throughout carried on with that strength of argument, force of reason and solidity of judgement', that instead of comical it 'may deserve the Epithete of the *most Rational History of the Government of the Moon*'.[14] Here was someone who would vigorously deny those allegations of insanity levelled at Cyrano. Even with the support of dedicated admirers from Russen to Rostand, and despite his important influence on writers of genius like Molière, Voltaire and Jonathan Swift, Cyrano's literary heritage has been obscured for a long time. He penned an experimental and successful comedy, an audacious and powerful tragedy, letters that ranged from the passionately seductive, through lyrical description and sparkling wit to the bitterest invective and a novel that pushed back the boundaries of inventiveness and hilarity. And yet none of this was enough to rival his most creative work of all – his life story. As often as Cyrano is misrepresented as a person, he is also undervalued as a writer.

After Russen, Cyrano's posthumous reputation continued to fluctuate for the next two hundred years; those who actually read his work were inspired and delighted, while those who contented themselves with repeating stale slanders continued to exaggerate his failings and to denigrate his talent. It was not until the advent of Rostand's play that the two extremes were reconciled. Rostand crafted a compelling story from the disparate elements of Cyrano's life and legend and, in doing so, unleashed an avalanche of renewed interest in his hero. In 1908, a decade on from the opening of the play, a reviewer for *The Times* declared that: 'Not to have seen Coquelin's Cyrano is to have failed in life.' There have been many more unmissably wonderful incarnations of the swashbuckling hero since then. In 1992, Robert Lindsay's wonderfully funny and touching performance was perfectly pitched between bravado and tenderness. Derek Jacobi's storming performance in the RSC's 1983 production inspired choreographer David Bintley to go away and create *Cyrano* the ballet.

Bintley's first attempt in 1991 was a costly flop for the Royal Ballet. However in February 2007 the Birmingham Royal Ballet staged his new version with a new score and an amended choreography. The new production was well reviewed, with particular praise being heaped on Robert Parker in the title role. In a neat little twist to the tale, this was to be Parker's last performance before leaving ballet to become a pilot. David Bintley explained his persistence in attempting to retell the story through dance, with a reference to the overwhelming appeal of Cyrano's legend: 'He's a magnificent character; he's endlessly fascinating.' It has been suggested that the failure of Bintley's first production stemmed partly from the importance of language to the play – it is after all a story about eloquence and poetry, written by a supremely eloquent poet.

In 1936, Franco Alfano staged an opera of *Cyrano de Bergerac* which struggled, to a lesser extent with the same fundamental difficulty. The work has endured all the same; Montpellier Opera's lively 2003 production, starring Roberto Alagna, was given a second run in 2006. Although Alagna and Parker both gave charismatic and appealing performances, both productions, whatever their successes, also inevitably highlighted this innate problem with all adaptations of Rostand. The original work is so flawless that, however rapturous the singing, however expressive the dancing, the necessary cuts and alterations diminish the piece.

On film, two interpretations in particular loom large. In 1950, George Clooney's uncle, the actor José Ferrer gained the extremely rare distinction of winning an Oscar and a Tony for the same part – Cyrano de Bergerac. He also reprised the role in 1964 for the French film adaptation of *Cyrano and D'Artagnan*. More recently, in 1990, Jean Paul Rappeneau directed a lavish production starring Gérard Depardieu in the title role. Depardieu excels in the scenes of bombast and fury but also offers a genuinely moving and nuanced portrayal. He is well supported by Anne Brochet, who manages to bring an appealing mixture of fragility and courage to the part of Roxane, and by Vincent Perez, whose Christian is no mere foil for Cyrano's blazing wit but a courageous and noble individual in his own right.

The comedian Steve Martin had long contemplated modernizing

the play, but it was a friend's suggestion that he give Cyrano a happy ending that finally triggered him to sit down and write a screenplay. The resulting romantic comedy *Roxanne* (1987) is an outstanding example of the genre. Cyrano is metamorphosed into the small-town fire-chief C. D. Bales (played by Martin at his mercurial best), and Roxane becomes an astrophysicist named Roxanne Kowalski (played by a radiant Darryl Hannah). In an even looser adaptation, the 1996 romantic comedy *The Truth about Cats and Dogs* by Audrey Wells, took Cyrano's crippling insecurity about his appearance and transposed it to a charming, wisecracking female lead, Janeane Garofalo. The most unusual film adaptation of them all has to be *Samurai Saga* (1960) starring Toshiro Mifune. The Cyrano character has transformed again, this time into a Samurai warrior, and his story is retold with all the passion and humour of the original. The autumn leaves that fall in the final scene are transformed into a dying fall of cherry blossom, and the Samurai code of courage, honour and self-sacrifice forms a fascinating reflection of Cyrano's own lofty ideals. It is an unexpected, but appropriate direction for the legend to have taken in its progress ever onwards and always 'towards the sky'.

Epilogue

On arriving in Bergerac by train, the first thing the traveller sees is a large hoarding advertising the local radio station Cyrano FM. The town centre is a short stroll away and other Cyrano-related distractions are on offer at every turn; see a film at the local Le Cyrano cinema, go for a drink in the Cyrano Hotel Bar, stay a night in the pretty Cyrano and Roxane-themed guest house, or just simply go for a wander down Cyrano Street. The fictional Cyrano's face is everywhere, and his name is used to sell everything from foie gras to window blinds. Local businesses are proud to identify themselves with a national hero; the 'Crémerie Cyrano' sells a variety of cheeses; 'Alu Cyrano' offers aluminium guttering; the 'Allo Cyrano' taxi company takes locals and tourists from A to B; 'Cyrano Colis' provides courier services, and so on and so forth. At the tourist office, the friendly staff are well used to enquiries about the city's adopted son. Visitor numbers are on the increase, particularly since the huge, international success of the film starring Gérard Depardieu. Every year, enthusiasts travel thousands of miles from all over the world to pay homage to their swashbuckling hero. In the tourist office, these pilgrims are gently disabused of the notion that they can see the house where Cyrano lived or Roxane's balcony, and then directed towards the two statues of Cyrano that grace the picturesque old town.

The first statue, by the contemporary artist Mauro Corda, is a recent addition, having been unveiled in July 2005. Cast in polychrome bronze, it stands 2.4 metres high and dominates the small square beside the Church of St Jacques, at the top of a hill. The square is surrounded by quaint half-timbered houses, and constantly circled by an ever-shifting tide of admiring, camera-wielding tourists. Cyrano's eyes are turned heavenward, reflecting his preoccupation with outer space, but also in order to give him a suitable dreamy, romantic air. His right hand rests lightly on the hilt of his gleaming sword and his large floppy hat is held loosely in his left. Corda used a model for Cyrano's imposing frame but created the face from his imagination; as he put it – 'there was no question of just sticking a Pinocchio nose on him'. A little further down the hill, in a quieter, flower-strewn, leafy square, the older statue is in a slightly sorry state. Cyrano's nose has been broken off and stolen (once again) and someone has attempted corrective surgery with a gigantic blob of chewing gum. This statue of Cyrano, the work of the sculptor Varoqueaux, has been a feature in the town since November 1977, and it would seem that familiarity has bred a degree of contempt.

In a little antique store opposite the statue there was a bundle of sentimental postcards from the 1920s for sale when I visited. Flicking through them, it became clear that they were all addressed to one man by a variety of different female admirers. When I remarked on the adoring tone of the letters and asked about buying the collection – the gentleman who had been engaged in a long haggling debate about rent with the owner of the shop asked me with a wink if I were planning on using them to get some tips, and 'doing a Cyrano'. The final paradox of Cyrano's story is that the real Cyrano is so totally overshadowed by his fictional counterpart, that the place where he is most vividly present in modern-day France is Bergerac – a city that the real Cyrano probably never even visited.

On leaving the town, I picked up a copy of French *Marie Claire* only to find an article about five female Cyranos, or 'Cyranettes', as the author dubbed them. The women had agreed to be photographed in profile showing off their dramatic features, for an article entitled 'I've got a big nose, so what?' All were attractive and successful, and unanimous in celebrating their large noses as a sign of their individuality. This inheritance from the original Cyrano has at least filtered down the ages intact. As for Roxane, it would not be until 1997 that the French novelist Amélie Nothomb would deliver her post-feminist revenge. In a reworking of the Cyrano legend, Nothomb tells the story of the hideously ugly anti-hero Epiphane Otos, and his murderous love for the deliriously beautiful Ethel. Nothomb's heroine soundly rejects Otos and, in doing so, points out the double standard he attempts to impose on her. He expects her to love him for his soul and to overlook his outward appearance, but he himself is capable of no such greatness since he has chosen her, with all her beauty for his adoration, rather than an ugly girl with a pure soul. The real Cyrano would have delighted in the searing honesty of Nothomb's vicious little satire.

Ever since Rostand, Cyrano has become a sort of shorthand for an endearing incompetence in affairs of the heart. Witness an episode of the radio comedy *Hancock's Half Hour*, entitled 'Cyrano de Hancock', in which Sid falls in love with Hancock's forbidding secretary, Miss Pugh. Hancock's attempts to help him win her nearly end in catastrophe, as he finds himself unwillingly led to the altar in Sid's place. Only the benign incompetence of the registrar, played by Kenneth Williams, can save him, and in the confusion Hancock is granted an eleventh-hour reprieve of sorts, when he finds himself married to the registrar instead of Miss Pugh.

There are myriad modern references to Cyrano: from the

Filipino mobile phone ad featuring 'Cyrano de Bitoy', to the frenetic *Sesame Street* character, who stars in the 'Cyranose de Bergerac' edition of Monsterpiece Theatre. American high-school students post Cyrano-inspired videos on the Internet – these range from a spoof history channel documentary to the re-enactment of a duel, with Cyrano played by a stuffed penguin and his opponent by a toy frog, to a delirious three-part sequel to the play. My personal favourite of all the numerous references to Cyrano that occur in other texts is probably the exchange between Madeleine 'the stars are God's daisy chain' Bassett and Bertie Wooster in P. G. Wodehouse's *Right Ho, Jeeves*, in which Madeleine tells Bertie that he is like a modern-day Cyrano. Bertie has been desperately trying to promote the cause of Madeleine's sweetheart, his rather hopeless newt-loving friend, Gussie Fink-Nottle, largely because if their engagement fails he will be forced to marry her himself.

> 'You have a splendid, chivalrous soul.'
>
> 'Oh, no.'
>
> 'Yes, you have. You remind me of Cyrano.'
>
> 'Who?'
>
> 'Cyrano de Bergerac.'
>
> 'The chap with the nose?'
>
> 'Yes.'
>
> I can't say I was too pleased. I felt the old beak furtively. It was a bit on the prominent side, perhaps, but, dash it, not in the Cyrano class.

Cyrano himself was a big fan of the nose gag, but it is still a little disheartening to realize that the man who was once a wild adventurer, explorer of the known and unknown universe, is now seen only as a funny-looking romantic failure. Father Garasse, nemesis of the freethinkers, wrote angrily about their need not to follow the expected path: 'never judging according to common understanding but always going off at tangent, swerving and forging a new path'. This refusal of the norm was the very quality that Cyrano's admirers most prized in him, a man who found the wide world too narrow for his lavish imagination:

> *The fire of his mind and his selfless daring,*
> *Roamed through the vast deserts of earth and sky,*
> *But finding them always of too narrow compass,*
> *He broke open their ramparts to pass into the universe.*

Audiences love the fictional Cyrano because he's a heroic failure, noble but cursed. The original Cyrano is sharper, funnier and, ironically, more modern than the romantic hero whose creation he inspired. The tragedy of the real Cyrano is that, despite his extraordinary independence of mind, his heroic courage, his sharp wit, his unfailing good humour and his riotous creativity, he is generally only remembered as 'the chap with the nose'. The combined extravagances of Cyrano's life and works can ultimately be refined to a single overriding message to humanity, paradoxical perhaps, coming from the dangerous duellist, but no less heartfelt for that. After condemning the hero of *The Voyage to the Sun* to death, for the crime of being human, the leader of the republic of birds (a dove) hears evidence that he once set free a caged bird. His liberation of a fellow creature redeems the condemned man. The judgement is reversed and he is sent on his way with the following blessing:

'Go in peace then and live joyfully.'

Notes

CHAPTER ONE

1. Rostand, quoted in Jean Suberville, *Edmond Rostand*, Paris, 1921, p.iii.
2. Edmond Rostand, *Cyrano de Bergerac*, trans. A. Burgess, Hutchinson, 1985, p.171.
3. William Archer, *Study and Stage: A Year-Book of Criticism*, London, 1899, p.50.
4. C. E. Montague, *Dramatic Values*, London, 1911, p.46.
5. Edmond Rostand, *Cyrano de Bergerac*, Paris, 1897.
6. Coquelin, Letter to Edmond Rostand, *Le Petit Parisien*, 1897.
7. Sarah Bernhardt, Letter to Constant Coquelin, *Le Figaro*, 29 December 1897.
8. William Archer, *Study and* Stage: *A Year-Book of Criticism*, London, 1899, p.50.
9. Quoted in Pierre Brun, *Cyrano de Bergerac – Gentilhomme Parisien, l'histoire et la légende*, p.6.
10. Pierre Brun, *Cyrano de Bergerac – Gentilhomme Parisien, l'histoire et la légende*, 1909, p.7.
11. Pierre Brun, *Savinien de Cyrano Bergerac – Gentilhomme Parisien, l'histoire et la légende d'après des documents inédits*, Paris, 1893, p.4.

CHAPTER TWO

1. First published by Professor M. Alcover in her article 'Le grand-père de Cyrano était-il sénonais?' in *La Lettre Clandestine*, no.13, Paris: Presses de l'Université de Paris-Sorbonne, 2005, pp.261–78
2. J. L. Flandrin, *La revue XVII siecle, Conference 1972–3*, quoted in P. Ariès, *L'enfant et la vie familiale sous L'Ancien Régime*, Editions du Seuil, 1973, p.15.
3. Anonymous, *Le Caquet de l'Accouchée*, 1622.
4. See Michel de Montaigne, 'De l'Affection des Pères aux enfants', *Essays*, II, Gallimard, 1965, pp.77–98.
5. Cyrano de Bergerac, *Les Etats et Empire de la Lune et du Soleil*, Paris: Folio, 2004, p.117.

   NB Cyrano's two-volume novel *The Other World* was published in two sections and is known by various titles. The title that Cyrano gave the work

The States and Empires of the Moon and Sun was a deliberate parody of a contemporary work of travel writing but this title was not used in the first posthumous publications. For the sake of simplicity the work will be referred to by the title of each volume as *The Voyage to the Moon* and *The Voyage to the Sun*, these being the names by which the works were most familiar to Cyrano's contemporaries.

6. Cyrano de Bergerac, *Les Etats et Empire de la Lune et du Soleil*, Paris: Folio, 2004, p.115.
7. Cyrano de Bergerac, *Les Etats et Empire de la Lune et du Soleil*, Paris: Folio, 2004, p.118.
8. Edmond Rostand, *Cyrano de Bergerac*, Flammarion, 1989, pp.116–17.
9. Edmond Rostand, *Cyrano de Bergerac*, trans. A. Burgess, Hutchinson, 1985, p.61.
10. See E. Magne, *Les Erreurs de documentation de Cyrano de Bergerac*, Paris, 1898.
11. Cyrano de Bergerac, Letter XI 'D'une Maison de Campagne' in *Les Oeuvres Comiques Galantes et Littéraires*, Paris, 1962, p.40.
12. King Louis XIII, quoted in M. Monestier, *Duels*, Paris, 1991, p.152.
13. Cyrano de Bergerac, Letter XVII 'D'un Songe', *Les Oeuvres Comiques Galantes et Littéraires*, Paris, 1962, p.80.
14. Héroard, *Journal sur L'Enfance et la Jeunesse de Louis XIII*, quoted in P. Ariès, *L'enfant et la vie familiale sous L'Ancien Régime* Editions du Seuil, 1973, p.79.
15. Henri Le Bret, 'Préface' (1657) In *Les Etats et Empire de la Lune et du Soleil*, Honoré Champion, 2004, p.483
16. Alexandre Dubois, *Journal d'un Curé de Campagne au XVIIe siècle*, Henri Platelle (ed.) Paris, 1965, p.29.
17. Alexandre Dubois, *Journal d'un Curé de Campagne au XVIIe siècle*, Paris, 1965, p.71.
18. Alexandre Dubois, *Journal d'un Curé de Campagne au XVIIe siècle*, Paris, 1965, p.130.
19. Père Lejeune, *Du devoir des pères*, 1620. Quoted in R. Briggs, *Communities of Belief*, Oxford: Clarendon Press, 1989.
20. Henri Le Bret, 'Préface' (1657) In *Les Etats et Empire de la Lune et du Soleil*, Honoré Champion, 2004, p.483
21. Cyrano de Bergerac, *Le Pédant Joué* in *Oeuvres Comiques, Galantes et Littéraires*, Paris, 1962, p.285.

CHAPTER THREE

1. Cyrano de Bergerac, *Les Etats et Empire de la Lune et du Soleil*, Paris: Folio, 2004, p.146.
2. Cyrano de Bergerac, *Les Etats et Empire de la Lune et du Soleil*, Paris: Folio, 2004, p.115.
3. Charles Sorel, *Histoire Comique de Francion*, Editions Gallimard, 1996, p.551.
4. Henri de la Trémoille, *Letter to his son*, 1662, quoted in J. Dewald, *Aristocratic*

experience and the origins of Modern Culture, University of California Press, 1993, p. 73.

5. Henri Le Bret, 'Préface' in *Les Etats et Empires de la Lune et du Soleil*, Honoré Champion, 2004, p.490
6. Théophile Gautier, *La France Littéraire* (1834): quoted in *Cyrano dans tous ses Etats,* ed. L. Calvié, Toulouse Anacharsis Editions, 2004, p.126.
7. Ibid., p.125.
8. Thomas Overbury, *Observations,* 1609, quoted in *France Observed in the 17th Century by British Travellers,* ed. J. Lough, Oriel Press, 1985, p.95.
9. Anonymous, *A New Journey*, 1715, quoted in *France Observed in the 17th Century by British Travellers*, ed. J. Lough, Oriel Press, 1985, p.106.
10. See Héroard, *Journal sur L'Enfance et la Jeunesse de Louis XIII*, 1868.
11. F. de Dainville, *La Naissance de L'Humanisme Moderne*, Paris, 1940, p.160.
12. Michel de Montaigne, *Essais* I, Gallimard, 1965, p.238.
13. Peter Heylyn, *Travels*, 1656, quoted in *France Observed in the 17th Century by British Travellers*, ed. J. Lough, Oriel Press, 1985, p.53.
14. James Howell, *Letters*, 1619, quoted in *France Observed in the 17th Century by British Travellers*, ed. J. Lough, Oriel Press, 1985, p.54.
15. Anonymous, *A New Journey*, 1715, quoted in *France Observed in the 17th Century by British Travellers*, ed. J. Lough, Oriel Press, 1985, p.107.
16. Maréchal de Caillière, *Les Fortunes de gens de qualité et des gentilhommes particuliers*, 1661, p.72.
17. Peter Heylyn, *Travels*, 1656. and J. Reresby, *Memoirs and Travels* quoted in *France Observed in the 17th Century by British Travellers*, ed. J. Lough, Oriel Press, 1985, p.92.
18. Maréchal de Caillière, *Les Fortunes de gens de qualité et des gentilhommes particuliers*, 1661, quoted in P. Ariès, *L'enfant et la vie familiale sous l'Ancien Régime*, Editions du Seuil, 1973, p.117.

CHAPTER FOUR

1. Nicolas Faret, *L'Honnête Homme ou l'art de plaire à la court*, 1630, quoted in J. Dewald, *Aristocratic experience and the origins of Modern Culture*, University of California Press, 1993, p.45.
2. Olivier de la Marche, *Traité de Duel,* 1436, quoted in Jean-Marie Constant, *La Noblesse française aux XVIe et XVIIe siècles*, Hachette, 1985, p.98
3. Ibid.
4. Ibid.
5. Henri Le Bret, 'Préface', in *Les Etats et Empires de la Lune et du Soleil*, Honoré Champion, 2004, p.484.
6. Théophile Gautier, *Le Capitaine Fracasse*, Paris, 1863, p.320.
7. Théophile Gautier, *Le Capitaine Fracasse*, Paris, 1863, p.320.
8. Jacques Prévot, *Cyrano de Bergerac Poète et Dramaturge*, 1978, p.7.
9. Jacques Prévot, *Cyrano de Bergerac Poète et Dramaturge*, 1978, p.7.
10. Pierre Charron, *Traité de la Sagesse*, Bk.III ch.iii, (1601) quoted in J. Cornette, *Le Roi de Guerre*, Paris, 1993, p.52.

11. Nicolas Faret, *L'Honnête Homme ou l'art de plaire à la court*, Paris, 1630, quoted in E. Schalk, *From Valor to Pedigree*, Princeton, 1986, p.145.
12. Pierre Fortin de la Hoguette, *Catéchisme royal*, Paris, 1650, p.16.
13. Corneille, *Le Cid*, ed. Eve, Cambridge University Press, 1924, p.10.

CHAPTER FIVE

1. Pierre Corneille, *Le Menteur*, 1643, Act I, sc.i, Magnard, 2002, p.21.
2. Le Bret, 'Préface' in *Les Etats et Empires de la Lune et du Soleil*, Honoré Champion, 2004, p.484.
3. Cardinal Richelieu, *Testament Politique*, quoted in F. Bluche, *Richelieu*, 2003, p.125.
4. Richelieu, *Mémoires*, quoted in M. Monestier, *Duels*, Paris, 1991, p.145.
5. J. Chenel de la Chapperonaye, *Revelations of the Solitary Hermit* (1617), quoted in F. Billacois, *The Duel: its Rise and Fall in Early Modern France*, Yale, 1990, p.83.
6. Quoted in R. J. Knecht, *Richelieu*, Longman, 1991, p.52.
7. Corneille, *Le Cid* (*a translation in Rhymed Couplets* by V. Cheng), University of Delaware Press, 1987, p.57.
8. Cyrano de Bergerac, *le Pédant Joué* in *Oeuvres Comiques, Galantes et Littéraires*, Paris, 1962, pp.278-9.
9. Quoted in M. Cuenin, *Le Duel sous L'Ancien Régime*, Paris, 1982, p.132.
10. Corneille, *Le Cid*, quoted in M. Cuenin, *Le Duel sous L'Ancien Régime*, Paris, 1982, p.115.
11. Lodowick Bryskett, *A Discourse of Civill Life*, New York: Da Capo Press, 1971, pp.64–5.
12. Molière, *Les Fâcheux (1661) in Oeuvres Complètes*, vol.1, Gallimard, 1983, p.378.
    Eraste: *On m'a vu soldat avant que courtisan;*
    J'ai servi quatorze ans, et je crois être en passe
    De pouvoir d'un tel pas me tirer avec grâce,
    Et de ne craindre point qu'a quelque lâcheté
    Le refus de mon bras me puisse être imputé.
    Un duel met les gens en mauvaise posture,
    Et notre roi n'est pas un monarque en peinture:
    Il sait faire obéir les plus grands de l'État,
    Et je trouve qu'il fait en digne potentat.
    Quand il faut le servir, j'ai du coeur pour le faire;
    Mais je ne m'en sens point quand il faut lui déplaire;
    Je me fais de son ordre une suprême loi:
    Pour lui déobéir cherche un autre que moi.
    Translation by H. van Laun, The Works of Molière, Edinburgh, 1875, p.107
13. Bussy-Rabutin, *Les Mémoires de Messire Roger de Rabutin, Comte de Bussy, Lieutenant Général des Armées du Roy et mestre de camp général de la cavalerie légère*, Paris, 1696, pp.27–8.
14. Comte de Forbin, *Mémoires du Comte de Forbin*, Paris, 1993, p.40.
15. René de Ceriziers, *Le Héros français ou l'idée du grand capitaine* (1645), quoted

in Briost, Drevillon, Serna, *Croiser le Fer – Violence et culture de l'épée dans la France Moderne*, 2002, p.270.

16. Jean de La Taille, *Discours Notable sur les Duels* (1607) quoted in M. Cuenin, *Le Duel sous L'Ancien Régime*, Paris, 1982, p.27.
17. Rostand, *Cyrano de Bergerac*, trans. A. Burgess, Hutchinson, 1985, p.37.

CHAPTER SIX

1. Cyrano de Bergerac, 'Lettre à M. Gerzan, sur son *Triomphe des Dames*' in *Oeuvres Comiques, Galantes et Littéraires*, Paris, 1962, p.65.
2. Quoted in F. Bluche, *Richelieu*, Paris, 2003, p.140.
3. Cyrano de Bergerac, Lettre 'Sur le Blocus d'une Ville' in *Oeuvres Comiques, Galantes et Littéraires*, Paris, 1962, p.114. NB. Professor M. Alcover makes a compelling case for a reading of this work as an account of the siege of Paris but Mouzon is the more traditionally accepted interpretation.
4. Cyrano de Bergerac, Lettre 'Contre les médecins' in *Oeuvres Comiques, Galantes et Littéraires*, Paris, 1962, p.171.
5. Michel de Montaigne, 'De la Liberté de Conscience', Essais II, Gallimard, 1965, p.434.
6. H. J. C. von Grimmelshausen, *The Adventures of Simplicius Simplicissimus* (translated by G. Schulz-Behrend), Camden House, Columbia, 1993, p.26.
7. H. J. C. von Grimmelshausen, *The Adventures of Simplicius Simplicissimus* (translated by G. Schulz-Behrend), Camden House, Columbia, 1993, p.26.
8. Quoted in *France Observed in the 17th Century by British Travellers*, ed. John Lough, Oriel Press, 1985, p.168.
9. Lady Fanshawe, *Memoirs*, quoted in *France Observed in the 17th Century by British Travellers*, ed. J. Lough, Oriel Press, 1985, p.167.
10. Cyrano de Bergerac, *Les Etats et Empire de la Lune et du Soleil*, Paris: Folio, 2004, p.106.
11. Quoted in *France Observed in the 17th Century by British Travellers*, ed. J. Lough, Oriel Press, 1985, p.95.
12. Quoted in G. Parker, *The Thirty Years War*, Routledge, 1997, p.270.
13. Cyrano de Bergerac, *Les Etats et Empire de la Lune et du Soleil*, Paris: Folio, 2004, p.106.
14. Cyrano de Bergerac, 'Contre les Frondeurs', *Oeuvres Comiques, Galantes et Littéraires*, Paris, 1962, pp.83–4.
15. Cyrano de Bergerac, *Les Etats et Empire de la Lune et du Soleil*, Paris, Folio, 2004, p.147.
16. Cyrano de Bergerac, *Les Etats et Empire de la Lune et du Soleil*, Paris, Folio, 2004, pp.147–8.
17. Archevêque d'Embrun, quoted in M. Cuenin, *Le Duel sous L'Ancien Régime*, Paris, 1982, p.165.

CHAPTER SEVEN

1. Le Bret, 'Préface' in *Les Etats et Empires de la Lune et du Soleil*, Honoré Champion, 2004. p.484.

2. Cyrano de Bergerac, *Les Etats et Empire de la Lune et du Soleil*, Paris: Folio, 2004, p.79.
3. Cyrano de Bergerac, *Les Etats et Empire de la Lune et du Soleil*, Paris: Folio, 2004, p.79.
4. Tristan L'Hermite, 'La Servitude' in *Le Page Disgracié,* ed. J. Serroy, Presse Universitaire de Grenoble, 1980, p.9.
5. Primi Visconti, quoted in W. D. Howarth, *Molière – A Playwright and his Audience,* Cambridge University Press, 1982, p.50.
6. Guez de Balzac, Letter (1637) quoted in W. D. Howarth, *Molière – A Playwright and his Audience*, Cambridge University Press, 1982, p.50.
7. Rostand, *Cyrano de Bergerac*, trans. A. Burgess, Hutchinson, 1985, p.44.
8. Cyrano de Bergerac, Lettre 'Le Duelliste' in *Oeuvres Comiques, Galantes et Littéraires*, Paris, 1962, p.68.
9. Cyrano de Bergerac, Lettre 'Contre un faux brave' in *Oeuvres Comiques, Galantes et Littéraires*, Paris, 1962, p.172.
10. Cyrano de Bergerac, Lettre 'Le Duelliste' in *Oeuvres Comiques, Galantes et Littéraires*, Paris, 1962, p.67.
11. Cyrano de Bergerac, Lettre 'Le Duelliste' in *Oeuvres Comiques, Galantes et Littéraires*, Paris, 1962, p.68.
12. Cyrano de Bergerac, Lettre 'Le Duelliste' in *Oeuvres Comiques, Galantes et Littéraires*, Paris, 1962, p.68.
13. E. Magne, *Le Chevalier de Lignières*, Paris, 1920, p.27.
14. Rostand, *Cyrano de Bergerac*, trans. A. Burgess, Hutchinson, 1985, pp.69–70.
15. Rostand, *Cyrano de Bergerac*, trans. A. Burgess, Hutchinson, 1985, pp.70–1.
16. Le Bret, 'Préface' in *Les Etats et Empires de la Lune et du Soleil*, Honoré Champion, 2004. p.485.
17. Fr. Garasse, *La Doctrine Curieuse des Beaux Esprits de ce temps*, Paris, 1624, p.5.
18. Théophile de Viau, *Théophile de Viau: un poète rebelle*, Paris: Guido Saba, 1999, p.18.
19. Molière, *Dom Juan*, translated by H. van Laun, *Dramatic Works of Molière*, Edinburgh, 1876, p.168.
20. Le Bret, 'Préface' in *Les Etats et Empires de la Lune et du Soleil*, Honoré Champion, 2004, p.484.

CHAPTER EIGHT

1. Rostand, *Cyrano de Bergerac*, trans A. Burgess, Hutchinson, 1985, p.79.
2. J. Prévot, *Cyrano de Bergerac – Poète et Dramaturge*, Paris, 1978, p.46.
3. Le Bret, 'Préface' in *Les Etats et Empires de la Lune et du Soleil*, Honoré Champion, 2004, p.491.
4. Le Sieur de Grimarest, *La vie de M. de Molière* (1707), Paris, 1955, p.39.
5. L.-R. Lefèvre, *La Vie de Cyrano de Bergerac*, Paris, 1927, p.139.
6. Cyrano de Bergerac, Lettre 'Pour une Dame Rousse', *Oeuvres Comiques, Galantes et Littéraires*, Paris, 1962, p.39
7. Cyrano de Bergerac, 'Lettre IV' in *Oeuvres Comiques, Galantes et Littéraires*, Paris, 1962, p.178.

8. Marie-Catherine Desjardins, Lettre, quoted in *Lettres d'Amour du XVIIe siècle*, ed. Rohou, Paris, 1994, p.288.
9. E. Magne, *Ninon de Lenclos*, Paris, 1925, p.40.
10. Marie de Gournay, *Égalité des hommes et des femmes* (1622), Paris, 1989, pp.108–9
11. Quoted in C. Dulong, *La Vie Quotidienne des femmes au Grand Siècle*, Hachette, 1984, p.48.
12. Mlle de Scudéry, Lettre, quoted in C. Dulong, *La Vie Quotidienne des femmes au Grand Siècle*, Hachette, 1984, p.146.
13. L'Abbé de Pure, *La Prétieuse ou le mystère des ruelles*, ed. Magne, Paris, 1939, see also 'des remèdes aux maux de mariage' pp.13–113.
14. Molière, *Les Femmes Savantes*, Hachette, 1920, p.68.
15. Guez de Balzac, quoted in D. Maland, *Culture and Society in Seventeenth Century France*, London, 1970, p.148.
16 Mme de Sévigné, quoted in C. Dulong, *La Vie Quotidienne des femmes au Grand Siècle*, Hachette, 1984, p.153.
17. Cyrano de Bergerac, *Les Etats et Empire de la Lune et du Soleil*, Paris: Folio, 2004, p.303.

CHAPTER NINE

1. J. Glanvill, *SaddLcismus Triumphatus or Philosophical Considerations touching Witches and Witchcraft*, London, 1682, p.2.
2. Cyrano de Bergerac, *Oeuvres Comiques, Galantes et Littéraires*, Paris, 1962, p.44.
3. Ibid, p.54.
4. Bouillau letter to Gassendi, quoted in M. Carmona, *Les Diables de Loudun*, Paris, 1988, p.71
5. Montaigne, 'De la Conscience', *Essais II*, Gallimard, 1965, p.57.
6. H. Boguet, *Discours execrable des sorciers, Lyon*, 1605 [unpaginated].
7. Cyrano de Bergerac, Lettre 'Contre les Sorciers', *Oeuvres Comiques, Galantes et Littéraires*, Paris, 1962, p.53.
8. Voltaire, quoted in Robert Muchembled, *Le Roi et la Sorcière*, Paris, 1993, p.15.

CHAPTER TEN

1. Susan Read Baker, 'Permutations of Parricide: Cyrano de Bergerac's *La Mort d'Agrippine* (1647)', *The French Review*, Vol. 65, No. 3 (Feb 1992), pp. 375–84.
2. Tallemant des Réaux, *Historiettes*, Paris, 1960, pp.886–7.
3. Father Garasse, quoted in J. S. Spink, *French Free Thought*, Toronto, 1960, p.9.
4. G. Naudé, *Apologie pour tous les grands hommes qui ont été faussement soupçonnés de magie*, in *Libertins du XVIIe siècle*, ed. Prévot, Gallimard, 1998, pp.169–71.
5. Cyrano de Bergerac, 'Entretiens Pointus', *Oeuvres Comiques, Galantes et Littéraires*, Paris, 1962, p.202.

6. Cyrano de Bergerac, *Les Etats et Empire de la Lune et du Soleil*, Paris: Folio, 2004, p.168.
7. Thomas Browne, *Hydriotaphia*, 1620, p.51.
8. Cyrano de Bergerac, *Les Etats et Empire de la Lune et du Soleil*, Paris: Folio, 2004, p.157.
9. René Pintard, *Le Libertinage Erudit*, Paris, 1943, p.26.
10. Guillaume de Catel, Lettre Catel à Peyresc, Feb 1619.
11. *Historiarium Galliae ab excessu Henrici IV*, libri XVIII, 1643.
12. *Interrogatoire de Mathieu Molé*, MS 1623-a.
13. Voltaire, *Lettre à l'Abbé d'Olivet*, 6 Jan 1736.
14. Cyrano de Bergerac, *Les Etats et Empire de la Lune et du Soleil*, Paris: Folio, 2004, p.167.
15. Cyrano de Bergerac, *Les Etats et Empire de la Lune et du Soleil*, Paris: Folio, 2004, p.167.

CHAPTER ELEVEN

1. Johannes Kepler, Letter to Galileo, April 1610.
2. Giordano Bruno, *The Ash-Wednesday Supper*, 1584, dialogue III.
3. Ibid.
4. Quoted in Jean Rocchi, *L'Errance et l'hérésie ou le destin de Giordano Bruno*, Paris, 1989, p.261.
5. Cyrano de Bergerac, *Les Etats et Empires de la Lune et du Soleil*, Folio, 2004, p.92.
6. Cyrano de Bergerac, *Les Etats et Empires de la Lune et du Soleil*, Folio, 2004, p.112.
7. Cyrano de Bergerac, *Les Etats et Empires de la Lune et du Soleil*, Folio, 2004, p.110.
8. Fr. Garasse, *La Doctrine Curieuse des beaux esprits de ce temps*, Paris, 1650, pp.229–30.
9. Cyrano de Bergerac, *Les Etats et Empires de la Lune et du Soleil*, Folio, 2004, p.53.
10. Johannes Kepler, *Conversations with Galileo's Sidereal Messenger*, trans. Rosen, New York, 1965, p.36.
11. Johannes Kepler, *Conversations with Galileo's Sidereal Messenger*, trans. Rosen, New York, 1965, p.43.

CHAPTER TWELVE

1. Quoted in Cyrano de Bergerac, *Les Etats et Empires de la Lune et du Soleil*, ed. M. Alcover, Champion, 2004, p.xxxvi.
2. See discussion of the attribution in M. Alcover, *Cyrano relu et corrigé*, Genève: Droz, 1990.
3. *Les Pensées de M. Dassoucy dans le Saint Office de Rome*, quoted in *Les Libertins du XVIIe siecle*, ed. Jacques Prévot, Gallimard, 1998.
4. Cyrano de Bergerac, *Les Etats et Empires de la Lune et du Soleil*, Folio, 2004, p.92.

5. Le Bret, 'Préface', in *Les Etats et Empire de la Lune et du Soleil*, Honoré Champion, 2004, p.483.
6. Charles Dassoucy, *Les Pensées de Monsieur Dassoucy dans le S. Office de Rome*, in *Les Libertins du XVIIe siècle*, ed. Prévot, Gallimard, 1998, p.899.
7. Francis Bacon, *Novum Organum*, London, 1905, p.54.
8. Johannes Kepler, *Somnium*, trans. E. Rosen, University of Wisconsin, 1967, p.33.
9. Lucian, *Certain Select Dialogues of Lucian together with his True History*, 1634, p.107. This quotation is taken from an English translation by Francis Hickes which appeared in 1634, in itself a significant indication of the contemporary enthusiasm for texts which were blurring the boundaries between truth and fiction.
10. Bernard de Bovier de Fontenelle, *A Discovery of New Worlds*, trans, A. Behn, London, 1688, b5r–b5v.
11. Kepler, *Conversations with Galileo's Sidereal Messenger*, trans Rosen, New York, 1965, p.5.
12. Ibid, p.5.
13. Cyrano de Bergerac, *Les Etats et Empires de la Lune et du Soleil*, Folio, 2004, p.109.
14. Cyrano de Bergerac, *Les Etats et Empires de la Lune et du Soleil*, Folio, 2004, p.235.
15. Cyrano de Bergerac, *Les Etats et Empires de la Lune et du Soleil*, Folio, 2004, p.282.
16. Dassoucy, 'Les Pensées de M. Dassoucy dans le S. Office de Rome' (1676) in *Les Etats et Empires de la Lune et du Soleil*, ed. Alcover, Honoré Champion, 2004, pp.528-9.
17. Cyrano de Bergerac, *Les Etats et Empires de la Lune et du Soleil*, Folio, 2004, p.235
18. Cyrano de Bergerac, *Les Etats et Empires de la Lune et du Soleil*, Folio, 2004, p.53.
19. Cyrano de Bergerac, *Les Etats et Empires de la Lune et du Soleil*, Folio, 2004, p.134.
20. Cyrano de Bergerac, *Les Etats et Empires de la Lune et du Soleil*, Folio, 2004, pp.134–5.
21. Dassoucy, 'Les Aventures de M. Dassoucy', in *Les Libertins du XVIIe siècle*, ed. Prévot, Gallimard, 1998, p.765.
22. Thomas Hobbes, *Leviathan*, Amsterdam, 1670, p.65.
23. Cyrano de Bergerac, *Oeuvres Comiques, Galantes et Littéraires*, Paris, 1962, p.29.
24. Cyrano de Bergerac, *Oeuvres Comiques, Galantes et Littéraires*, Paris, 1962, p.40.
25. *Je veux faire des vers qui ne soient pas contraints,*
Promener mon esprit par de petits desseins,
Chercher des lieux secrets où rien ne me déplaise,
Employer tout une heure à me mirer dans l'eau,
Ouïr comme en songeant la course d'un ruisseau,

Écrire dans les bois, m'interrompre, me taire,
Composer un quatrain sans songer à le faire.

Théophile de Viau, 'l'Elegie à une Dame' in G. Saba, *Théophile de Viau: un poète rebelle*, Paris, 1999, p.6

26. Cyrano de Bergerac, Lettre 'D'une Maison de Campagne', *Oeuvres Comiques, Galantes et Littéraires*, Paris, 1962, p.40.
27. Cyrano de Bergerac, *Les Etats et Empires de la Lune et du Soleil*, Folio, 2004, p.141. This phrase was initially censored and therefore did not appear in the 1657 edition of the text.

CHAPTER THIRTEEN

1. Henri Le Bret, 'Préface' in *Les Etats et Empire de la Lune et du Soleil*, Honoré Champion, 2004, p.483
2. Cyrano de Bergerac, *Les Etats et Empires de la Lune et du Soleil*, Folio, 2004, p.109.
3. Cyrano de Bergerac, *Les Etats et Empires de la Lune et du Soleil*, Folio, 2004, p.249.
4. Cyrano de Bergerac, *Les Etats et Empires de la Lune et du Soleil*, Folio, 2004, p.143.
5. Dassoucy, in *Les Libertins du XVIIe siècle*, vol I, ed. Prévot, Gallimard, 1998, p.880.
6. Cyrano de Bergerac, *Les Etats et Empires de la Lune et du Soleil*, Folio, 2004, p.156.
7. *Les Libertins de XVIIe siècle*, ed. Prévot, Gallimard, 1998, p.880.
8. Dassoucy, in *Les Libertins de XVIIe siècle*, ed. Prévot, Gallimard, 1998, p.885.
9. Dassoucy, in *Les Libertins de XVIIe siècle*, ed. Prévot, Gallimard, 1998, p.879.
10. Cyrano de Bergerac, *Les Etats et Empires de la Lune et du Soleil*, Folio, 2004, p.92.
11. Montigny, 'Lettre à Eraste', quoted in 'Introduction' to *Les Etats et Empires de la Lune et du Soleil*, ed. M. Alcover, Honoré Champion, 2004, p.xxxiv.
12. Le Bret, 'Préface' in *Les Etats et Empire de la Lune et du Soleil,* Honoré Champion, 2004, p.487.
13. Cyrano de Bergerac, *Les Etats et Empires de la Lune et du Soleil*, Folio, 2004, p.141.
14. Cyrano de Bergerac, *Les Etats et Empires de la Lune et du Soleil*, Folio, 2004, p.239.
15. Cyrano de Bergerac, quoted in 'Introduction' to *Les Etats et Empires de la Lune et du Soleil*, ed. M. Alcover, Honoré Champion, 2004, p.liv.
16. Cyrano de Bergerac, Lettre 'Contre un Ingrat', *Oeuvres Comiques, Galantes et Littéraires*, Paris, 1962, p.122
17. Cyrano de Bergerac, Lettre 'Contre un Ingrat', *Oeuvres Comiques, Galantes et Littéraires*, Paris, 1962, pp.123–4.
18. Cyrano de Bergerac, *Les Etats et Empires de la Lune et du Soleil*, Folio, 2004, p.236.

CHAPTER FOURTEEN

1. Le Bret, 'Préface' in *Les Etats et Empires de la Lune et du Soleil,* Honoré Champion, 2004, p.485.
2. Edmond Rostand, *Cyrano de Bergerac,* trans. A. Burgess, Hutchinson, 1985, p.170.

3. Le Sieur de Grimarest, *La vie de M. de Molière* (1705), ed. Mongredien, 1955, Paris, p.39
4. Cyrano de Bergerac, *Les Etats et Empires de la Lune et du Soleil*, Folio, 2004, p.89.
5. Professor Madeleine Alcover's detailed analysis of the texts proves the attribution baseless. See M. Alcover, 'Stylistique et critique d'attribution: Requiem pour les mazarinades défuntes de Cyrano', *La Lettre Clandestine*, no.13 (pp.233–59) Paris: Presses de l'Université de Paris-Sorbonne, 2004.
6. Cyrano de Bergerac, *Oeuvres Comiques, Galantes et Littéraires*, Paris, 1962, p.137.
7. *The Referee*, London, 25 May 1902, quoted in Hobart Ryland, *The Sources of the Play Cyrano de Bergerac*, Institut des Etudes Françaises, vol. 70–1, 1936. p.83.
8. Quoted in Hobart Ryland, *The Sources of the Play Cyrano de Bergerac*, Institut des Etudes Françaises, vol. 70–1, 1936. p.83.
9. Rosemunde Gérard, *Edmond Rostand*, Paris: Bibliothèque-Charpentier, 1935, p.11.
10. A. M. Burrage, *War is War*, by Ex-Private X, London, 1930, pp.57–8.
11. Burrage, *War is War*, by Ex-Private X, London, 1930, p.7.

CHAPTER FIFTEEN

1. M. de Cyrano Bergerac, *Satyrical Characters and handsome descriptions in Letters written to severall Persons of Quality*, London, 1658, A3r.
2. Quoted in M. Alcover, 'Cyrano *In Carcere*', *Papers on French Seventeenth Century Literature*, XXI, 41, 1994, p.402.
3. John Evelyn, *Diaries*, quoted in *France Observed in the 17th Century by British Travellers*, ed. Lough, Oriel Press, 1985, p.95.
4. Cyrano de Bergerac, *Les Etats et Empires de la Lune et du Soleil*, Paris, Folio, 2004, p.79.
5. Edmond Rostand, *Cyrano de Bergerac*, trans. A. Burgess, Hutchinson, 1985, p.169.
6. Quoted in Cyrano de Bergerac, *Les Etats et Empires de la Lune et du Soleil*. ed. M. Alcover, Champion, 2004. p.lxii [translation by Julie Labay].
7. Cyrano de Bergerac, 'Contre un jésuite assassin et médisant', *Lettres d'amour et d'humeur*, Librio, 2004, p.88.
8. Quoted in Michel Foucault, *L'Histoire de la Folie à l'âge classique*, Gallimard, 1972, p.112
9. Cyrano de Bergerac, *Les Etats et Empires de la Lune et du Soleil*, Honoré Champion, 2004. p.168.
10. Cyrano de Bergerac, *Les Etats et Empires de la Lune et du Soleil*, Honoré Champion, 2004. p.198.
11. Michel Foucault, *L'Histoire de la Folie à l'âge classique*, Gallimard, 1972, p.150.

CHAPTER SIXTEEN

1. Rediscovered thanks to the painstaking research of Professor Madeleine Alcover and published in her edition of *Les Etats et Empires de la Lune et du Soleil*, Honoré Champion, 2004, pp.477–93.

2. Le Bret, 'Préface' in *Les Etats et Empires de la Lune et du Soleil*, Honoré Champion, 2004, p.490.
3. Le Bret, 'Epître à Messire Tanneguy Renault des Boisclairs' in *Les Etats et Empires de la Lune et du Soleil*, Honoré Champion, 2004, p.478.
4. Although not impossible as the example of the Chevalier de Roquelaure demonstrates. However, Roquelaure also benefited from the fact that he was closely related to several of his prosecutors. A notable exception to the difficulty in obtaining a release from prison would be in the case of imprisonment for debt, but as we have seen there is no reason to suppose that Cyrano's finances were in that grievous a state.
5. M. S. Arsenal quoted in Michel Foucault, *L'Histoire de la Folie à l'âge classique*, Gallimard, 1972, p.129.
6. Le Bret, 'Epître à Messire Tanneguy Renault des Boisclairs' in *Les Etats et Empires de la Lune et du Soleil*, Honoré Champion, 2004, p.478.
7. Charles de Sercy, 'Epître à M. de Cyrano de Mauvières', in *Les Etats et Empires de la Lune et du Soleil*, Honoré Champion, 2004, p.494.
8. Charles de Sercy, 'Epître à M. de Cyrano de Mauvières', in *Les Etats et Empires de la Lune et du Soleil*, Honoré Champion, 2004, p.495.
9. Fr. Garasse, *La Doctrine Curieuse*, Paris, 1624, p.209.
10. Cyrano de Bergerac, 'Contre un Poltron', *Oeuvres Comiques, Galantes et Littéraires*, Paris, 1962, p.117.
11. Molière, *Dom Juan*, translated by H. van Laun, *The Dramatic Works of Molière*, Edinburgh, 1876, p.134.
12. Gilles Ménage, *Menagiana*, Paris, 1693, quoted in M. Alcover, 'Cyrano *In Carcere*', *Papers on French Seventeenth Century Literature*, XXI, 41, 1994, p.403.
13. Ibid.
14. D. Russen, *Iter Lunare*, London, 1703, p.3.

Select Bibliography

Alcover, M., 'Cyrano *In Carcere*', *Papers on French Seventeenth Century Literature*, XXI, 41, 1994.

Alcover, M., *Cyrano relu et corrigé*, Genève, 1990.

Alcover, M., *La Pensée Philosophique et scientifique de Cyrano de Bergerac*, Paris, 1970.

Alcover, M., 'Le grand-père de Cyrano était-il sénonais?', *La Lettre Clandestine*, no.14, (pp.261–78) Paris: Presses de l'Université de Paris-Sorbonne, 2005.

Alcover, M., 'Sisyphe au Parnasse: La réception des oeuvres de Cyrano aux XVIIe et XVIIIe siècles, *Oeuvres et Critiques*, XX, 3 (pp.219–50) Tübingen, 1995.

Alcover, M., 'Stylistique et critique d'attribution: Requiem pour les mazarinades défuntes de Cyrano', *La Lettre Clandestine*, no.13 (pp.233–59) Paris: Presses de l'Université de Paris-Sorbonne, 2004.

Alcover, M., 'Un gay trio: Cyrano, Chapelle, Dassoucy', *Actes du 4e colloque du Centre International de Rencontres sur le XVIIe siècle, Université de Miami, Biblio*, 17 (117), (pp.265–75) Tübingen, 1999.

Anonymous, *Le Caquet de l'Accouchée*, Paris, 1622.

Anonymous, *Le Combat de Cirano de Bergerac avec le singe de Brioché Au bout du Pont Neuf*, Paris, 1704.

Apostolides, J-M., *Cyrano qui fut tout et qui fut rien*, Paris, 2006.

Archer, W., *Study and* Stage*: a year-book of criticism*, London, 1899.

Aries, P., *L'enfant et la vie familiale sous L'Ancien Régime*, Editions du Seuil, 1973.

Bacon, F., *Novum Organum*, London, 1905.

Barrière-Flavy, C., *La Chronique Criminelle d'une Grande Province sous Louis XIV: les drames et les désordres les plus sensationnels du Languedoc au XVIIIe siècle d'après les archives du Parlemet de Toulouse*, Paris: Editions Occitania, 1926.

Billacois, F., *The Duel: its Rise and Fall in Early Modern France*, Yale UP, 1990.

Bireley, R., *The Jesuits and the Thirty Years War: Kings, Courts and Confessors*, Cambridge University Press, 2003.

Bluche, F., *Richelieu*, Paris, 2003.

Boguet, H., *Discours execrable des sorciers*, Lyon, 1605.

Briggs, R., *Communities of Belief*, Oxford: Clarendon, 1989.

Briggs, R., *Early Modern France 1560–1715*, Oxford: OUP, 1998.

Briost, Drevillon, Serna, *Croiser le Fer – Violence et culture de l'épée dans la France Moderne*, 2002.

Brissette, P., *La malediction littéraire – Du poète crotté au génie malheureux*, Montreal, 2005.
Browne, T., *Hydriotaphia*, 1620.
Brun, P., *Savinien de Cyrano Bergerac – Gentilhomme Parisien, l'histoire et la légende d'après des documents inédits*, Paris, 1893.
Bruno, G., *Oeuvres Complètes* (trans. Yves Hersaut) Paris, 1993.
Bryskett, L., *A Discourse of Civill Life*, New York: Da Capo Press, 1970.
Burrage, A. M., *War is War*, London, 1930.
Bussy-Rabutin, *Les Mémoires de Messire Roger de Rabutin, Comte de Bussy, Lieutenant Général des Armées du Roy et mestre de camp général de la cavalerie légère*, Paris, 1696.
Caillière, Maréchal de, *Les Fortunes de gens de qualité et des gentilhommes particuliers*, 1661.
Calvié, L., *Cyrano dans tous ses Etats*, Toulouse: Anacharsis Editions, 2004.
Carmona, M., *Les Diables de Loudun*, Paris, 1988.
Charron, P., *Traité de la Sagesse*, Paris, 1601.
Constant, J-M., *La noblesse Française aux XVIe et XVIIe siècles*, Hachette, 1985.
Corneille, P., *Le Cid*, Cambridge: CUP, 1924.
Corneille, P., *Le Cid* (*a translation in Rhymed Couplets* by V. Cheng), University of Delaware Press, 1987.
Corneille, P., *Le Menteur*, Magnard, 2002.
Cornette, J., *Le Roi de Guerre*, Paris, 1993.
Cuenin, M., *Le Duel sous L'Ancien Régime*, Paris, 1982.
Cyrano de Bergerac, S., *L'Autre Monde ou Les Estats et Empires de la Lune*, ed. M. Alcover, Paris: Champion, 1977.
Cyrano de Bergerac, S., *Les Etats et Empires de la Lune et du Soleil*, ed. M. Alcover, Paris: Honoré Champion, 2004.
Cyrano de Bergerac, S., *Les Etats et Empire de la Lune et du Soleil*, ed. Prévot, Paris: Folio, 2004.
Cyrano de Bergerac, S., *Les Etats et Empires du Soleil*, ed. B. Parmentier, Flammarion, 2003.
Cyrano de Bergerac, S., *Les Oeuvres Comiques Galantes et Littéraires*, Paris, 1962.
Cyrano de Bergerac, S., *Lettres d'amour et d'humeur*, Librio, 2004.
Cyrano de Bergerac, S., *Oeuvres*, ed. Lacroix, Paris, 1858.
Cyrano de Bergerac, S., *Oeuvres Complètes*, ed. Erba, Paris: Honoré Champion, 2001.
Cyrano de Bergerac, S., *Satyrical Characters and handsome descriptions in Letters written to severall Persons of Qualilty*, London, 1658.
Cyrano de Bergerac, S., *Selenarchia* (trans. St Serf) London, 1659.
Cyrano de Bergerac, S., *Voyages to the Moon and the Sun*, trans. Aldington, London: Folio Society, 1991.
Dainville, F. de, *La Naissance de l'Humanisme Moderne*, Paris, 1940.
Dewald, J., *Aristocratic experience and the origins of Modern Culture*, University of California Press, 1993.
Dubois, A., *Journal d'un Curé de Campagne au XVIIe siècle*, ed. Platelle, Paris, 1965.

Dulong, C., *La Vie Quotidienne des femmes au Grand Siècle*, Hachette, 1984.
Faret, N., *L'Honnête Homme ou l'art de plaire à la court*, Paris, 1630.
Fontenelle, B. le B. de, *A Discovery of New Worlds*, trans, A. Behn, London, 1688.
Forbin, Comte de, *Mémoires du Comte de Forbin*, Paris, 1993.
Fortin de la Hoguette, P., *Catéchisme royal*, Paris, 1650.
Foucault, D., *Giulio Cesare Vanini – Un Philosophe Libertin dans l'Europe Baroque*, Paris, 2003.
Foucault, M., *L'Histoire de la Folie à l'âge classique*, Gallimard, 1972.
Garasse, Fr., *La Doctrine Curieuse des beaux esprits de ce temps*, Paris, 1624.
Gautier, T., *Le Capitaine Fracasse*, Paris, 1863.
Gérard, R., *Edmond Rostand*, Paris: Bibliothèque-Charpentier, 1935.
Glanvill, J., *Saddumismus Triumphatus or Philosophical Considerations touching Witches and Witchcraft*, London, 1682.
Godwin, F., *The Man in the Moon*, London, 1638.
Gournay, M. de, *Égalité des hommes et des femmes*, Paris, 1989.
Grimarest, le sieur de, *La vie de M. de Molière*, Paris, 1955.
Grimmelshausen, H. J. C. von, *The Adventures of Simplicius Simplicissimus* (trans Schulz-Behrend), Camden House, Columbia, 1993.
Hayden, D., *Pox, Genius, Madness and the Mysteries of Syphilis*, Oxford, 2003.
Héroard, *Journal sur l'Enfance et la Jeunesse de Louis XIII*, 1868.
Hobbes, T., *Leviathan*, Amsterdam, 1670.
Howarth, W. D., *Molière – A Playwright and his Audience*, Cambridge University Press, 1982.
Jones, H., *Pierre Gassendi 1592–1655 – An Intellectual Biography*, Nieuwkoop, 1981.
Kepler, J., *Conversations with Galileo's Sidereal Messenger* (trans. Rosen), New York, 1965.
Kepler, J., *Somnium* (trans. Rosen), University of Wisconsin, 1967.
Knecht, R. J., *Richelieu*, Longman, 1991.
Koyré, A., *Du monde clos à l'univers infini*, Gallimard, 1988.
Lachèvre, F., *Cyrano de Bergerac – Notice Biographique*, Paris: Honoré Champion, 1920.
Lefèvre, L.-R., *La Vie de Cyrano de Bergerac*, Paris, 1927.
Lejeune, *Du devoir des pères*, 1620.
L'Hermite, T., *Le Page Disgracié*, Presse Universitaire de Grenoble, 1980.
Lloyd, S., *The Man Who Was Cyrano*, Indiana: Unlimited, 2002.
Lough, J. (ed.), *France Observed in the 17th Century by British Travellers*, Oriel Press, 1985.
Lucian, *Certain Select Dialogues of Lucian together with his True History* (trans. Hickes), 1634.
Magne, E., *Le Chevalier de Lignières*, Paris, 1920.
Magne, E., *Les Erreurs de documentation de Cyrano de Bergerac*, Paris, 1898.
Magne, E., *Ninon de Lenclos*, Paris, 1925.
Maland, D., *Culture and Society in Seventeenth Century France*, London, 1970.
Mandrou, R., *Magistrats et Sorciers en France au XVIIe siècle*, Paris: Seuil, 1980.
Marche, O. de la, *Traité de Duel*, 1436.

Maurel-Indart, H., *Du Plagiat*, Paris, 1999.
Ménage, G., *Menagiana*, Paris, 1715.
Michaut, G., *La Jeunesse de Molière*, Paris, 1922.
Molière, *Les Femmes Savantes*, Hachette, 1920.
Molière, *Oeuvres Complètes*, Gallimard, 1983.
Molière, *The Works of Molière* (trans. H. van Laun) Edinburgh, 1875.
Monestier, M., *Duels*, Paris, 1991.
Mongrédien, G., *Cyrano de Bergerac*, Paris, 1964.
Montague, C. E., *Dramatic Values*, London, 1911.
Montaigne, M. de, *Essays*, Gallimard, 1965.
Muchembled, R., *Le Roi et la Sorcière*, Paris, 1993.
Naudé, G., *Apologie pour tous les grands hommes qui ont été faussement soupçonnés de magie*, Paris, 1625.
Parker, G., *The Thirty Years War*, Routledge, 1997.
Petitfils, J-C., *Le véritable d'Artagnan*, Paris, 2002.
Pintard, R., *Le Libertinage Erudit*, Paris, 1943.
Prévot, J., *Cyrano de Bergerac – Poète et dramaturge*, Paris, 1978.
Prévot, J., *Cyrano de Bergerac romancier*, Paris, 1977.
Prévot, J., (ed.) *Les Libertins du XVIIe siècle*, Gallimard, 1998.
Pure, L'Abbé de, *La Prétieuse ou le mystère des ruelles*, Paris, 1939.
Quétel, C., *Le Mal de Naples – Histoire de la Syphilis*, Paris, 1986.
Ranum, O., *La Fronde*, Seuil, Paris, 1995.
Read Baker, S., 'Permutations of Parricide: Cyrano de Bergerac's *La Mort d'Agrippine*', *The French Review*, Vol. 65, No. 3 (Feb 1992), pp. 375–84.
Réaux, T. des, *Historiettes*, Paris, 1960.
Rizza, C., *Libertinage et Littérature*, Schena, 1996.
Rocchi, J., *L'Errance et l'hérésie ou le destin de Giordano Bruno*, Paris, 1989.
Rochester, J. Wilmot Earl of, *Rochester's Poems*, Shakespeare Head Press, 1984.
Rohou, *Lettres d'Amour du XVIIe siècle*, Paris, 1994.
Rostand, E., *Cyrano de Bergerac*, Flammarion, 1989.
Rostand E., *Cyrano de Bergerac*, trans. A. Burgess, Hutchinson, 1985.
Russen, D., *Iter Lunare*, London, 1703.
Ryland, H., *The sources of the play Cyrano de Bergerac*, Institut des Etudes Françaises, vol. 70–1, 1936.
Saba, G., *Théophile de Viau: un poète rebelle*, Paris, 1999.
Sacchi, H., *La Guerre des Trente Ans*, Paris: L'Harmattan, 1999.
Schalk, E., *From Valor to Pedigree*, Princeton UP, 1986.
Sorel, C., *Histoire Comique de Francion*, Editions Gallimard, 1996.
Spink, J. S. *French Free Thought*, Toronto, 1960.
Suberville, J., *Edmond Rostand*, Paris, 1921.
Verciani, L., *Le moi et ses diables*, Paris, 2001.
Wilkins, J., *A Discovery of a New World, or A Discourse tending to prove that 'tis Probable there may be another Habitable World in the Moon*, London, 1638.

／

Acknowledgments

My heartfelt thanks to: Sarah Reece for being my first reader and best source of encouragement; Jim Gill my wonderful agent for his invaluable help in the early stages and continued support; Andrew Gordon my editor for his insightful comments, his precision and his patience; Professor Alcover for her prompt and detailed response to my questions and for the vital archival research she has undertaken in order to establish a clearer, more detailed picture of the real Cyrano; Sophie Trouilhet pour Mauvières, Paris et pour sa amitié précieuse; Dr Christian Belin and Dr Charles Whitworth for their kind help and support; Dr Robin Robbins for telling me to look for the gap on my shelf; M. Le Comte et Mme La Comtesse de Bryas merci pour votre accueil; Julie Labaye warmest thanks for invaluable translation assistance – tu es un ange; Lisa Mathieu for her excellent Master's thesis on the Chevalier de Roquelaure; Rob Bartlett for his belief in happy endings; thanks to Max Addyman for finding that elusive quotation for me; Mrs Jane Menon for always being there; Nandita Menon for her kind hospitality at La Trufière; Aliye and Nicole for New York; Delilah Seale for her invaluable help and kindness; Bruno for tea and sympathy; Olivier L'Hôte merci pour la musique et l'audace; Dr Nick Hughes – thanks for research assistance and for drinking those cappuccinos so that I didn't have to. Thanks to Karen and Joseph for their kind hospitality. Fabien Gaillard, merci pour la très belle coloration de gravure. Maître Fredairgues, mon maître d'escrime, merci pour vos conseils et votre enthousiasme pour ce projet.

Many thanks to the wonderful staff of the British Library reading rooms in London and Boston Spa. Merci également aux bibliothécaires à la Bibliothèque Nationale et à la Bibliothèque Mazarine à Paris, ainsi que ceux de la Bibliothèque de l'Université Paul Valéry III et de la Médiathèque Emile Zola à Montpellier.

I have been lucky enough to be taught by lots of brilliant and dedicated women over the years and would therefore like to thank all my teachers. Special mention must go to Mrs Hughes who worked so hard for us and whose efforts I didn't appreciate at the time. Also in fond memory of Mrs Small, a brilliant history teacher and Dr Avril Bruten, a true original. Special thanks also to Professor Isabel Rivers for attempting to instil discipline and academic rigour into me at an important early stage and to Ann Wordsworth for her inspirational teaching. Love and thanks to all my family and friends not already singled out above. But above all else, infinite, grovelling thanks to my parents for their unfailing support and generosity.

Index

Index